Simon Fraser

In Search of Modern British Columbia

Best wishes
to
Joan and Charlie

Logan Lake, 2008

Stephen Hume

IN SEARCH OF MODERN BRITISH COLUMBIA

Based on the series in the *Vancouver Sun*

STEPHEN HUME

HARBOUR PUBLISHING

1 2 3 4 5 — 12 11 10 09 08

Harbour Publishing Co. Ltd
P.O. Box 219, Madeira Park, BC, V0N 2H0
www.harbourpublishing.com

Edited by Susan Mayse.
Indexed by Hugh Morrison.
Text and map design by Roger Handling, Terra Firma Digital Arts.
Dust jacket design by Anna Comfort.
Printed in China.

Additional image credits: front cover Simon Fraser portrait, image PDP02258 courtesy of Royal BC Museum, BC Archives; front cover background image, Bill Keay/*Vancouver Sun*; front flap, detail of John Innes, "Simon Fraser in the Fraser Canyon on His Journey to the Sea," A.D. 1808 [1925], Simon Fraser University Collection, commissioned by Native Sons of British Columbia; back cover, Bill Keay/*Vancouver Sun*; back flap author photo, Mark Van Manen/*Vancouver Sun*; endsheets, Map of the Northwest Territory of the Province of Canada by David Thompson (1770–1857). [1814] (Archives of Ontario. F 443, R-C(U), AO 1541); title page, "Canoe Manned by Voyageurs Passing a Waterfall," Frances Anne Hopkins fonds, Library and Archives Canada, accession number 1989-401-1, C-002771.

Harbour Publishing acknowledges financial support from the Government of Canada through the Book Publishing Industry Development Program and the Canada Council for the Arts, and from the Province of British Columbia through the BC Arts Council and the Book Publishing Tax Credit.

Library and Archives Canada Cataloguing in Publication

Hume, Stephen, 1947–
Simon Fraser : in search of modern British Columbia / Stephen Hume.

Includes index.
ISBN 978-1-55017-434-2

1. Fraser, Simon, 1776-1862. 2. Northwest, Canadian—Discovery and exploration.
I. Title.
FC3212.1.F73H85 2008 971.1'02 C2008-900033-1

For Dusty, a born traveller

TABLE OF CONTENTS

Simon Fraser, who rose to prominence in the fur trade and then subsided into relative obscurity, explored the great western river that now bears his name. *Image PDP02258 courtesy of Royal BC Museum, BC Archives*

FOREWORD

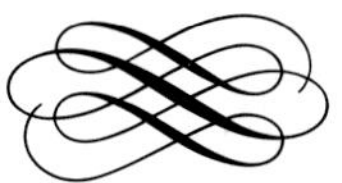

This book began as a one-paragraph memo and somehow grew to more than three hundred pages. What follows is not history in the scholarly sense of that discipline. There are no cross-indexed footnotes citing the precise source of every snippet of information. Nor is this a conventional biography. I had neither the resources nor the inclination to write one. It is simply a curious reporter's story, a bit more personal than some, perhaps more detailed than most, but nonetheless just the narrative of an epic life and the times it spanned.

None of it would have been possible without the support of Patricia Graham and Chris Rose, editor-in-chief and special projects editor respectively at the *Vancouver Sun.* Patricia and the *Sun* made available the resources necessary for a journey that eventually covered 20,000 kilometres and took four years to complete, then stood behind a story that came to consume scores of news pages. Chris managed the logistics of canoe trips, jetboats and long silences from the bush punctuated by sudden floods of text. More important, he patiently pointed out the trail ahead for a story that often threatened to go wild and run away. He prodded it back to life when it occasionally threatened to go into hibernation.

Nor would it have been possible without my daughter Heledd, who provided companionship and the occasional adept bow paddle on some of the loneliest legs of the journey. Nor without the advice of my wife and fellow writer, Susan Mayse, as perceptive an advisor on matters literary as one might hope to find.

Bill Keay taught me how to stalk a lynx while burdened with camera gear. Mark Van Manen proved that a latté can be sweet-talked out of any establishment with a pot of coffee, including a heavy equipment garage. Research librarian Kate Bird demonstrated her skill as a document sleuth nonpareil, locating amazing things in the most obscure places. Sonny McHalsie took me on a tour of the Sto:lo mythic world that would have been totally inaccessible if I'd had to rely on anthropologists alone. Barbara Rogers shared her vast knowledge and corrected my errors. Others who helped are mentioned in the book. To those I failed to mention, my profound thanks.

Readers should be aware of the special problem of spellings. The languages and dialects of the peoples of the region Simon Fraser named New Caledonia did not take written form until the late nineteenth century, when Father Adrian Gabriel Morice devised a system of syllabics and compiled a dictionary and grammar.

North West Company fur traders who first encountered these languages—almost always with the assistance of Métis, Cree or other First Nations interpreters—were not linguists. Often they had minimal schooling in the grammar and spelling of their own language.

The traders' renderings into English of personal and place names, filtered through another aboriginal language or translated first into French and then back into English, became attempts to invent spellings they thought resembled unfamiliar sounds they often had difficulty pronouncing.

It's small wonder, therefore, that fur traders frequently misheard pronunciations, mangled them in an attempt to transliterate and subsequently provided spellings which were exceedingly variable, often changing from one trader's journal to another and sometimes from one entry to another in the same journal.

Over the centuries, spellings and orthographies evolved—and are still evolving—as linguists refine their understanding and First Nations assert greater control over their own cultural heritage as it makes its transition from oral to written form. For a non-linguist like me, it can become confusing. I'm doubtless guilty myself of some mangling and misunderstanding, so for that I'll beg indulgence in advance.

To provide consistency both for myself and for those not familiar with these rapidly changing conventions, I have relied primarily upon personal and place name spellings set out in Morice, spellings given for traditional place names by provincial governments which consult with First Nations, and spellings preferred by various First Nations authorities. I've sought to apply common sense throughout in choosing the spellings that seem most likely to be understood by the broadest number of readers while respecting First Nations desires to exercise sovereignty over their rich linguistic culture.

Stephen Hume
North Saanich, 2008

Simon Fraser

1

THE BIRTH OF A PROVINCE

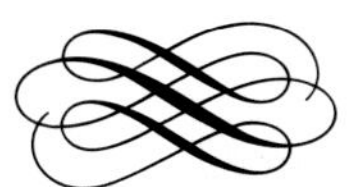

On a fall afternoon about two hundred years ago, when the air was crisp with that sharp taste of snow that signals every winter's march into central British Columbia, a sturdy, auburn-haired man stepped from a flimsy canoe onto a willow-clad tongue of land between two fast-running streams at the northwest end of what we now call McLeod Lake.

His name was Simon Fraser. He was not yet thirty. And pressed into the soft ground with his footprints, almost nine hundred kilometres north of Greater Vancouver's glowing pillars of glass and steel, were the seeds of an enterprise that would grow into today's great province.

The narrow lake before him extended to the southeast, nestled into a trough where the Nechako Plateau butts up against the Misinchinka mountain range, a western outrider of the towering northern Rockies. Then as now—as the dwindling days of 1805 closed in on the lean winter months ahead—a dark forest crowded it, displaying an occasional flare of autumn foliage.

Beyond the lake, the land rose to a distant range of hills. Behind Fraser, what we now call the Pack River twisted away into the trees, seeking its confluence to the northwest with the Parsnip, itself a muscular fork of the mighty Peace River that rolled relentlessly northeast through its forbidding canyons toward Athabasca Lake and ultimately the Arctic Ocean.

Even today there's a stillness about the place that almost belies what sprang from the seeds Fraser planted here so long ago. The glossy lake that now carries my

This view down McLeod Lake differs little from the one that greeted Simon Fraser when he stepped ashore somewhere near this vantage point in 1805. *Stephen Hume*

own reflection, the motionless trees and the enormous, crushing silence are disturbed only by the faint blat of a truck using its engine to brake on nearby Highway 97. There's no hint of the megalopolis in the southwestern corner of the province that illuminates the night sky for hundreds of kilometres around, its neon canyons pulsing with electricity generated from these same fast-flowing rivers.

Back then Fraser stood at the farthest end of a tenuous transportation route. It reached back across a wild and dangerous continent. News of his arrival—travelling at the speed that river currents allowed, seldom faster than a man could walk—would take a full year to reach the company's directors in distant Montreal. Their acknowledgment and further instructions would take another year to come back, then one more year for his reply and the latest financial accounting. A three-year turnaround seems almost unimaginable in our age of instant messaging.

While far off Europe seethed with a titanic conflict—Nelson would smash the French fleet at Trafalgar on October 21, and Napoleon would crush the allies' army at Austerlitz on December 2—Fraser was left to worry in blessed ignorance about his increasingly leaky canoes and whether he could secure enough fish and game from this unknown country to see his voyageurs, hired hands, guides and hunters through the hungry days that surely lay ahead.

It was late in the season, but we can be reasonably sure it wasn't late in the day when Fraser made his decision to build a trading post here at McLeod Lake. After thirteen years on the northern frontier, he was a seasoned wilderness traveller.

Fraser would want plenty of light to make camp. Night would be blacker and stars brighter than anyone now living can imagine, save for the few who have been to the upper edges of the atmosphere. In 1805 the haze from the "dark satanic mills" of the coal-fired Industrial Revolution had not yet begun to obscure the skies.

Whether or not his eye lingered upon the esthetic qualities of the view, it must have noted the spot's advantages. A near-constant breeze from the lake would blow summer mosquitoes and black flies off the point. Clean running water was abundant. There would be fish in the lake—Trout Lake, it was called by the Tse'Khene people he'd already encountered—and it was well-positioned for further exploration. Indeed, he already knew of other lakes off to the west.

Fraser's canoe was held together with spruce-root stitching, its birchbark skin little thicker than the cardboard in a pizza box and its seams waterproofed with sticky black pitch. The slight craft had already carried him nearly four thousand kilometres to this spot, and had itself been carried over spine-popping portages where newcomers discovered the trail was marked upon the naked bedrock by sweat dripping from the burdened men just ahead of them.

By comparison, my own six-metre canoe, a bit battered after thirty years of paddling but nonetheless sound for its adventures, is a space-age marvel of nearly puncture-proof aluminum. A knife-edge keel keeps it tracking true and my shatterproof aluminum paddles with plastic blades are far more efficient than wooden ones with their tendency to splinter on rocky bottoms. Its classic shape may be the same as its birchbark ancestor, but its materials reflect the technological gulf that separates my time from Fraser's.

Fraser lived in a world powered by wind, water and muscle. Medicine was rudimentary and relied on principles and practices we now know to be wrong, even life-threatening. His world was illuminated by open flame. Information travelled at what scholars estimate was an average pace of 2.4 km/h. He navigated by the stars, the seasonal rising and setting of the sun, the length of shadows and the direction of flowing water. His only weather reports were broadcast by the sky.

I communicate by cellphone and send emails on a wireless hand-held computer. I can count on the triangulated signals from satellites to locate me within a few metres of my true position. I get my weather report over a portable radio that reports changing weather conditions by the hour and even alerts me to sudden hazards with an automated alarm, and its information comes from someone in a concrete bunker in Vancouver whose computers analyze photographs taken from space. Fraser's messages to and from Montreal took years to conclude, but mine are immediate. Ground that he took months to cover I can traverse in a few hours.

24. McLEOD LAKE
Some time in the late fall of 1805, probably late October or early November — the North West Company journal covering this precise period appears to be lost — Simon Fraser established a trading post on McLeod Lake. It was to prove the birthplace of BC, the oldest continuously inhabited European settlement west of the Rocky Mountains, north of Spanish colonies in California and south of Russian outposts in Alaska.

23. ROCKY MOUNTAIN PORTAGE HOUSE
Simon Fraser established this fort at the foot of the steep portage around the impassable Peace River Canyon in 1805 and it became a key staging post for his later explorations west of the Rocky Mountains. Located near present day Hudson's Hope, it marked the gateway through the Rockies, rich new trading territories and made possible the early commercial infrastructure in British Columbia's interior that made possible the birth of a new province.

22. FORT ST. JOHN
Rocky Mountain Fort, the first European settlement in what's now British Columbia, was established at the confluence of the Moberly and Peace Rivers near here about 1798 but was abandoned by 1805 and replaced by Fort St. John at the confluence of the Beatton and Peace Rivers in 1806. Traders withdrew to Fort Dunvegan in present day Alberta after the clerk and four voyageurs were murdered in 1823.

21. FORT CHIPEWYAN
The first fort was built near the western end of Lake Athabasca in 1788. Alexander Mackenzie had taken charge of the Athabasca District for the North West Company and in this year his old mentor, Peter Pond, turned over to Mackenzie his maps and observations about a possible route to the Pacific and retired from the fur trade. Dubbed the "Athens of the North," Fort Chipewyan became an important hub for further expansion across the north and west. From here Mackenzie launched his two famous voyages of exploration to the Arctic and to the Pacific.

20. METHYE PORTAGE
At the north end of Lac La Loche, Peter Pond carried his canoes over a rise of land beyond which the rivers ran north to the Arctic Ocean. He was the first non-native known to have crossed the portage which put him on the Clearwater River and a long downstream run through what are now Alberta's oil sands to Lake Athabasca River. The way to the northwest was open.

19. LA LOCHE
Following rivers upstream from the north end of Lac Île-à-la-Crosse, Peter Pond was here in 1778 with four canoes in search of the elusive route to the fabled Athabasca district from which Cree middlemen sometimes obtained luxurious pelts from Chipewyan trappers. Today La Loche is a first nations community of just over 2,100. In Simon Fraser's time this was the farthest reach of the watersheds draining east to Hudson Bay.

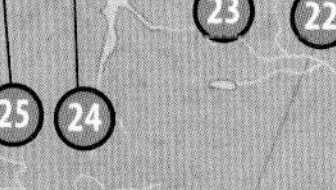

25. FORT ST. JAMES
On the south end of Stuart Lake, in an accommodation with the Carrier Chief Kwah, Fraser builds the trading post in 1806 that will become the administrative capital of New Caledonia. From here will grow the trading and transportation network around which BC will take shape.

26. LEON CREEK
On June 10, 1808, Fraser's party cached its canoes here and continued on foot, guided from First Nation to First Nation through almost impassable canyons along a series of trails, ladders, suspension bridges and flimsy scaffoldings of poles lashed together with vines and rawhide.

16. AMISK LAKE
The rock-choked Sturgeonweir River links this body of water just west of the Manitoba border near Flin Flon to both the Churchill River to the north and the route to Montreal to the south. It was the fur trade's long-sought gateway to the North. The first trading post was established in 1774 by the Frobisher brothers who later were founding partners in the North West Company.

28. MUSQUEAM
At the still-occupied village near the present University of BC campus, Fraser first saw the Pacific on July 2, 1808, but was forced to beat a hasty retreat back up the river when confronted by apparently angry Musqueam warriors.

27. LOWER RIVER
Somewhere above the North Arm of the river at New Westminster, Fraser appropriated a canoe for his final run to the sea. He returned the canoe but ill-feeling from the incident would dog the expedition for the rest of the journey.

15. THE PAS
The first European to see the immense swampy estuary where the Saskatchewan flows into Cedar Lake near the Manitoba boundary was probably Henry Kelsey who wintered in 1690 during an expedition deep into the unmapped Prairies. Arctic explorer Samuel Hearne would later push west to establish Cumberland House, the HBC's first inland trading post which proved a key to expansion into the northwest.

14. GRAND RAPIDS
Situated where the Saskatchewan River enters Lake Winnipeg from Cedar Lake, the fort founded by the French in the early 18th century was eventually abandoned but the portage remained strategically crucial. The river, which branches north and south near Prince Albert, Sask., provided a direct water route to the Rocky Mountains from the Yellowhead to the Crowsnest as well as a link to the northern watersheds of the Churchill River system.

13. WINNIPEG RIVER
At least eight fur trade forts were scattered along the turbulent lower section of the river where it leaves western Ontario on its way to Lake Winnipeg, the remnants of a gigantic ice age lake that spans almost all the present province of Manitoba. From it, there were river routes to Hudson Bay, the Canadian Prairies, the Arctic and the Great Lakes. A route from Montreal to the legendary furs of the northwest was in place.

12. RAT PORTAGE
After passing up Rainy River past Fort St. Pierre, established in 1731 by Christophe Dufrost de La Jemerais, a nephew of Pierre Gaultier de La Verendrye, fur traders reached Lake of the Woods. At Rat Portage they crossed to the Winnipeg River and it was here that they passed from the eastern woodlands of the rugged Canadian Shield into the vastness of the Great Plains.

Simon Fraser's World

1. MAPLETOWN
Simon Fraser was born in this rural district straddling what's now the New York-Vermont boundary in 1776 just six weeks before the Declaration of Independence launched a revolutionary war between the British and the American colonies. That same summer independent fur traders from Montreal decided to set up a forward supply base on Lake Superior to compete with the Hudson's Bay Company.

2. BENNINGTON
American rebels crush a British force of professional soldiers in a decisive battle in 1777 that foreshadows the defeat of General John Burgoyne's northern army at Saratoga a few weeks later. Simon Fraser's Loyalist father dies of "illuse" in a rebel prison at Albany, setting the stage for his persecuted widow's flight to Canada with seven children.

3. BOSTON
The main commercial centre of the New England colonies was a hotbed of revolutionary sentiment and the site of a major psychological victory when British troops "won" the Battle of Bunker Hill but only after rebel forces had inflicted such carnage that thoughts of an easy suppression of the rebellion abruptly evaporated.

4. NEW YORK
Initially loyal to the British, New York authorities provided Simon Fraser's father with title to his farm but its right to do so was challenged by rebel Vermont and 60 of his best acres were expropriated. It was from New York that many of the loyalists who migrated to Canada embarked.

5. LACHINE
Situated above the awesome rapids on the St. Lawrence River that provided its name, this settlement upstream from Montreal became the staging point for canoe brigades which left each spring carrying trade goods to the distant interior and returned in the fall with thousands of valuable furs from the unmapped heart of the continent.

6. OTTAWA VALLEY
This rift in the ancient rocks of the Canadian Shield — likely explored by Étienne Brûlé for his mentor Samuel Champlain — led fur traders to the Mattawa River and a route to the Great Lakes that despite arduous portages still cut weeks of travel from the circuitous route up the St. Lawrence, through Lake Ontario and Lake Erie and then back up the length of Lake Huron.

7. LAKE NIPISSING
In the upper reaches of the Mattawa River, fur traders crossed a height of land just east of this lake which marked a divide beyond which waters drained westward into the Great Lakes. Crossing the lake from North Bay, their canoes reached the French River which carried them downstream to the northern shore of Lake Huron and clear paddling to the west.

8. SAULT STE. MARIE
Situated on a short river that flows from Lake Superior to Lake Huron, this was a strategic point in east-west travel controlled by the Ojibwa peoples for millennia before the first Europeans arrived. It proved strategic for the newcomers, too — French, British, Americans all sought to control what was a portal to rich territories to the west.

9. AGAWA BAY
Eerie rock paintings adorn a rock face that looked down on the fur brigades as they paddled past. The images evoke powerful stories of supernatural spirits as well as the almost superhuman deeds of warrior chiefs which are corroborated by other sources. They remind everyone that the history of the west did not begin with the arrival of Europeans.

10. FORT WILLIAM
French fur traders built the first forts in the 17th century but the site was abandoned when the North West Company found a shorter route to the west at Grand Portage in what's now Minnesota. However, when the new U.S.-Canada border passed north of their base, the company built again on the old site and it was there in 1805 that Simon Fraser was assigned to take the fur trade beyond the Rockies and find a route to the Pacific.

11. GRAND PORTAGE
Simon Fraser visited "the great carrying place" on his first journey west. Here brigades from Montreal and fur traders who had wintered deep in the interior met each summer in the annual "rendezvous" to exchange trade items and furs and to resupply the distant outposts. Senior partners met to discuss business, clerks like Fraser got their assignments and employees and guests were hosted at sumptuous banquets and balls.

17. LA RONGE
Free trader Peter Pond was on Lac La Ronge in 1781 when he was implicated in the shooting death of a competitor, Jean-Etienne Waden, and later returned to the region as a partner in the North West Company with Alexander Mackenzie as his clerk whom he tutored in the fur trade and doubtless told of his theories about a river in the Athabasca region leading to the Pacific. Today it's the biggest community in northern Saskatchewan.

18. ÎLE-À-LA-CROSSE
Thomas Frobisher established a trading post on Lac Île-à-la-Crosse in the year Simon Fraser was born. It took its name from the lacrosse games that the Cree peoples occasionally played on a peninsula in the lake. Traders travelled northwest to Peter Pond Lake. Among those who served at Île-à-la-Crosse was Sir James Douglas who would later preside over the creation of the colony of British Columbia.

Although the original buildings erected by Simon Fraser at what he called the Trout Lake Post on McLeod Lake in 1805 are long lost, later buildings shared many features. *Image PDP02818 courtesy of Royal BC Museum, BC Archives*

Yet that frail bark canoe had taken him safely down thundering chutes where white crosses gleaming on the riverbanks marked the graves of the drowned, those who miscalculated by a hair or hesitated for a second. It had carried him across quaking, mosquito-infested muskegs, into gorges so deep and gloomy they seemed like gates to the underworld, and onward into unmapped territory occupied by peoples who had never met a European and might prefer to kill him rather than invite him to dinner.

Fraser wasn't the first white man to penetrate this region of what is now BC. Alexander Mackenzie had passed through on his famous dash to the Pacific thirteen years earlier. In 1794, a fort had been built not far from present-day Fort St. John, although it was soon to be abandoned. John Finlay had briefly ventured through the Peace River canyon in 1797 and up the north fork that now bears his name. David Thompson had explored the Peace in 1804, establishing a base on the east side of the Rockies before turning his attention southward to the Kootenays and a route to the Columbia River. One of Fraser's associates, James McDougall, had then made a quick reconnaissance of the country to the west that Fraser now surveyed. But of this bold few, Fraser was perhaps the most important. He was the first to come with clear intentions of creating a permanent European presence at this farthest reach of the known world. From the commercial enterprise he launched would unfold a truly astonishing future.

When Fraser stepped ashore on the little promontory at McLeod Lake, he was fulfilling instructions from his board of directors. At a meeting on the Great Lakes earlier that year, he had been ordered to expand the North West Company's trading interests beyond the Rocky Mountains and to commercially exploit, if possible, the territory Mackenzie had briefly traversed on his exploratory mission to the Pacific Ocean.

Although the fur trade would reign for only another fifty years in the province, it would lay down the infrastructure of transportation routes, supply depots, permanent settlements, geographical knowledge, and perhaps most important, an emerging psychology of place. This would ensure British sovereignty over the region in the face of American expansionism. It would also facilitate the development of resources that began with the Fraser River gold rush in 1858.

In ten generations, the seeds sown by Fraser would blossom into one of the country's largest provincial economies, its most important western port, a global player in world commodity markets, a crucial component in the North American energy grid, home to leading edge high-tech industries of the information age, great universities and a metropolitan area whose population now is more than six times greater than all of Canada's population in 1805.

Fraser was a seminal figure in our province's creation story, yet few of us know much about the man.

"Simon Fraser is the most neglected of the major explorers of Canada. No biography of him has been written, and the versions of his writings that have been printed hitherto are without exception inaccurate," observed the eminent historian W. Kaye Lamb in the introduction to a collection of Fraser's letters, journals and other documents published in 1960.

Almost fifty years later, University of Victoria history professor John Lutz said Fraser was a casualty of changing fashions in the scholarly end of the discipline.

"The ferment of the sixties led to a challenge to the white male world view of history," Lutz said. "There was a growing interest in aboriginal views. These explorers were seen to have been engaged in a colonial enterprise in which one perspective was emphasized at the expense of the other, and so there was a retreat from biography, from the focus on white male leaders. Except for juvenile literature, explorers are out of fashion."

Which helps explain why for most of us, Fraser is little more than a name on a teacher's blackboard, at best dimly remembered from a cursory answer to some school exam question.

So who was Simon Fraser?

My search for an answer to this question would eventually lead me across the continent and simultaneously backward through time, deep into the historical

The search for Simon Fraser began in the archives of the university that now bears his name where some surviving papers are held, including letters and notes on his family history. *Ian Lindsay/*Vancouver Sun

roots of a political landscape we take for granted, but that bears almost no resemblance to that of two hundred years ago.

The trail would lead through dusty libraries, across once-bloody battlefields and through a geography utterly transformed by industry, technology and population from what Fraser knew—yet in many places I would find that landscape eerily unchanged.

My search began with documents: Fraser's own letters and journals, his last will and testament, a petition to the government from his mother for assistance, another seeking a pension for one of his daughters, a letter from his son proudly outlining his father's accomplishments half a century afterward.

But these soon petered out. Working for a daily newspaper, I didn't have an academic's luxury of grant-funded decades to scour obscure archives and pore over land transaction records. Besides, my intention was not to write the unwritten scholarly biography or densely footnoted history, but simply to tell Fraser's story in a way that would bring him and his times to life for readers in this largely unremarked bicentennial of the real birth of BC.

Soon the dearth of primary documents forced me toward secondary sources, but these too proved disappointing. Most historians—apart from Lamb, who collected his transcripts from original documents—provided only a few paragraphs here, an aside there, at best a page or two reciting the known facts.

In Fraser's era, records were kept in two ways. They existed as stories in an oral tradition, passed from generation to generation until the details were burnished away and only the mythic shape remained, sometimes conflated with different events. Or they might be handwritten with a quill pen and preserved in handmade ledgers; these were heavy, subject to the ravages of mice, mildew, fire, accident and the human tendency for later generations infatuated with new technology to toss them out as useless clutter. When the great Victorian explorer, linguist and ethnologist Richard Burton died, for example, his wife—offended by some of his accounts—burned many of his surviving unpublished papers.

A new bookcase in my office gradually filled to overflowing with more than 350 books, some in French, a few in Spanish, many gleaned from elsewhere in my library of British Columbiana, some hunted down and ordered by email from antiquarian booksellers on the other side of the continent, a few photocopied at libraries that held noncirculating copies of rare limited editions.

In coil-backed notebooks, more than fifteen hundred handwritten pages accumulated. I jotted my entries in libraries, museums, special collections and used bookstores. I scribbled in coffee shops, in canoes, sitting on logs beside old fur brigade trails, sheltering from sleet in the stone ruins of a long-abandoned fort and sitting in beer parlours where somebody taking notes was the funniest thing anyone had seen for a long time. Once, pulled over on the shoulder of a dirt road suddenly turned to gumbo, I made notes as I waited out a torrential rainstorm.

Photocopied references went into one, then two, then four bulging D-ring binders, a lawyer's accordion file and a banker's box. Photographs gradually expanded to fill 130 pages of a 200-page portfolio, then 222 megabytes of digital computer files.

Still the man proved as elusive as the Scarlet Pimpernel. We don't even have a verifiable likeness of Fraser, just a photograph of what was purported to be a portrait in the possession of a now forgotten family member who produced it in 1908 on the hundredth anniversary of the explorer's famous voyage to the Pacific. Mystery also surrounds the fate of journals and letters known to have survived the explorer's death.

Lamb recounts a story from early BC librarian and historian E.O.S. Scholefield, who in turn tells the tale of Simon Fraser's son John, then working prospects in the Cariboo goldfields. John Fraser was a close friend of prominent Victoria resident Dr. Israel Wood Powell, after whom both Powell River and Vancouver's Powell Street are named.

On a visit to Victoria sometime between 1863 and 1865, Scholefield says, young Fraser gave to Powell for safekeeping a thick bundle of his late father's journals and letters. Powell kept the papers for years after the son's death at Barkerville but eventually turned them over to Fraser's relatives in eastern Canada. A granddaughter apparently eventually sold them through a dealer in Ottawa, but details of the deal could never be determined. No one knows where the invaluable documents went. Possibly they reside in a private collection held by someone who doesn't know their historic value. Perhaps, like Burton's papers, they've since been destroyed through ignorance or neglect.

Luckily for posterity, Fraser's own handwritten account of his voyage of exploration survived, and the Toronto Public Library acquired it. American historian H.H. Bancroft had transcripts made of some fragments from the lost bundle of papers during a visit to Victoria in 1878, although Lamb laments the ignorance and lack of interest by the hired copyist, who filled them with errors.

Fraser's few surviving letters show he could be amiable, but he was also as tough as nails and ruthless when necessary. He expected results, and he got them. He was a natural leader, born to the hard and sometimes brutal life at the far edge of the known. He had a flinty eye for the bottom line but could be smooth, too, and on occasion must have been a fast talker—and quick to seize the calculated risk if the potential payback looked good. And he was a patriot. He was already sixty-one when he joined a volunteer infantry unit raised during the Rebellion of 1837, suffering a serious lifelong injury on active service. Yet, however reasonable, much of this is admittedly a writer's speculation.

If Fraser's character seems elusive, the formal record offers eloquent hints. He'd started in his era's equivalent of the stockroom—apprenticed at sixteen as a clerk to a North West Company fur warehouse in Montreal—but by the time he set out

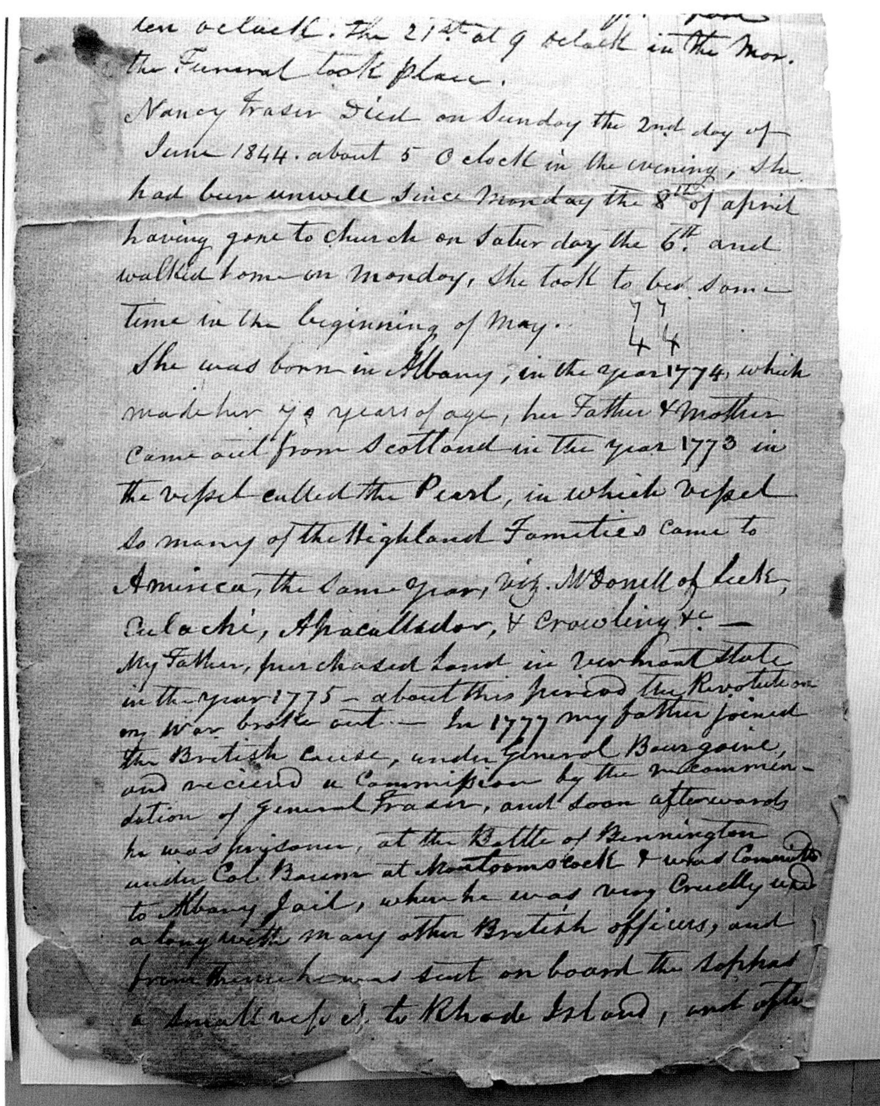
ten oclock. the 21st at 9 oclock in the Mor.
the Funeral took place.
Nancy Fraser Died on Sunday the 2nd day of
June 1844. about 5 Oclock in the evening, She
had been unwell Since Monday the 8th of april
having gone to church on Saturday the 6th and
walked home on Monday, She took to bed Some
time in the beginning of May.
She was born in Albany, in the year 1774, which
made her 70 years of age, her Father & Mother
Came out from Scotland in the year 1773 in
the vessel called the Pearl, in which vessel
So many of the Highland Families Came to
America, the same year, viz. McDonell of Leek,
Culachie, Aberchalder, & Crowlinny &c. —
My Father, purchased land in Vermont State
in the year 1775 — about this period the Revolutionary War broke out — In 1777 my father joined
the British Cause, under General Bourgoine,
and recieved a Commission by the recommen-
dation of General Fraser, and soon afterwards
he was prisoner, at the Battle of Bennington
under Col. Baum at [illegible] & was Committed
to Albany Jail, where he was very Cruelly used
along with many other British officers, and
from thence he was sent on board the [illegible]
a small vessel to Rhode Island, and after

This fragile document in Simon Fraser's swooping copperplate hand, includes details of his father's fateful enlistment with a Loyalist regiment during the American Revolution. *Ian Lindsay/Vancouver Sun*

for what he would call New Caledonia, he had already risen to a full partnership in one of the biggest, most profitable corporations of the day. Think of a grade ten student now dropping out of school to take a keyboarding job with Microsoft, who within a decade emerges as a partner.

At McLeod Lake, in the uncharted heart of a largely unexplored continent, his pale blue eyes ever alert for warning signs of an ambush or the onslaught of a startled grizzly bear—both ever-present possibilities—this aggressive young entrepreneur launched the daring enterprise from which modern BC would be forged.

Yet while this young businessman ensured the rise of this province, I found Fraser little more than a footnote to much of the formal work by both academics and popular historians. The exceptions were Lamb and Senator L.F.R. Masson—a distant relative of Alexander Mackenzie—who in 1889 published important early fur-trade documents.

A sketch of the explorer's life is included in an American museum curator's book published in 1950, but John Spargo's treatment runs to a scant thirty-nine pages, and most of the narrative bears upon Daniel Williams Harmon, an American contemporary in the fur trade.

A thirty-two-page Canadian pamphlet by Vernon Llewellyn Denton sold for ten cents in 1928. A few popular kids' books, by the likes of historian Walter Noble Sage, mostly focus on Fraser's dramatic journey to the sea. Vancouver's Barbara Rogers diligently sifted through obscure and fragmentary records—she found four Simon Frasers simultaneously active in the fur trade, not to mention the confusing fact that several famous relatives shared the patronym—and assembled four well-researched articles for the *British Columbia Genealogist* in 1989 and 1990.

But the man who founded BC generally commands only a few pages here and there, even in major works such as Margaret Ormsby's sweeping *British Columbia: A History* or Peter Newman's extraordinary, wonderfully accessible multivolume history of the fur trade and its role in shaping today's Canada, *Company of Adventurers.*

To be sure, many British Columbians know that our great, defining river bears Fraser's name. If we check the *Gazetteer of Canada,* we discover thirty-six other geographical features in the province do too. We know he has a university named for him, an elementary school, a street or two, and less directly, a health authority, a sustainable stewardship organization, a conservative think tank and a famous—or infamous, depending upon point of view—beer parlour.

I went up the mountain to Simon Fraser University to read some of the original letters held there, trying to glean some sense of the man from the elegant, sweeping copperplate script on documents that his fingers had touched so long ago. Archivist Frances Fournier told me, however, I was the first person to ask to see them since they'd come into the collections decades earlier.

Even after a drowsy morning in a silent library, straining to decipher a fading alien hand that neatly lined family connections and lineages onto crumbling pages older than Canada, I still nursed that vexing question I'd started with—just who was Simon Fraser, anyway?

He seems a curious candidate for nonentity, particularly considering the high drama of his life and the way its adventurous arc parallels the momentous events that shaped our province, our country and our continent.

The Highland clearances by which Scottish clan society was shattered and dispersed after a failed Roman Catholic rebellion against Protestant English rule, the American Revolution, the Napoleonic Wars, the Loyalist migrations that reconfigured Canada, the War of 1812, the sequential eclipse of France and Spain and

Russia in North America, the meteoric ascendance of the United States, its own Civil War and bloody campaigns of ethnic cleansing against native Indian nations, the violent annexation of territory from Mexico, bushwhackings and blood feuds in a wild Canadian west that makes the American myth seem tame by comparison, the rise and fall of fur empires on a lawless frontier, the Industrial Revolution, the destruction of the bison (often popularly called the buffalo) and the settling of the Prairies, the loss of the Oregon Territory, the steps leading to the eventual union of New Caledonia with Vancouver Island to create British Columbia: all these occurred within the span of Simon Fraser's long and eventful—yet remarkably obscure—life.

His predecessor in exploring the far northwest, Mackenzie, is justly lionized as the first to reach the Pacific Ocean overland in 1793. Thompson, the buckskin-clad geographer who explored and mapped most of the western Prairies and the Rocky Mountains, deserves his new biography. Fraser's American counterparts, Meriwether Lewis and William Clark, who also crossed the Rockies—from the Missouri River to the mouth of the Columbia—in 1805, attract a great national clamour in the US.

Library of Congress catalogues list more than ten thousand titles that refer to Lewis and Clark. Run a simple keyword search there for Simon Fraser and you get a handful—mostly referring to the university of the same name.

Some say Fraser's place in history is minor because his own great voyage of exploration, the journey that confirmed that the Fraser and the Columbia were different rivers—immensely important industrial intelligence in its time—was a commercial failure. He didn't find a quick, viable river route from the fur-rich Interior to the sea, which would have meant faster shipment and vastly greater profitability. But neither did Mackenzie. Fort Clatsop, where Lewis and Clark wintered at the Columbia's mouth, was soon abandoned.

The settlement at Trout Lake Post, however, which Fraser founded several months before Lewis and Clark put up their defensive palisades, still exists. Later named Fort McLeod in honour of Fraser's friend, it justly claims to be the oldest continuously inhabited European settlement in what is now Canada's westernmost province.

For the epicentre of so much history, McLeod Lake is a humble place today. It has a combined gas station, liquor outlet, post office and general store in an old Hudson's Bay Company building that was moved more than half a century ago from the original site on the west bank of the river outlet to Highway 97.

Up a spur road lies the Tse'Khene settlement of McLeod Lake, a tidy, forward-looking community of several hundred that coalesced when nomadic hunting bands settled near the fur-trade post. The main industry is now logging through the band's Duz Cho company, although prospects for oil and gas development seem increasingly bright.

Yet what began here two hundred years ago in this quiet, dispersed settlement

First Nations bands travelled among seasonal camps to exploit available resources but later settled in villages, often associated with fur-trade posts like McLeod Lake. *Image I-58057 courtesy of Royal BC Museum, BC Archives*

of about 250 souls, most of them Tse'Khene as in Fraser's day, would lead to the economic powerhouse that pumps out wealth on a scale that even the explorer's wealthiest senior partners could not have imagined.

When officers of the North West Company instructed Fraser to set up business on the western side of the Rockies, the bustling metropolis of Montreal had a population of fewer than ten thousand, smaller than present-day Parksville. New York City was about the size of present-day Prince George—minuscule in comparison to the more than four million people who now inhabit the province.

The real provincial gross domestic product for BC in 2005, for example, was more than thirteen times greater than the real GDP for the entire United States in 1805. Today, BC's real GDP is close to four times that of the entire United Kingdom two hundred years ago.

It was from the tiny post on Trout Lake—in the region Fraser named New Caledonia after a romanticized homeland that people of Scots ancestry like him knew only from stories—that he would establish Fort St. James and Fort Fraser, which would in turn spawn Fort George, Fort Alexandria, Fort Kamloops, Fort Langley and Fort Victoria. This network of trading posts became the sturdy framework for permanent communities upon which the muscle and sinew of BC's economy outside the Lower Mainland would grow.

From here Fraser would later mount his unsurpassed reconnaissance down the turbulent river that bears his name, all the way to tidewater and back in a stunning seventy-one days. Most of us would find this feat daunting even with outboard engines, metal-skinned canoes and trailers to assist on the portages.

Other factors shaped BC, of course. These included the geopolitical jockeying of British and Spanish empires at Nootka Sound, the struggle by a newly independent United States to wrest control of the territory north of California from the despised British, the waxing and waning of Russian imperial influence on the north coast, the discovery of coal on Vancouver Island that rendered it a vital supply depot in the Pacific just at the time the powerful Royal Navy changed from sail to steam, and the great gold rush that flooded up the Fraser River in 1858.

But we can safely say that the moment Fraser landed on the north end of what is now McLeod Lake and decided to build a permanent trading post, he set in relentless motion the commercial events from which our province would fashion itself.

Eventually I laid aside my books and papers and turned to the land for my sense of the elusive Simon Fraser. Since my search had to start somewhere, I decided the narrow, windy point where the young explorer first stepped ashore was the place to begin his story. The auburn-haired explorer's long, eventful life seemed an ideal metaphor for this important thread in the creation myth from which we tirelessly braid the rich, complex and pluralistic tapestry of our present.

As creation stories go, BC's is dramatic. In an immediate sense, it sprang from a bitter struggle among powerful merchants for domination of North America's fur trade, the largest and most lucrative industry of its era. That struggle also resonated with sectarian strife between Protestants and Roman Catholics, long-simmering animosities between Scots and English rooted in the Jacobite rebellions of the eighteenth century, England's subsequent dismantling of Scotland's clan system and the driving of Highlanders into wholesale emigrations.

Many displaced Scots wound up in the New World. As independent traders, there they banded together to form the North West Company and quickly wrested much of the fur trade from the Hudson's Bay Company, an English enterprise with an exclusive royal charter to trade in Rupert's Land, the vast watershed surrounding Hudson Bay. The Nor'Westers competed by going farther into unknown country, taking greater risks and being hardier in harsh conditions.

Simon Fraser and his companions seized the business initiative by going to the Indians rather than waiting for the Indians to come to them. They set up distant forts and intercepted the highest quality furs before they could reach the Hudson's Bay traders, shipping them back to Canada along their own immense, intricate and improbable transportation network of rivers and lakes. Ultimately the Scottish upstarts from Montreal cut deeply into English profits and triggered a growing tension between the corporate giants.

All this took place in the midst of a larger matrix of tensions. A collision of global empires and their geopolitical interests was reconfiguring the world. The British, the French, the Spanish, the Russians and the United States—that fusion of former colonies that had emerged from the American Revolutionary War—all

Author Stephen Hume beaches his canoe on McLeod Lake not far from where it empties into the Pack River at the windy point where Simon Fraser established British Columbia's first permanent European settlement.
Mark Van Manen/Vancouver Sun

jockeyed for control of territories that in some ways were as distant from their capitals as the dark side of the moon.

But that was then. My search was in the present.

As I drove Highway 97, winding north from the quintessential pulp mill town of Prince George through the northern Rockies to Hudson's Hope, Fraser's landing point on McLeod Lake seemed a hopelessly unpretentious birthplace for such a huge economic engine.

Today a dusty, nondescript little historic cairn rests in a patch of weeds on the highway margin, flanked by the raw earth of a pullout for heavy equipment, gas pumps and the small general store. Inside I got directions to what remains of the HBC fort that succeeded the North West Company post first established by Fraser. It lay just off the spur road to the Tse'Khene community of McLeod Lake.

When I first visited, the historic site sign had rotted off its supports. I retrieved it from the lank grass and propped it up against the whitewashed board-and-batten siding of the Hudson's Bay Company ice house, cool and quiet in a meadow loud with bees.

Some distance behind me, a black bear browsed on green shoots in a slough. If I'd known she had a pair of cubs in the underbrush, I wouldn't have been quite so cavalier about getting out of my car and walking down to the breezy point where Fraser had landed two hundred years ago.

The old cemetery I passed on the way was so overgrown that only the white tops of the few century-old grave markers peeped above the waving grass. Davitt Fisher, who died September 1, 1904, aged eight and his brother, Peter, who died December 14, 1905, aged eleven—they were a mystery for another day. Farther out on the point, where the original fort had stood, piles of trash surrounded an abandoned shack, its floors littered with garbage and debris. Even here, standing where he had once stood, I had no real sense of his presence and no clear answer to my question: Who was this largely uncelebrated founder of BC?

Out there, the lake darkened as it had for him on that earlier afternoon. Shadows pooled blue and long at the forest's edge. When I left, the chunky sound of my car door slamming echoed across the lake, spooking the bear and her cubs.

If I hoped to find my answer in the landscape, I decided, I'd have to turn east—more than five thousand kilometres southeast as the crow flies—and search for Simon Fraser in the distant country place where he was born.

Simon Fraser

2

IN THE CRADLE OF REVOLUTION

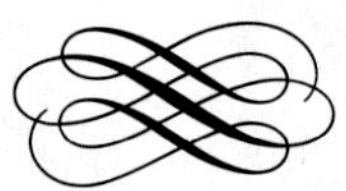

A blade of the palest silver, daybreak slides between velvety heavens and the dark rim of Vermont's Green Mountains just as the dawn chorus erupts. These songbirds, nestled in sugar maples, hickory and butternut trees, thickets of witch hazel and other unfamiliar shrubs of the eastern woodland, have been waiting out the chilly night with me.

There is an eerie, almost orchestral quality to that wall of sound. It belies the plunge in songbird populations down the entire Atlantic seaboard of the United States as pollutants accumulate and habitats erode. Indeed, this symphony of bird calls seems strangely oversized for a countryside that to me appears so small. These "mountains" would barely qualify as foothills back home. We'd call the "rivers" creeks. And the flora and fauna feel alien to a visitor from the brooding silence of New Caledonia's boreal forests where the grizzly and the raven rule.

My search for Simon Fraser had led me to the far side of the continent and into a historical sensibility as different from mine as the terrain east of the Rockies is from the western reaches. His presence seemed as ephemeral here as elsewhere.

Mapletown no longer exists in any real sense. These shadowed fields and the dim resonance of a name on a road sign are all that linger from a complicated past. For some it hearkens to a golden age of liberty and ideals, for others, just more empty echoes of greed and hypocrisy.

In BC our historic sense revolves around the fur trade and the gold rush, Spanish captains and British admirals, American hustlers and Haida chiefs, railway tycoons and immigrants from Asia. Here in the hinterlands of New York and Vermont, it revolves around philosophical arguments from the Age of Reason. The big exhibition at the small-town museum just up the road is entitled Independence of Thought, Freedom of Speech—although I note the roadsides are festooned with identical yellow ribbons and signs that say Honk 4 R Troops, while the *Bennington Banner* reports a student has just been sent home from school for wearing a T-shirt with an antiwar message on it. Free speech for some but not for others—Simon Fraser would identify with that irony. In some ways, with its lip service to ideals of individual liberty in the midst of a crude public insistence upon conformity and like-mindedness, the present evokes the conflicted past of Fraser's childhood.

This was the crucible of the American Revolution that reconfigured the political and economic future of North America. The struggle scarred Fraser's early life and propelled him into the career that would create BC. I was soon to discover just how deeply Fraser's own birth pangs were entangled with those of the newly minted American republic.

Bennington, Vermont, a few kilometres from where Simon Fraser was born, painted in 1791, six years after the Fraser family fled persecution for Canada. *Ralph Earle, Bennington Museum*

On twisting, frequently unmarked backcountry roads, I had travelled into upstate New York. Then, on my final day, I'd risen in the wee hours and made my way here. Now I waited out the night in a quixotic attempt to witness this landscape as it might have appeared to Fraser. I wanted to sense the little-changed shape of hills and valleys as they emerged into first light from a primordial darkness that I'd persuaded myself could symbolize both his murky past and the great chronometer of the heavens.

It proved a vain endeavour. Just a few hours' drive down the Hudson River from here was the twenty-four-hour illuminated throb of New York City, Newark and Jersey City. A few hours to the southeast lay Boston, and to the north Montreal. To the west were Albany, Syracuse and Buffalo. Unlike the skies above Fraser's world of tiny, scattered settlements lit only by fire, the stars in my firmament competed with the blinking lights of red-eye shuttles inbound with their cargos of bleary business suits for Kennedy and LaGuardia airports. And where his stars glittered like crystals, mine were dimmed by an irreducible habitation glow from more than fifty million people who now inhabit the northeastern United States.

BC's great explorer was American by birth, so I had come here, to the real heartland in which the US was formed. Its industrial muscle made possible its present status as the most awesome military and economic power the world has seen. I'd timed my arrival for May 20, the day he was born in 1776, hoping to see the place as his family must have seen it as they rose to tend their livestock. Their farm was little more than a hardscrabble clearing notched into the edge of a wild and precarious frontier.

Exactly how many of Fraser's siblings were on the farm when he was born is unclear. His brother William, the oldest, was in his late twenties and already homesteading for himself. His sister Nancy, born in Albany in 1774 and still a toddler, was certainly there. So was another older brother, Angus, who is identified in later records. We can be sure that his mother, Isabella Grant was there. Or was it Isobel? The spelling changes. The educated and literate daughter of a minor Highland aristocrat who had married at eighteen, she was forty-two when Simon, her ninth child, was born.

The average life expectancy for women at the time was thirty-five. On the North American frontier, five of every thousand otherwise healthy pregnant women died in childbirth, and about 30 percent of their children failed to reach the age of twenty-one. Even today, with the wonders of modern obstetrics, pregnancies over forty are considered high-risk. Isabella Grant had two in quick succession in the absence of any medical care that we would consider remotely adequate.

For Fraser's remarkable mother, daughter of the Laird of Daldregan, the land must have seemed vastly different from the domesticated valley bottoms of Scotland. Much of it had yet to be wrested from the forest, still inhabited by fierce predators and powerful warring tribes.

The American part of my quest for Simon Fraser had actually begun not here in New York, but across the state boundary in Bennington, Vermont. In the few surviving papers found in Fraser's own hand, some notes say he was born in Vermont not far from Bennington. I'd begun by combing through records housed in a silent library that smelled of parchment and old leather bindings. Its ceiling-high bookshelves held New England directories dating from the seventeenth century. Furthermore, John Spargo, a curator of the Bennington Museum who retired half a century ago, had gathered scraps of information and correspondence regarding Fraser. He'd mentioned these in his obscure, idiosyncratic but nonetheless fascinating little book, *Two Bennington-born Explorers and Makers of Modern Canada.*

Today this sleepy colonial town is a small community, about the size of Summerland. It lies in a broad, flat valley surrounded by sheltering hills, with Mt. Glastenbury to the north and Mt. Greylock to the south. Mature maples and chestnut trees line its streets, and the town is an interesting jumble of architectural styles. Buildings from the prerevolutionary era still stand. Georgian portico gives way to early Victorian gingerbread, which in turn yields to industrial robber-baron ostentation and finally postmodern cubes of brick and glass.

Superficially the town resembles one of those nostalgic Norman Rockwell paintings of New England, the kind of place where the high school sprinter makes the local newspaper for finishing ninth in the hundred-metre final. The *Banner* devotes half a page to that day's lunch menus in school cafeterias: At Sacred Heart, cheeseburgers; at Grace Christian, fish sticks; at Shaftsbury, Sloppy Joes with peas; at Mt. Anthony, chicken fajitas.

Yet if the town today seems tranquil, even bucolic, in Bennington many of the events took shape that led to rebellion against British colonial authority and eventually to civil war. This would force Fraser's ultimate emigration to Canada.

Ethan Allen and the Green Mountain Boys, one of the tough citizen militias that played a key role in the American Revolution, gathered here and plotted resistance in the Catamount Tavern. They were angry at a deepening dispute over the legitimacy of land titles. Homespun democrats from New Hampshire who had settled themselves on the frontier defied staunch Tory monarchists from New York who considered the pioneers squatters and by nature "vulgar, insolent, cunning and litigious."

Before 1760 the region had been largely depopulated by a century of bloody raids and counter-raids up and down Lake Champlain and the Mohawk Valley by the French, the British and various Indian confederacies. "Indian Massacre Road" still wanders across the map, and the gruesome butchering of Dutch settlers at Schenectady by French and Hurons stands as one of the more appalling atrocities in the sorry annals of warfare.

Land grants on this remote frontier had initially been made by Benning Wentworth, the colonial governor of New Hampshire, described by his counterpart in

Massachusetts as a "contemptible simpleton" who made his money selling booze and gunpowder and shocked society by marrying a beautiful young serving girl while in his dotage.

"He was such a scoundrel," Bennington's friendly and extraordinarily well-informed librarian Tyler Resch told me with a laugh. He was dapper in his blue shirt and tan chinos, clearly the master of his archive. "He was so scandalous nobody has written a biography, because everything he did was underhanded and illegal."

Not surprisingly, Governor Wentworth's authority to make grants was subsequently challenged by the prosperous landed gentry, expanding up the Hudson River valley from New York. When King George III granted legitimacy to New York grants at the expense of those handed out by New Hampshire's disreputable governor, secessionist settlers from what is now Vermont went on a rampage. They burned barns, pulled down fences, tore the roofs off houses and intimidated the "Yorkers" who claimed title on the basis of the British Crown's ruling.

Things became so turbulent that Gen. Thomas Gage, commander-in-chief of British forces in North America, was sent to restore order. Soldiers were slain in an exchange of fire with the insurgents. So in 1766, almost a decade before the mythic "shot heard round the world" at Lexington, the shooting war had already begun over a series of land grabs right where Fraser's father chose to settle his large and growing family.

In that sense, the rebellion was well on the boil in Bennington by the time Allen mustered other secessionists in 1772 to form the Green Mountain Boys. This hardy militia would later surprise and capture the stone fortress at Ticonderoga from the British on Lake Champlain, one of the great morale-building propaganda coups of the conflict.

Another such event was a fierce battle in 1777 on the outskirts of Bennington. There a ragtag army of New England volunteers surprised and destroyed a large force of German mercenaries, Indians and Loyalists, setting the stage for the humiliating surrender of an entire British army at Saratoga a few weeks later and the entry of the French into the war on the side of the rebels. It proved a crucial turning point.

One who fought in the debacle at Bennington was the BC explorer's father, also named Simon Fraser. He'd been given a commission as captain, an odd appointment for a settler who'd been in the country for only three years and a soldier for less than six weeks. Perhaps his rapid promotion from lieutenant spoke more to clan connections and a military family than to personal prowess at arms—or perhaps it spoke to the same silver tongue that would later bless his youngest son in the fur trade.

Two of Simon Fraser Sr.'s brothers had served under Gen. James Wolfe in the conquest of Quebec. John Fraser had stayed on as a high-ranking official in Montreal with powerful army connections. Another kinsman, a brigadier-general also named Simon Fraser, commanded the British army's advance guard as it marched from Canada toward New York.

While planning the resistance that would so plague the British at Bennington, Allen had taken lodging at the Walloomsac Inn, where US presidents Thomas Jefferson and James Madison—contemporaries of Fraser who both later influenced his great western adventure—once took their rest. On my way into town, I paused outside the weathered, ramshackle old structure, one of the many bits of living history that endure from Fraser's time. Built in 1764, it was a working inn as late as 1990 and is still in use, although it served as a private residence when I passed by.

The Bennington Museum was open the day I pulled in and took a room at a motel just down the street, but the library was closed. So I spent a pleasant afternoon on the publisher's nickel taking in an exhibition of folk paintings by Anna Mary Robertson Moses.

Grandma Moses was born in 1860 during Simon Fraser's lifetime. She began supporting herself as a hired farm hand at the age of twelve, married another farm hand in 1887 and bore ten children before she began painting scenes from rural life at the age of seventy-eight. Her one-woman show in New York in 1940 caused a sensation, and she produced more than a thousand paintings and illustrations before she died at 101. It struck me that many of her portrayals of country life probably differed little from the experiences of Fraser's kin.

Then I took a stroll before supper through the town's leafy streets, admired the gleaming colonial-era architecture in the earliest part of town and stopped by the Old First Church. The earliest Protestant church in the state had convened as a congregation for the first time in 1762.

In this church a 1791 convention ratified Vermont's admission to the United States, making it the first state to surrender its sovereignty as an independent republic. It joined the original thirteen colonies that had declared their independence on July 4, 1776, when Fraser was still in his swaddling clothes, a baby just shy of seven weeks old.

In the cemetery I found the graves of seventy-five revolutionaries killed during the Battle of Bennington. A marker commemorated an unknown number of British redcoats and Hessian mercenaries who died of their wounds while being held captive at the meeting house. The prisoners' meals were provided by the Walloomsac Inn. There the hospitality ended. Those who died were unceremoniously tumbled into a mass grave. Many others killed in the fighting had already been tossed into an unmarked pit on the battlefield.

On a less combative note, I also came across the graves of the great American poet Robert Frost and his wife, Elinor Miriam White, continuing their cosmic journey, "Together wing to wing and oar to oar."

The next morning Resch found a 1779 map of the region and aided my attempts to locate the original Fraser homestead. We struggled to decipher from minuscule

In 1774, the Fraser homestead at Mapletown, New York, was a tiny notch on a violent frontier. Today it is tranquil farm fields and woodlands flanked by a highway bypass. *Christina Florada*/Vancouver Sun

copperplate script the locations of property owned by people more than ten generations earlier.

"It was very confused jurisdictionally at the time," Resch explained. "You can see the Vermont townsites are here and then the New York townsites are all jumbled in there, too."

The farm where Simon Fraser was born, it turned out, was right at the centre of all this confusion. It had been in New Hampshire before the revolution, but when the war ended, it wound up straddling the present boundary that separates New York from Vermont. The portion on which the original farm house had stood was just across the border in New York.

What that house had been like, nobody could say. Photographs of surviving eighteenth-century farm houses taken in the late nineteenth century indicate most rural homes of the period were probably rough but neat structures of hand-squared logs, yet others were finished with milled lumber and painted. These looked closer to contemporary suburban homes than the stereotypes of dime-store pulp fiction and its descendant, network television.

The Hoosick Township Historical Society plaque wrongly marks not the birthplace of Simon Fraser but the site of a trading post run by kinsman Hugh Fraser. *Christina Florada*/Vancouver Sun

Next we consulted a map showing today's roads, comparing them with the roads of 230 years ago. To help me find my way to Fraser's birthplace, Resch offered prosaic modern directions: head down secondary Highway 7 toward Troy and New York's capital city of Albany, look for an abandoned gas station and an old cemetery at an unmarked junction, turn right on East Hoosick Road, take a left on Mapletown Road and look on the right side just before the turnoff for Burgess Road. I did this and found myself navigating through a deeply rural quilt of rolling fields and rustling woods. Then I came to the modest birthplace of Simon Fraser.

A shade-dappled meadow made a small opening in the hardwood trees. Across the road, a little creek rose in a boggy bottom and chuckled away toward its ultimate confluence with the Hudson River, in Fraser's time the main transportation corridor to New York and civilization. Two huge lilacs drooped with blooms that scented the spring air.

At one end of the meadow, behind a thick hedge, stood a white clapboard house. The yard was weedy and overgrown, the veranda piled high with what looked like old furniture. A battered rural mailbox had Waller scrawled on one side. Nobody answered when I knocked. But I did find one indication that I was at the right spot. A rusted metal plaque in the roadside weeds marked the site where the explorer of the far Canadian west was born.

Marker or no marker, something wasn't right. This was too far from the New York–Vermont boundary. Historian W. Kaye Lamb said the records showed clearly that a large piece—close to a quarter of the Fraser farm—had been lopped off by the later settling of the border. Wherever the parcel was, it couldn't be more than a kilometre from the boundary and was likely much less.

I backtracked to the secondary road and took another road that paralleled the state border. Sure enough, it connected with a road that ran east as though it were an extension of Mapletown Road and then continued into Bennington County. Here I saw nothing but farm fields, brush, woods and wetlands, but logic argued that this must be the homestead site, about two kilometres east of the plaque.

Charles Filkins, curator of the Hoosick District Historical Society's museum, cleared up my confusion with matter-of-fact precision. He explained that the historical marker—put up for the US bicentennial celebrations in 1976—was misplaced. A local historian had mistaken Hugh Fraser, one of Simon's relatives who ran a trading post on the old Mapletown Road from 1750, for the explorer's father. Just to make sure things were absolutely clear, Filkins provided historical maps, a contemporary map that showed the present roads and satellite images courtesy of the US Geological Survey on which he marked the Fraser homestead.

"There was a house down there in 1854 but it was gone by 1862," Filkins told me. "It could have been a [log] cabin, but it could have been a [frame] house too. It would have been over a mile to the nearest sawmill, so my guess is that it would have been a cabin. Whatever the building was, it was gone by 1862.

"Simon Fraser got his land from a guy named Alexander Caulden, who had been the lieutenant-governor and the acting governor of New York," Wilkins told me when I phoned later for details. "He was the one who was in the squabble with Benning Wentworth over the New Hampshire land grants."

That helps explain some of his father's later troubles with the Vermont rebels, and perhaps his decision to side with the New York authorities from whom he leased his land. One thing is clear from the sparse available records—young Simon was born into a world of trouble.

Simon Fraser

3

SCATTERED POEMS AND FLYING FAMILIES

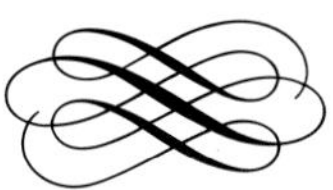

His father had left the Scottish Highlands with his wife, six children and 425 other clansmen, and sailed aboard the immigrant ship *Pearl* in 1773. After the Scots' successive rebellions to restore the Roman Catholic Stuart kings to the throne, the Protestant English were dismantling the clan system. They drove Highlanders into a global diaspora as indentured labour on plantations, into military service to expand the empire or as settlers to colonize frontiers where the English wanted a greater presence.

For an eighteenth-century voyage, the Frasers' passage must have been thankfully uneventful. It took them only six weeks to sail from Fort William on the west coast of Scotland to New York, a journey that frequently stretched into months if the weather was stormy.

Today we look back with astonishment upon the dangers of travel by sail, the foul conditions below decks, the wretched, weevil-infested rations at sea, the casual acceptance of inevitable casualties. Corpses were wrapped in canvas with a cannon ball, a last stitch of sailmaker's twine was passed through the nose to make sure they were really dead, and then they were consigned to the deep. In Simon Fraser's time, however, such vessels were the high-tech passenger jets of their day—an unbelievably swift and easy method of transportation in contrast to the slowness of travel by foot over rough, muddy, bandit-haunted roads. And it's all a matter of perspective. Travellers from the 1700s might look with equal astonishment and horror at the ease with which we accept the annual toll of deaths and maimings from automobile accidents.

Spargo's research at Bennington indicates that when Fraser arrived, he already had kinsmen in the area. One of his father's cousins had settled in 1764. About a year after disembarking, Simon Fraser Sr. leased 65 hectares (a quarter-section, or 160 acres) of land, 45 hectares (about 110 acres) of it already cleared. He cleared another five after taking possession.

The elder Fraser wasn't poor by the standards of the time. He'd paid the equivalent of more than forty thousand dollars in today's dollars for improvements that included a farm house and some outbuildings. One of the few surviving contemporary accounts—a claim for compensation incurred as a consequence of military service—numbers the Fraser farm's livestock at twenty-four sheep, twenty head of cattle that included six oxen for plowing, hauling and other heavy work, and three horses that included a colt. Chickens and pigs weren't mentioned, but were so essential to frontier life that they were almost certainly present too.

Simon Fraser Sr. had a classical education—"cultivated" is how one clan history describes his literary tastes—and so did his wife, Isabella Grant. In fact, according to one history of the Fraser clan, the family brought to America a library of rare old Gaelic literature collected by his mother. This offers a caution against making assumptions based on rustic appearances and stereotypes of untutored pioneers.

Yet life would have been arduous, particularly for Isabella and her daughters, whose tasks would have included carding, spinning and weaving wool for clothing, churning butter, washing clothes for a family of ten, making soap, making candles and educating the younger children in the absence of schools. The sons would have been clearing land, putting in subsistence crops, caring for the livestock and supplementing the larder with hunting and fishing.

Unfortunately for Fraser, his acquisition of property under New York title put him smack in the middle of the jurisdictional dispute with New Hampshire. Less than a year after taking residence, almost twenty-five hectares of his best cropland was declared part of what is now Vermont, and his New York title to it was voided.

Complicating matters was religion.

The Vermont secessionists were mostly New England Protestants of the same Puritan stock as Oliver Cromwell, who had beheaded Charles I. Indeed, a Moses Dunbar was arrested in Connecticut for converting from the Congregational to the Anglican faith and executed for treason in 1777. But the Scottish immigrants were Roman Catholics fresh from persecution by Protestants in their homeland for twice trying to restore the Stuart line to the throne. Many of their clansmen had subsequently enlisted in regiments such as the 71st and the 78th Fraser's Highlanders to show their loyalty and to ease the pressure on their families and kin. They were deployed to the far ends of the empire, the Frasers winding up in British North America.

It's not surprising, therefore, that when formal hostilities finally commenced, many of these systematically marginalized frontier Scots—Simon Fraser included—threatened and abused by their bellicose Protestant neighbours, chose to enlist with the British army sent to protect their land rights rather than joining the local militias that had been afflicting them.

In 1777 British Gen. John Burgoyne conceived a plan for driving from Montreal down Lake Champlain, the blood-soaked route of the French and Indian Wars, to link up with a British garrison at New York. Simon Fraser Sr. enlisted in July with the Queen's Loyal Rangers under a local commander, Lt. Col. John Peters. His eldest son William served in Montreal with Sir John Johnson's regiment, the King's Royal Regiment of New York. The elder Fraser's brother John had retired from the British army in Montreal, and his relative and neighbour, the trader Hugh Fraser of Mapletown, had fled there in 1776.

"Burgoyne was coming down from Canada. Some were for the King. Some were imbued with the spirit of the American Revolution. Some didn't know which way to go. It was a time of great uncertainty and turmoil," Resch explained.

Burgoyne planned to separate the New England rebels from the more southerly colonists, leaving his professional army to mop up at will. He advanced south with 10,000 men, including 1,000 Indians, Canadian militia units and two regiments recruited among local Loyalists. He recaptured Fort Ticonderoga and advanced steadily southward.

But the army moved slowly and consumed ten tonnes of supplies a day, all of it brought through hostile territory. Near Bennington, against the advice of both Brig. Gen. Fraser and Lt. Col. Peters, he divided his army. He sent the Indians and more than seven hundred regulars, mercenaries and Loyalists with Simon Fraser's father, promoted to captain—and according to family notes in his son's handwriting, now "Superintendant of Indians"—to capture military stores.

Instead of a small, easily overwhelmed garrison at a stores depot, they encountered fourteen hundred rebel soldiers from New Hampshire bolstered by six hundred of the Green Mountain Boys. The rebels were commanded by a seasoned veteran of wars with the French, Brig. John Stark. He rallied his troops with the cry, "There they are, boys! We beat them today, or Molly Stark sleeps a widow tonight!"

When I went to find the battlefield, the historic site was still closed for the season. I had to hike in, but I had the site completely to myself. The day was warm, and wildflowers nodded in the breeze. Standing at the spot where Fraser's father, his Loyalist clansmen and the Indians had faced the rebels, I tried to imagine the two withering volleys that had mowed down two hundred men in an instant, then the storming of redoubts on Hessian Hill that had overwhelmed the survivors in brutal hand-to-hand fighting.

The morning of August 16, 1777, had dawned stormy and ominous for the

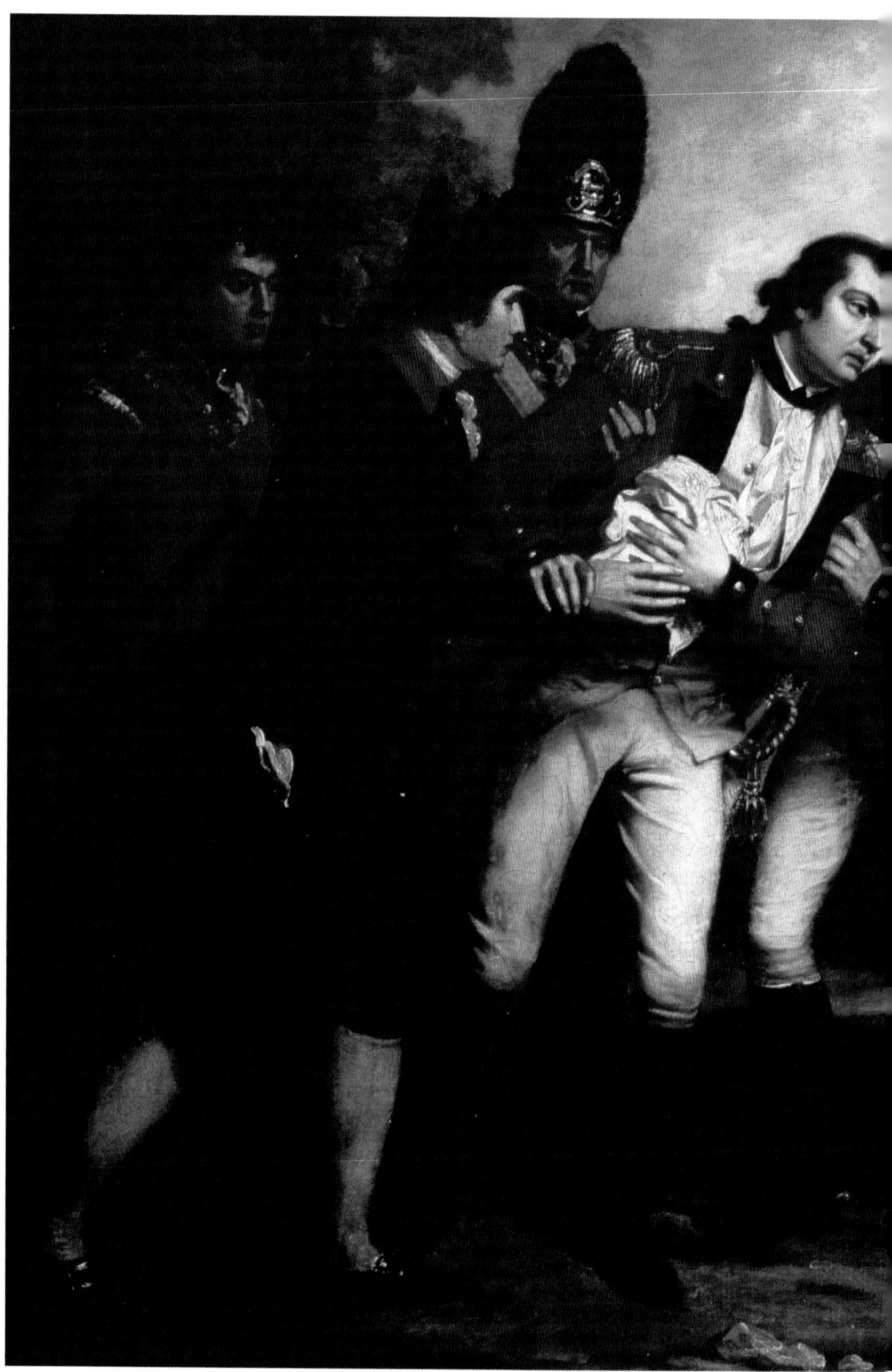

Brigadier-General Simon Fraser, warned General "Gentleman Johnny" Burgoyne that the American rebels could fight. He was slain by a sniper before the British surrendered. *Samuel Woodforde, Library and Archives Canada, accession number 1990-366xDAP, C-147401*

British army under the command of "Gentleman Johnny" Burgoyne that was marching down the Hudson River.

The campaign had started well, but things had begun to go awry. Burgoyne's army was moving much more slowly than planned and was short of supplies. A supporting force driving south from Lake Ontario had been forced to retreat. The army in New York that was supposed to come up the Hudson River had instead gone haring off to the south in hot pursuit of the rebels in Gen. George Washington's Continental Army.

A few days earlier, the newly commissioned Capt. Fraser's unit had been detached from the main army and sent toward the town of Bennington. Its mission was to capture and secure a storehouse reported to be full of supplies that Burgoyne's army now desperately needed. But the weather had not cooperated.

The previous day and all night, torrential rains had swollen the creeks and soaked the ground where Capt. Fraser and six hundred other troops had been ordered to dig in. They were preparing for an attack by what they had just learned was a brigade-strength force of rebels. The British expedition now learned it was outnumbered by more than three to one by American troops seasoned during the French and Indian Wars and earlier fighting in Boston.

Capt. Fraser had enlisted a month earlier with the Loyalist regiment raised by local settler John Peters. Now they were drawn up for battle just a few kilometres from the homestead on the New York–Vermont border where Fraser's wife, Isabella, waited anxiously with their children—including the youngest son, Simon, not quite fifteen months old. The civil war had come home with a vengeance.

Things had been difficult for Capt. Fraser for the past few days. He was nominally Superintendent of Indians but his commander, Lt. Col. Friedrich Baum, a mercenary hired by the British who spoke no English, had already sent a dispatch to Gen. Burgoyne complaining "the savages cannot be controlled; they ruin and take everything they please."

This was particularly galling since an additional objective of Baum's expedition away from the main army had been to raise the support of other Loyalists. Instead, as eyewitness John Wallace observed, "women and children are flying before the enemy with there Effects, women crying, sum walking . . . sum Rideing on horses with there Children at there Brests. Sum before, sum behind, tyed to there mothers."

In fact the assumption that more Loyalist support could be raised had been a subject of great contention within Burgoyne's general staff.

One local landholder—who stood to benefit from having a military road cut through his property—had assured Burgoyne that Loyalists outnumbered rebels five to one in the region and would join the cause instantly. Burgoyne thought the American rebels would not fight professionals.

Disagreement came from both Brig. Gen. Simon Fraser, a kinsman of Capt. Fraser and a veteran of North American campaigns, and Lt. Col. Peters, who had raised the Loyalist regiment that Capt. Fraser had joined. They'd seen the Americans fight before.

In an exchange sufficiently tumultuous to be remembered by those who overheard it, Burgoyne abruptly overruled the advice from his most experienced field officers and dispatched the expeditionary force. This included about two hundred German heavy dragoons who'd been forced to dismount for lack of horses but still carried long, cumbersome cavalry sabres that weighed more than five kilograms.

"I am ready to obey your orders, Gen. Burgoyne," Lt. Col. Peters had told his commander, "but we shall not return."

Now the expedition dug in to await attack by an overwhelming force.

What happened next was convincingly determined in 1989 when a team from the Division of Research and Collections of the New York State Museum undertook a remarkable survey. They combed hundreds of records for eyewitness accounts and analyzed a contemporary map of the British positions, drawn afterward by Lt. Desmaretz Durnford of the British Corps of Engineers.

They superimposed the young British officer's map upon the present landscape. Then they applied modern archeological and survey techniques to recreate both the events and the countryside that existed during the events of that fateful day 212 years before.

The result was *War over Walloomscoick: Land Use and Settlement Pattern on the Bennington Battlefield—1777*, published as Bulletin No. 473 of the New York State Museum. It represents an astonishing and utterly fascinating example of forensic history. I've relied on it to recreate a sketch of the events.

Thus we know, because the researchers walked through the events of the battle as recounted by survivors, that when the assault came, it caught the defenders of the Tory redoubt by surprise. The attackers had taken advantage of a small ravine that hid them from view until the last minute. The sound of their approach would have been drowned in the roar of streams in spate. When the rebels appeared, they popped into view right beneath the Loyalist's guns.

One eyewitness recalled getting off one hurried volley, then being overwhelmed in hand-to-hand fighting when the rebels, instead of firing back, charged up the hill and over the breastworks before the defenders could finish reloading.

Military experts later pointed out that trained British regulars could have reloaded and fired four volleys in the time available and that the inexperience of the Loyalist volunteers likely made the difference in outcome.

Survivors later recounted the fearsome noise of bullets shredding the underbrush, tree trunks and their companions, and the savagery of the fighting.

Surgeon J.F. Wasmus with the German unit, who took shelter behind a large oak tree while tending the wounded, reported "the cannon shot balls and grapeshots, sometimes to the right, sometimes to the left and then again forward into the bush . . . the enemy came rushing over our entrenchment and three quickly took aim and fired at me. I again fell to the ground behind the tree and the bullets were dreadful, whistling over and beyond me."

Lt. Col. Peters realized that the man who had just stabbed a bayonet into his left breast was his wife's cousin and an old school playmate. He nevertheless shot him dead.

Another account by one of the attacking force's officers tells how one rebel named William Clement parried a Tory bayonet thrust while he came over the redoubt "and drove his own through his opponent's eye and head with such force that the bayonet came off and remained in the Tory's head. When they buried the slain, the soldiers told Clement to take the bayonet out of the man's head, but he swore he would never touch it again, and the body was buried in that condition."

Capt. Fraser's Indians quickly abandoned a lost cause, slipped silently into the forest and returned to Burgoyne. The Tory loyalists ran, leaving more than half their contingent of 291 behind, either dead or wounded. The rebel attackers overran the German positions, mortally wounded the commander, and hunted down and killed or captured the survivors who sought shelter in the woods. There many of the wounded perished.

It was a poor country. The victors often stripped the dead and dying of their clothing and valuables, and for days after the battle the naked bodies of British and German soldiers were found.

When a relief column from Burgoyne's army arrived, it also was driven off in heavy fighting.

According to his explorer son's later accounts, Capt. Fraser was wounded and taken prisoner on the battlefield at Bennington. If he was indeed captured at the battle and not afterward as some accounts suggest, a large painting in the Bennington Museum shows what happened that day.

To the jeers of the rebels, the Tory survivors were roped together and prodded into line with bayonets behind a black servant or slave who was, to add to the symbolic humiliation of the vanquished, mounted on a horse. Then they were led away to a dreadful captivity under conditions that Capt. Fraser would not survive.

Where his body lies remains a mystery.

"The Battle of Bennington was a crucial engagement for morale—on both sides," Resch said. Rebel confidence soared while it dawned on the British that they were in serious danger of losing the war. A few weeks later Burgoyne, outmanoeuvred and outfought, surrendered most of his army at Saratoga.

Simon Fraser Sr., his family's papers insist, was wounded and captured on the battlefield along with 152 other Loyalist prisoners who were led off as the victors taunted them. But Spargo claims that local court records indicate he escaped and was arrested later on his farm. What's not in dispute is that he was thrown in prison. Like so many captives on both sides, he was so "ill-used" that, despite a petition from neighbours pleading for his release, he died there early in 1779.

Capt. Fraser's fate was not unusual for captives before the Geneva Convention. The British maintained prison hulks off New York where conditions were horrific, and many prisoners died of malnutrition and disease. The Americans did the same at Albany. At one Connecticut prison camp, the rebels confined their British captives in their own filth in the wet, cold, lightless shafts of an abandoned copper mine, twenty metres below ground.

Fraser's widow Isabella, in poor health and with seven children to fend for—her eldest son was in Canada serving with the British army—suffered dire consequences. American neighbours looted the farm and stripped it of its livestock and utensils, even its furniture. They destroyed her books and her rare old Gaelic poetry manuscripts.

There was little redress. In 1778 Massachusetts passed an act of banishment for Loyalists. In more remote regions, people took the law into their own hands. One New England Loyalist named John Roberts was simply strung up and left kicking as he strangled to death in front of his wife and ten children.

Shortly after Isabella Fraser's husband died in captivity, New York passed a law of forfeiture that forced the wives and children of absent Loyalists to leave their homes because the rebel colonies refused to support these destitute families.

It's a reminder that for all the deliberate myth making, the American Revolution was as much about greed and savage self-interest as it was about high-minded ideas. Farms were looted for provisions by both sides, households were appropriated to billet officers, and women and girls—left alone while the men were away fighting—frequently suffered violence.

In his iconoclastic *A People's History of the American Revolution,* Ray Raphael tells how Loyalists complained that when Flora MacDonald's daughters were apprehended in 1777, rebels put "their swords into their bosoms, split down their silk dresses and, taking them out into their yard, stripped them of all their clothing."

On the other hand, Raphael also cites a British officer who wrote back to Britain that his men were "as riotous as satyrs" and that "a girl cannot step into the bushes to pluck a rose without running the most imminent risk of being ravished, and they are so little accustomed to these vigorous methods that they don't bear them with the proper resignation." According to depositions cited by Raphael, a number of those expected to suffer rape by soldiers with the "proper resignation" were as young as ten.

Small wonder, then, that as the officers on both sides strutted and the armies marched and counter-marched, the roads were choked with women, children and old people in flight from both sides.

When the American Revolutionary War finally ended in 1783, Fraser's widow was fifty, already an old woman by the standards of her day, and in ailing health. But she prepared to emigrate again. Early one morning in the spring of 1784, with her seven surviving children—Simon was eight, Nancy was ten—Isabella began the trek to a difficult new life on an even wilder frontier.

As the light of dawn flooded over the sweet corner of New York where he was born so long ago—a place once steeped in a bitter history that's been burnished into softness by the passing centuries—my search for Simon Fraser now turned north, to Canada.

4

PORTAL TO THE WILD NORTHWEST

Once a rutted wagon track, Boulevard St-Joseph snakes through Lachine toward the incandescent pillars that tower above Montreal's old quarter. Each one houses a business or residential community larger in population than the whole city that stood there two hundred years earlier. Not until the early 1800s would Canada's second-largest city exceed nine thousand inhabitants.

Today what began as Ville Marie, a raw frontier village clinging to a precarious existence on the banks of the turbulent St. Lawrence River, is the glittering heart of North America's most sophisticated metropolis. The world's second-biggest French-speaking city is simultaneously Francophone and Anglophone, immigrant and native, American and European, oldest and newest, constantly energized and renewed by the urgent tensions and expectations of its complicated urban life.

And it was in Lachine, now a largely Francophone borough of close to forty thousand—one in three of them singles—that the next phase in my search for Simon Fraser took shape.

A lovely green strip park reclaimed from industry meanders between the boulevard and the river beneath leafy trees. On the sunny afternoon I arrived, grey-headed cyclists and pretty girls wearing in-line roller skates were gliding lazily through the park's cool, rustling corridor. Their path ran beside the quiet 181-year-old Lachine Canal, decommissioned with the opening of the St. Lawrence Seaway in 1959. Its

The Montreal from which Simon Fraser headed west to the fur trade in 1792, shown here in a painting by George Heriot, had a population of less than 9,000. *George Heriot, Library and Archives Canada, accession number 1989-470-5R, C-012755*

locks were the high technology of their day. They provided a crucial shipping link to the Great Lakes, ended the reign of the canoe on eastern waterways, and were a key to the economic future of Canada and the near-explosive development of the West.

There was even a nostalgic personal twist to my visit. My mother-in-law—lifelong fan of the Canadiens hockey team, as skilled with a witty riposte as Henri Richard was with the puck, still missed years after her death on Vancouver Island—was born here in 1915. Her birthplace reminded me of how this fractious country is knit together by blood and memory and entangled histories it frequently tries not to acknowledge.

Lachine resonates with such history. One night in 1689 just up the street, an Iroquois war party retaliated for earlier ill-judged attacks by slaughtering two hundred French settlers and carrying away another hundred as prisoners. They were never heard from again. And from this spot in 1682, René-Robert Cavelier, Sieur de La Salle, began a quixotic search for the Northwest Passage to China. Like Alexander Mackenzie's hopes a century later, La Salle's dream of an easy route to the Orient soon evaporated. Hence the name La Chine—French for China—bestowed on his settlement with cool irony by his contemporaries. Yet La Salle, like Mackenzie, Fraser and Thompson, did find a great new river. He followed the Mississippi to the

Gulf of Mexico, where he was murdered in a mutiny.

Subsumed eventually into Montreal's two centuries of urban sprawl, Lachine really owes its existence not to La Salle's obsessions but to the violent stretch of water that it flanks. The mighty St. Lawrence spills over a series of ledges in the bedrock, falling the height of a two-storey building over a descent of just five kilometres.

Heading downstream, even seasoned travellers found the rapids a terrifying prospect. For canoes heading upriver, they were impossible to negotiate. And so Lachine came into being at the top of the old portage, serving as a storage depot and expediting point for anyone embarking for the continent's distant interior along the ancient river routes. Samuel Champlain, Étienne Brûlé, the La Vérendryes—both father and sons—Pierre-Esprit Radisson, Peter Pond, Thomas Frobisher, Mackenzie, Thompson—all passed through Lachine.

At the head of these rapids squats a gloomy structure of stolid grey stone. It's not a pretty piece of architecture. The simple hipped roof and narrow, many-paned windows are tarted up with a red timber trim. This fails to disguise its Caliban-like contrast with the graceful, soaring lines and silver domes of the convent of the Sisters of St. Anne just across the boulevard. The nuns themselves are yet another link of flesh and blood connecting Quebec to distant British Columbia.

It was from here in March 1858 that sisters Mary of the Sacred Heart, Mary Angèle, Mary Lumena and Mary Conception were persuaded by Bishop Modeste Demers to open a school at tiny Fort Victoria on the opposite coast. They sailed for

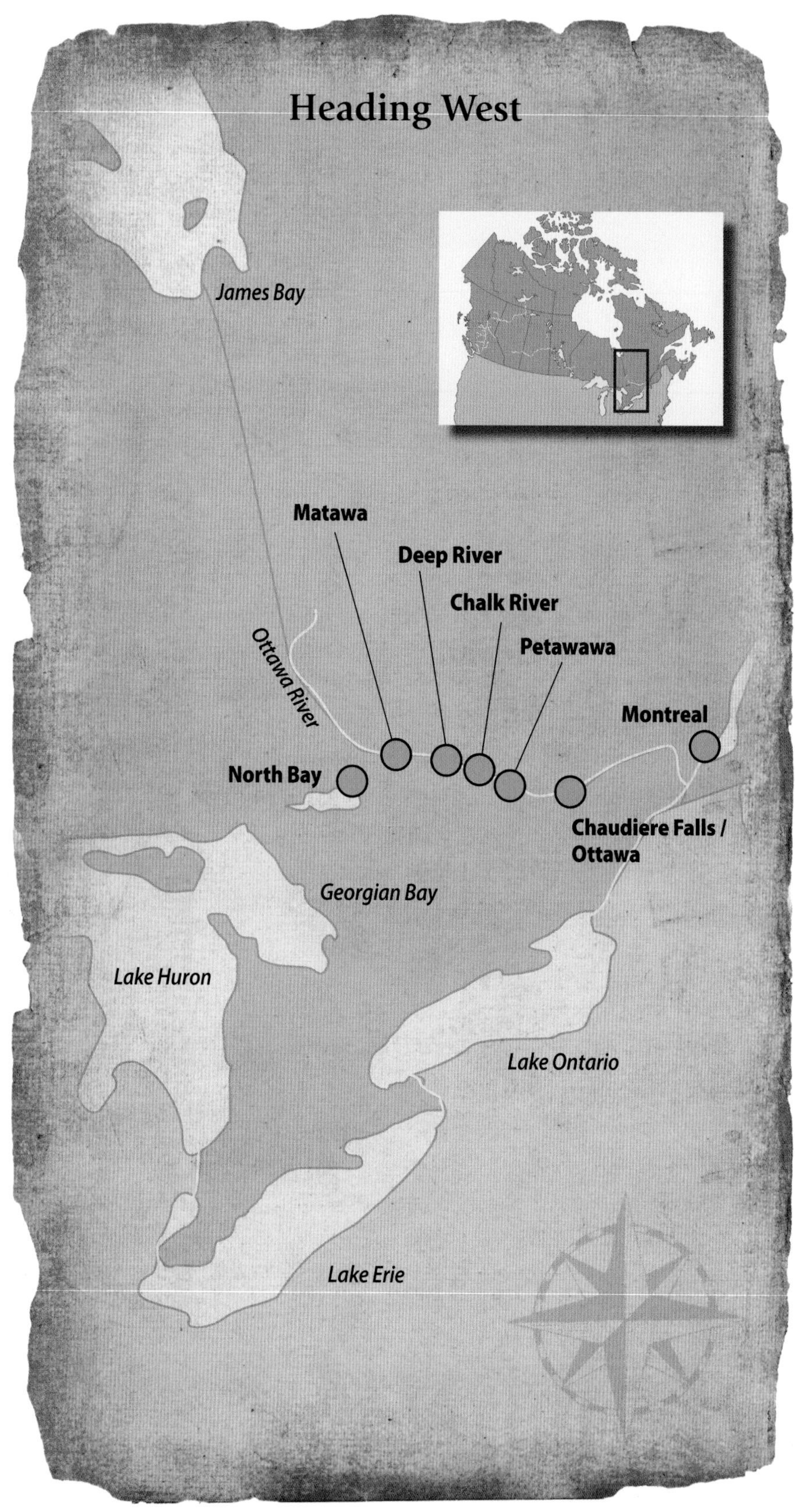
Heading West
James Bay
Matawa
Deep River
Chalk River
Petawawa
Ottawa River
Montreal
North Bay
Chaudiere Falls / Ottawa
Georgian Bay
Lake Huron
Lake Ontario
Lake Erie

Travellers portaged around Lachine Rapids on the St. Lawrence River, a terrifying barrier on the fur-trade route from Montreal to the uncharted interior of North America. *Julie Oliver/Ottawa Citizen*

This stone warehouse once owned by the North West Company still stands at Lachine. Spring brigades departed here for the head of Lake Superior while Simon Fraser was a schoolboy. *Pierre Obendrauf/Montreal Gazette*

Panama, crossed the isthmus with its clouds of fever-bearing mosquitoes, caught another ship north and arrived on Vancouver Island on June 5. By June 7, they were already teaching classes in a fourteen-year-old log cabin. That first schoolhouse, the forerunner of an education system that would culminate in more than a dozen colleges and universities, still stands just east of the Royal BC Museum in Victoria.

If the stone building across from the convent seems grimly utilitarian, that was its purpose from inception. Except for a period when it was inhabited by employees of the holy sisters, this was strictly an industrial site, a grimy, working warehouse in the fur trade.

The warehouse was Mile Zero on the fur-trade route that would lead Simon Fraser more than forty-five hundred kilometres across a trackless continent, all the way to the Backbone of the World—the Shining Mountains first seen by Europeans only thirty-three years before his birth—and then beyond them, beyond what we call the Rockies, into the still unexplored country he would call New Caledonia, to found what is now BC.

It was from there, from the precise spot that the swift and agile *canot du nord* and larger, heavily laden *canot de maître* of the North West Company's fur brigades set out each year for what the French traders called the *Pays d'en Haut*, the Upper Country—a wilderness where they obtained furs. They were bound for the western end of Lake Superior and the annual rendezvous with the wintering partners, those hardy traders who stayed year-round at the remote outposts. They came down from the north only to deliver their bales of furs, discuss strategy, do a little socializing and pick up the next season's supplies and trade goods.

The last surviving warehouse of the North West Company, whose dour presence

Lachine National Historic Site houses a major collection of fur-trade artifacts and demonstrates how demand in Europe created a globe-spanning mercantile colossus. *Lachine National Historic Site*

looms where the canoe brigades embarked each spring, is now a national historic site that houses an engaging museum on the fur-trade era.

A young Simon Fraser once walked here among rowdy voyageurs, fur-clad coureurs de bois, Indians in beaded leggings and what Peter Newman called "merchant princes" wearing brocaded waistcoats and turned-back cuffs. I came here for a quick lesson in history and economics.

First I examined the birchbark replica of a big *canot de Montréal* or Montreal canoe—another name for the *canot de maître*—built by César Newashish of the Attikamek people. Next I looked over the exhibits of baled pelts, crates of trade goods, barrels of lard and sacks of peas that would have comprised a typical cargo. Some eighteenth-century balance sheets gave me an idea of the financial and logistical magnitude of the enterprise.

Then park staffers Robert Bilodeau and Caroline Vezina gave me the short course in Fur Trade 101.

"This is the last warehouse left in Montreal, so it is really the last witness to that magnificent era," Bilodeau told me. "It's a small museum but it is densely packed with artifacts."

Dense was an understatement. I found examples of tools and weapons, explanations of aboriginal cultures, native Indian-European colonist relations, the transition from French to British control, a Victorian-era photograph of the Henley Inn just up the road where the voyageurs drank, an array of beaver hats depicting changing fashions, Sir Alexander Mackenzie's dinner plate decorated with his coat of arms, James McGill's gold medal commemorating his first journey to the northwest in 1766 and various interactive computer displays.

The story of the fur trade begins, as does much North American history, in class-conscious seventeenth- and eighteenth-century Europe and Asia where dress was a key indicator of social status.

Ermine, the white winter coat of the weasel, was a symbol of European royalty and was reserved for the bluest of the blue blood. Fashionable members of the elite and those who aspired to the upper crust opted for the next best thing. They adorned themselves with rare and exotic furs like lynx, white fox, mink and otter.

The quality, size and cost of hats manufactured from the most expensive felts had also made a public statement since late feudal times about the wearer's wealth and social rank. Because of its matting characteristics, beaver fur proved ideal for making the best felt.

There was a growing problem, however. Aristocrats and their bourgeois imitators from a rapidly expanding and upwardly mobile middle class of prosperous merchants, tradesmen and professionals had created an insatiable demand for furs that stripped Europe's forests and wetlands of fur-bearing animals.

All across Europe, the quantity and quality of available furs had slid into a steep and accelerating decline. Beaver, whose pelts provided the ultimate in durable, waterproof hat felt, were already wiped out in Western Europe. In Russia and Scandinavia, extinction loomed.

In a classic example of market economics, growing demand for shrinking supplies drove fur prices to astronomical levels that further emphasized the wealth of those buyers who could afford to wear them.

"Canada proved a treasure house of vast new supplies, and the furs from the north were best of all," Bilodeau said. "Due to the harsh climate, they were silkier and thicker."

As in Europe, the easily accessible resources were quickly exploited and exhausted, which encouraged merchants to finance the exploration of a dangerous and largely unknown interior, the upcountry or *Pays d'en Haut.*

What's more, the combination of demand and high prices made it economically worthwhile for traders, despite long turnaround times, to undertake the risks of travelling great distances to obtain prime quality furs and then transporting them thousands of kilometres to market.

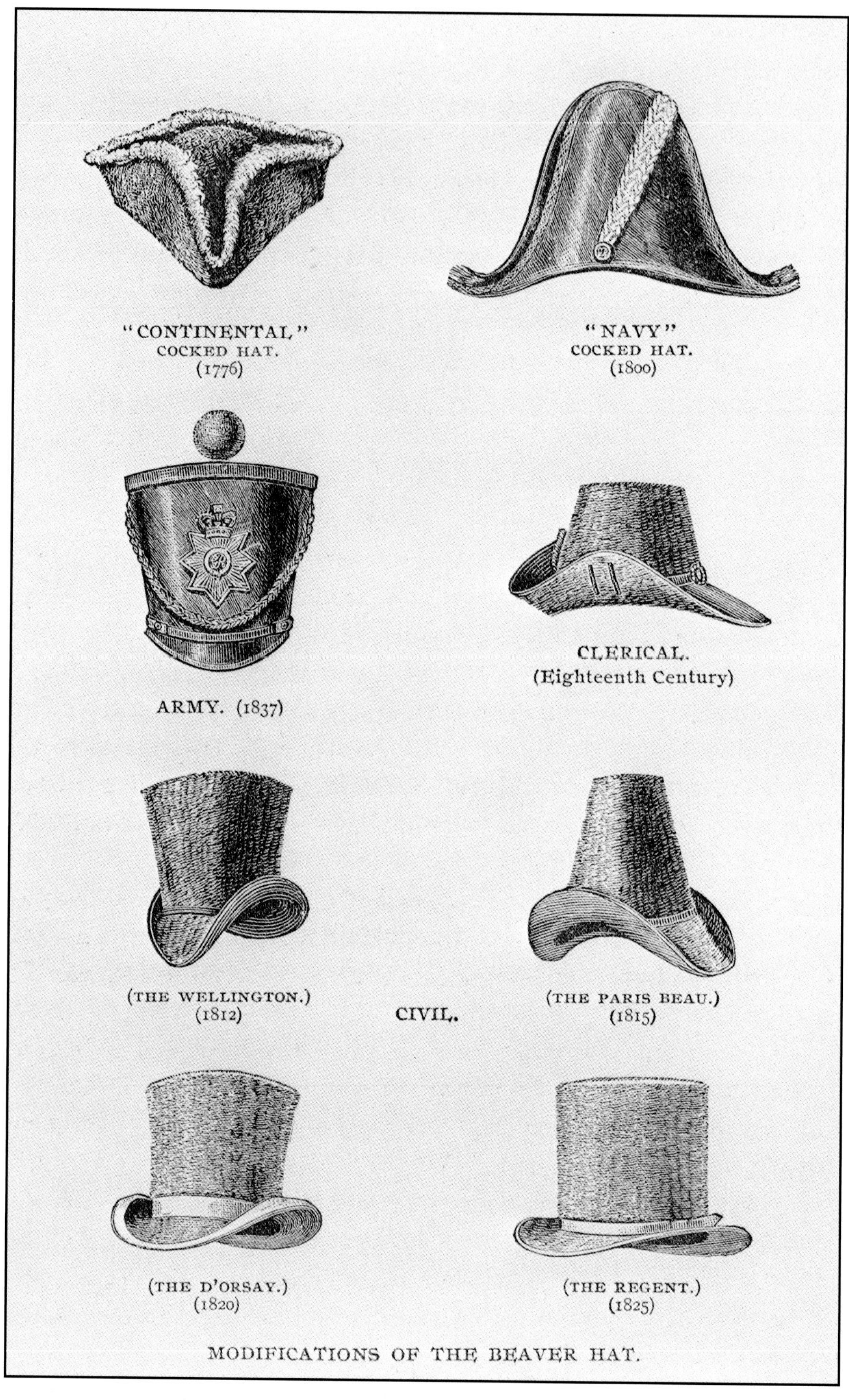

Changing fashions in headwear created insatiable demand for quality furs that generated fierce competition in North America, luring traders deeper into an unmapped and often hostile continent. *1892, Library and Archives Canada, C-017338*

Mackenzie outlined the lag time between investment and return for trading in the far west in 1798:

"The orders for the goods are sent to this country (England) 25th October, 1796; they are shipped from London, March, 1797; they arrive in Montreal, June, 1797; they are made up in the course of that summer and winter; they are sent from Montreal in May, 1798; they arrive in the Indian country, and are exchanged for furs the following winter, 1798–99; which furs come to Montreal September, 1799; and are shipped for London, where they are sold in March or April and paid for in May or June, 1800."

Nevertheless, profits could be so substantial that investors accepted the risks. When the fur trade was at its zenith and Fraser left Lachine for his apprenticeship in the Athabasca district, the value of a single bearskin sold in London was equivalent to the combined annual wages for more than a dozen housemaids. One otter pelt sold for as much as the combined annual wages of three footmen.

By comparison, in Montreal three beaver pelts would buy the services of a middle-seat canoeman for the whole voyage to Grand Portage and back. Twenty-one muskrat would pay a whole eight-man crew.

One bale of furs normally contained seventy beaver pelts, and the voyageurs' big *canot de maître* could typically carry sixty-four bales. Thus the value of 4,480 prime northern pelts in one shipment would be sufficient to cover the costs of all 1,120 canoemen that Mackenzie says the North West Company employed in 1798. And that year, Mackenzie says, the company shipped 106,000 beaver pelts, 17,000 muskrats and 2,100 bearskins.

The astonishing cost-benefit ratio explains both the traders' determination to accept the difficulties of trading over such enormous distances and their need to keep expanding into new territories where prime furs were abundant and relatively easy to procure.

It also explains the intense competition that arose between the Hudson's Bay Company—which had a royal charter to trade into Rupert's Land, the territory around the bay from which it took its name—and the North West Company, in which French, Scottish and a few American and English traders formed a Montreal-based cartel to trade beyond the HBC's jurisdiction and carry trade goods to Indians who had previously had to carry furs to coastal forts.

Trade requires two parties to the transaction. The aboriginal cultures of North America's interior were the other half of the equation, and the equation was much better balanced in Fraser's time than it is today.

For one thing, aboriginal populations had not yet fully experienced the series of epidemics—beginning with smallpox but including measles, influenza and tuberculosis—that would devastate and decapitate their societies.

Aboriginal peoples were still formidable in a military sense. They controlled the supply lines and had the capacity to cut them at any time they chose, they operated in their own territory while Europeans had to mount protracted expeditions to get there, and in many ways the traders relied upon them for sustenance during the long, harsh winters.

A modern stereotype portrays these aboriginal cultures entirely as victims of an unfair and predatory trade. But many were shrewd traders in their own right and didn't hesitate to play the competing North West Company and the Hudson's Bay Company against one another to their own advantage.

First Nations also clearly profited substantially from the enterprise, including through what today we would call technology transfers that yielded substantial productivity gains within their own economies.

It's a commonly advanced assumption, for example, that traders gave aboriginal people trinkets, liquor and weapons in exchange for extremely valuable furs.

True, the furs had a value for Europeans that aboriginal peoples did not share. On the other hand, the value to Europeans was so high that to win and keep trading clients, they had to provide goods that aboriginal suppliers wanted in exchange.

And what they wanted, according to an analysis done at the Canadian Museum of Civilization, was not booze, beads and bullets—although these were desirable commodities too—but woven fabrics for making and decorating clothing, durable metal utensils like cooking pots, kettles and cups, and edged weapons and tools like axes, adzes and knives that were more efficient and lasted longer than their bone and stone implements.

Examine the trading accounts of the North West Company and the Hudson's Bay Company and it quickly becomes evident that the greatest demand was not for rum but for cloth. According to the Museum of Civilization, bolts of fabric comprised 60 percent of the volume of goods traded from Europeans to Indians at the peak of the fur trade.

And who wanted fabric? Aboriginal women. Why? Because it eliminated an enormous amount of labour they had previously had to expend on making clothing from leather. Skins had to be scraped, tanned and softened by chewing before they could be properly worked and sewed with thread made from sinew, bark or root fibre.

Cloth did not displace leather or furs but it allowed women to produce more and better clothing with less expenditure of time and labour. The modern mukluk with its moosehide moccasin attached to a stroud legging over a thick duffle liner—still the best footwear for cold, dry winter conditions—is an example of the hybrid technologies that emerged and endured.

After fabric, 25 percent of the trade volume was in guns, powder, shot and edged weapons. Once again, this technology transfer resulted in immediate productivity gains for hunters.

These items accounted for 85 percent of the trade goods demanded in exchange for furs that to aboriginal people represented a surplus resource of little value except in terms of what it could be exchanged for at a trading post. By contrast, luxury items like liquor amounted to only 6 percent of the goods traded, tobacco only 2 percent and trade jewellery about 3 percent.

Today marketers make much of the fact that despite their absence from boardrooms and some trades and professions, women are responsible for 83 percent of the consumer purchases that drive our retail economy. Judging from the fur trade two hundred years ago, aboriginal women's desires and decisions had a similar influence on the economy of their time.

But by the mid-nineteenth century, fashions had begun to change in Europe, and demand for furs slackened. Agriculture, forestry, mining and manufacturing emerged as major engines of Canada's economic growth as the fur trade slipped into a long, gradual decline and eventual near eclipse.

As early as 1831, just a decade after the North West Company's merger with the Hudson's Bay Company created a fur-trade monopoly, the decline was already evident to Alexander Caulfield Anderson, buried in the beautiful little rural church-

Circa 1890, fur trader Colin Fraser bales precious pelts at Fort Chipewyan in a setting that changed little between his time and Simon Fraser's a century before. *Library and Archives Canada, accession number 1947-009 NPC, C-001229*

yard of St. Stephen's Anglican Church just outside Victoria.

The fur trader would later explore British Columbia's southern Interior, find an all-Canadian route for fur brigades to Fort Langley and secure the province for James Douglas in his schemes to oppose American expansion.

"This point in earlier times had been a very important station of the North West Company," he wrote. "Hence larger fleets of canoes were dispatched every spring to the head of Lake Superior, the point of rendezvous where magnates of the Interior annually assembled . . . but at the period of which I write, much of the glory of Lachine had departed."

In the park where I strolled, young Simon had also certainly walked as a lad, first on visits downriver to the big city to see his uncle and his cousins—two of whom on his mother's side were already in the fur trade—later to attend school and then to take his apprenticeship.

At the time the fur trade was the biggest commercial enterprise on the continent. Its urgent bustle must have had a magnetic effect on a sturdy boy from the backwoods living in a household full of older sisters. Probably it held the same appeal to a small boy that airports and train stations would in another age, offering a magic portal to exotic places and great adventures.

Simon Fraser

5

THE YEAR OF FATEFUL EVENTS

I'd made my way to Lachine driving north on the secondary roads from Fraser's birthplace in Mapletown, NY, taking the same route he most likely took as an eight-year-old refugee. In that bitter and chaotic spring of 1784, the year of the Loyalist migrations, he travelled with his ailing mother to safety in Canada.

First they went to Fort Edward on which Gen. John Burgoyne had squandered so much time that it proved fatal both to his plans and to Simon's father. Next they went to Fort Anne, until then the strategic "Gateway to the North" and the site of five crucial forts between 1690 and 1777. Today it's reduced to an old well at a dusty crossroads among rickety secondhand stores that style themselves antique emporiums.

Then the family would have trudged to Fort William Henry, its fame resurrected by James Fennimore Cooper's novel and in recent years by the movie *Last of the Mohicans.* Next they'd have gone on to Fort George, today resplendent as a tacky summer playground for New York City's middle class. Its sprawl of gift shops sell T-shirts with tasteless slogans and hot pink bikinis of a scantiness that the Fraser sisters and their mother could not have imagined. From there they would likely travel by boat down Lake George, perhaps overnighting in the shelter of the great star-shaped battlements of Fort Ticonderoga, and finally hike to yet another fort in this bloody corridor, Crown Point on the south end of Lake Champlain. Then they would re-embark for the last leg down the lake and the Richelieu River to the St. Lawrence, Montreal and the haven of Canada.

Founded in 1784 by Roman Catholic Scots in the fur trade, St. Andrew's Church went through three incarnations, ending as the neo-Gothic structure from which Simon Fraser was buried in 1862. *Rachele Labreque/* Vancouver Sun

Why choose this route rather than going down the Hudson River through Albany to New York and travel on by sailing ship to Nova Scotia, as so many Loyalists did in that desperate summer? Pure conjecture on my part, it's a best guess based on an absence of records and a considered balance of probabilities.

This had been the overland route from New York to Canada for a century before the American Revolution. I also knew—from oblique references gleaned from a Royal Commission on the Losses and Services of American Loyalists forced to flee after the war—that from 1784 to 1786, Isabella Fraser lived in Coteau-du-Lac, Quebec, with her eldest son, William, although other sources suggest he'd been in Kingston when the Frasers decided to come to Canada.

On the other hand, historian W. Kaye Lamb notes that Simon's older brother Angus travelled to Montreal in the spring of 1784, and his uncle John Fraser provided fifty *Louis d'or* to help his sister-in-law move her family. It was a considerable sum for the time with a purchasing power of close to five thousand dollars today, so it's certainly possible they travelled by ship.

Murky records notwithstanding, Isabella Fraser ended her journey at Coteau-du-Lac, right on the border that now separates Quebec from Ontario. It's just up the St. Lawrence River from its confluence with the Richelieu. It's also where William's regiment had been deployed from 1779 to 1781 to construct a canal past dangerous rapids. His commanding officer, Sir John Johnson, undertook to settle his Loyalist troops there after the war was lost. Johnson built his own home at Williamstown, only a few kilometres from where Fraser would later settle. It seemed logical to me that she would make for safety with her adult son by taking the most direct, and for all its hardships, the safest and most secure route.

On February 24, 1786, "Widow Fraser, now sickly and helpless," wrote the British commission set up to adjudicate claims by dispossessed Loyalists and indemnify them for losses. Isabella Fraser asked compensation for property confiscated after the death of her husband while being abused by his American captors at the Albany jail. By December 19, 1787, William was testifying to the commission, which took evidence in Montreal, that he was now acting on behalf of his younger siblings in the claim and that they were all living with him at Coteau-du-Lac.

Sources for this information include Lamb's book, which collected the surviving letters and journals of Simon Fraser, and the notes kept by Daniel Parker Coke, a British MP who served on the Royal Commission. They were annotated, cross-indexed and published in 1971. In addition, I pored over a remarkable volume outlining actual claims for compensation by Loyalists. They were painstakingly transcribed from the British Public Records Office by Peter Wilson Coldham and published by the National Genealogical Society in the US in 1980. These documents recount events in discursive legalese, but the plain-spoken memorials from witnesses offer a chilling window into the greed and violence with which the Loyalists were dispossessed of their property by their neighbours and erstwhile friends.

Young Simon had been seven in 1783, the year the Loyalist exodus began. It was to be a year of fateful events that would shape his future in several ways. On February 20, three months to the day before his seventh birthday, the British and the American rebels ended the war. By September 3, the Peace of Paris set out the terms for independence. Included under Articles 4, 5 and 6 were provisions ensuring that Loyalists would be treated justly and that all persons with an interest in previously confiscated lands would be entitled to full redress under the law. To the horror of Loyalists, however, the new rulers of the independent states found they had little power to enforce these noble sentiments and seemed little inclined to try.

"It was impossible under any circumstances to obtain redress in the American courts, either in the person of an assignee, or an original creditor," four claimants later wrote in a bitter letter to the Earl of Liverpool and British MP Nicholas Vansittart.

Indeed, once British authority was withdrawn, there was an orgy of Loyalist land seizures by other farmers. For all the high-minded language of the treaty, many took the postrevolutionary chaos as an opportunity to settle old scores, loot, rob and grab land—all justified with rhetoric about liberty and freedom. Those who objected were often subjected to violence. Some were arrested and even sold into servitude, forced to work their neighbours' land as near-slave labour.

"The Treaty of Paris, as expected, went unheeded. In many communities throughout the country, the victorious patriots—some still angry, some coveting land, some just exercising the power now at their command—made it clear that loyalists would find no peace among them," writes Ray Raphael in *A People's History of the American Revolution.*

Peter Oliver, who lived through those difficult times, wrote in the appendix to his own history of the events a description of the fate of one seventy-year-old man who was dragged from his bed and beaten. When his nephew, a Dr. Abner Beebe, intervened on his behalf:

"He was assaulted by a mob, stripped naked and hot pitch was poured upon him, which blistered his skin. He was then carried to a hog sty and rubbed over with hog's dung. They threw the hog's dung in his face and rammed some of it down his throat; and in that condition exposed (him) to a company of women. His house was attacked, his windows broke, when one of his children was sick, and a child of his went into distraction upon his treatment."

Much testimony later heard by the Royal Commission recounted similar experiences.

Simon Baxter, who had been captured with Burgoyne's army at Saratoga, was released after the war. He went home to his family but was seized, tied to a tree, jabbed with bayonets and flogged. His back was left "worse than I ever saw a soldier's back."

T. Hassard wrote in July 1783 that when he went to see his family and collect his possessions, he was "seased upon and put into prison for five days, and my vessel seased upon and broken open and plundered and my chest broken open and plundered and abused. Threatened to take my life and made me pay them the most exstravagant charges."

Samuel Anderson, who led sixty-four men to fight with Simon Fraser's father at Bennington and was one of only eight to survive, subsequently had his property seized and sold "by the people of Vermont." A war widow with small children said she was forced to pay rent for living on her own farm. Abraham Bristoll wrote that he'd been dragged from his house, which was plundered, leaving his family in "deplorable circumstances." After losing his harvest, he and his family were banished, with nowhere to go, without food or clothing, and his minor son James was sold as a slave.

Predictably, near panic ensued. By the spring of 1784, the year the Fraser family set out for Quebec, nearly thirty thousand people desperately sought transport out of America.

Canniff Haight, born in 1825, gave a speech to the United Empire Loyalists' Association of Ontario that I found in a rare, self-published 1897 edition of only a thousand copies. He quotes an unnamed British officer describing the refugees in terms that evoke those last searing images of Saigon as the Americans abandoned South Vietnam to the Viet Cong and the North Vietnamese:

"To describe their situation upon the evacuation is scarcely possible. There were old grey-headed men and women, husbands and wives with large families of little children, women with infants at their breasts, poor widows whose husbands had lost their lives in the service of King and country, with a dozen half-starved bantlings tagging at their skirts, taking leave of their friends. . . . In every street were to be seen men, women and children wringing their hands, lamenting the situation of those who were about leaving the country and the more dreadful situation of such who were either unable to leave or were determined rather than run the risk of starving in distant lands to throw themselves upon and trust to the mercy of their persecutors.

"The rebels, like so many furies or rather devils, entered the town and a scene ensued the very repetition of which is shocking to the ears of humanity. The loyalists were seized, hove into dungeons, prisons and provosts. Some were tied up and whipped, others were tarred and feathered, some were dragged to horse ponds and drenched till near dead, others were carried about the town in carts with labels on their backs and breasts with the word 'Tory' in capitals written thereon. All of the loyalists were turned out of their houses and obliged to sleep in the streets and fields. . . . A universal plunder of the friends of government took place."

Such stories must have been daunting for Isabella Fraser, without doubt a tough woman, but now aged fifty in a time when less than 2 percent of the population reached sixty-five. Her husband had been cruelly misused and had died in the custody of those seizing power. Her house had been looted, her livestock driven off and her crops stolen. Her nearest kinsman in Albany, Hugh Fraser, had likewise been driven off his property.

In this context, her decision to take her seven children to Quebec where she had a son, a prosperous brother-in-law and relatives on her own side of the family, seems eminently reasonable despite the risks of the overland journey.

If this cruel, violent upheaval suddenly changed the course of Simon Fraser's life, it also brought him to Canada and thus changed the course of our own history. Loyalists who travelled by sea from the New England ports flooded into the unsettled regions of Nova Scotia. New Brunswick was carved out of the territory to accommodate them in 1784. Other overlanders like the Frasers settled in Quebec, a number in what are now the Eastern Townships and others farther up the St. Lawrence River in areas where there was no European settlement.

For many the first three years of settlement in Canada were grim. The newcomers survived by eating roots, wild plants and bark stripped from trees, say Nick Mika and Helma Mika in their book *United Empire Loyalists: Pioneers of Upper Canada.*

"They were basically war refugees like people from Bosnia or Rwanda today," historian Peter McLeod at the Canadian War Museum explained when I asked him about the event. "About 40,000 of them came into Canada over about one year."

The impact was immediate and enormous. Almost overnight, he said, what was formerly New France was transformed from what had been a unilingual culture to a bilingual culture. Unsettled areas were settled. Canada itself would soon be irrevocably changed, divided into two provinces in 1791—Lower Canada was essentially old Quebec, and Upper Canada was essentially new Ontario—thus laying foundations for the eventual confederation from which the country we now share would grow.

Perhaps most important, these newcomers represented a massive infusion of intellectual and entrepreneurial capital. This powerfully energized and empowered the smaller British colonies to the north of the new republic that had displaced so many inhabitants.

Ottawa poet and playwright Tony Cosier, when he wrote his play *The First Man on the Rideau,* became intimate with these settlers who created Upper Canada. He told me about them over coffee in a bistro in Bytown, the national capital's old quarter.

"The stone house we live in was built by a Loyalist—John Chester," he said. "The next property over was built by Benedict Arnold's brother, Henry Arnold. They were people of property. They didn't just want to acquire land, they wanted control. There was a poor class of refugees, of course. However, it was not just poor guys coming off the boat. A lot of these people were the cream of the crop and they quickly set up a new elite society. These were mill owners and property holders."

British authorities used the Loyalist immigrants for their own strategic purposes, Cosier explained. Land was provided to former soldiers, but many units—including Butler's Rangers and the King's Royal Regiment in which William Fraser served and that terrorized Americans during the war—were settled in a pattern that created trained and instantly available military establishments as a buffer along the porous borders with American states.

"They had formed the militias that confronted the Americans," he said, "now they provided a home army that was already organized. So what you've got is a privileged group of people coming in just before the big influx of poor Irish and poor Scots. The intermarriage between these Loyalist communities was just like royal families. You now had a ruling aristocracy in place. You had a military aristocracy in place. And they were all in place before the labouring classes came in large numbers."

Among those taking land grants in what is now eastern Ontario were Simon's

Dour Montreal residence of fur magnate Simon McTavish, driving force behind the North West Company's challenge to the Hudson's Bay Company, photographed in the early 1890s. *McCord Museum, MP00018221*

two older brothers, William and Angus, who filed for eighty-hectare lots on the Rivière aux Raisins in what is now St. Andrew's West, just outside Cornwall. This is where Isabella appears to have settled for the remainder of her life, and it's where Simon himself finally homesteaded on retirement from the fur trade.

Meanwhile, another momentous event had occurred in 1783 that would also redirect Simon Fraser's life. Up in Montreal, a group of canny Scots entrepreneurs had long been working with French and other independent fur traders to circumvent the Hudson's Bay Company's attempt to monopolize the fur trade. Now they banded together to form a new enterprise, the North West Company. It would use the river systems explored by Brûlé, La Salle, Frobisher and Pond to penetrate to the heart of the continent. The business strategy was audacious: its traders would intercept the flow of furs before they travelled to the London-based competition's forts along the coastlines.

The genius behind the new company was Simon McTavish, destined to become the wealthiest man in Montreal. McTavish's brother-in-law was Hugh Fraser, a kinsman of Simon's father. Both were certainly acquaintances of John Fraser, Simon's uncle. Two of Isabella Fraser's brothers, Peter and Donald, were already serving

Alexander Mackenzie was the first fur trader to venture west of the Rocky Mountains and reach the Pacific in 1793. Simon Fraser followed his route up the Peace River. *Image PDP02244 courtesy of Royal BC Museum, BC Archives*

The battered compass that guided Alexander Mackenzie north to the Arctic Ocean and westward to the Pacific is now held by the Nor'Wester & Loyalist Museum in Williamstown, Ontario. *Rachele Labreque/*Vancouver Sun

in the fur trade. So when Simon, who had been educated at home by his mother and older sisters—quite well, too, judging from the general literacy of his later journals—was sent to Montreal in 1790 to be formally educated under the direction of his uncle John, he fell into a ready-made network of family relationships that involved the fur trade.

The adventures and disasters of traders would have provided dinner talk and casual conversation. The trade provided the commercial backdrop to social life. Young Simon's relatives were deeply involved in the financing, resupply and management of various aspects of the business. His uncle's friends had been traders in the remote northwest, and Lachine was steeped in the history of explorers such as Brûlé, the consummate coureur de bois, and La Salle, the bold if incompetent visionary.

Montreal society was also electrified by the exploits of another young partner in the company. Alexander Mackenzie had just returned from his discovery of an immense and previously unknown river in the northwest that had carried him to the Arctic Ocean. Now he was embarked on another attempt to reach the Pacific.

Can it be surprising that young Simon, a fourteen-year-old schoolboy, might have been irresistibly drawn from his books to this camp at Lachine? There the voyageurs prepared for their long spring journey, and in the fall they returned with their rich harvest of furs and tales of exploits in places that weren't even on most European maps. In 1792, at the age of sixteen, hardy enough to have survived all that he had, Simon would sign up for an apprenticeship as a clerk with the booming North West Company. Eventually he would walk the wagon track to Lachine himself, embark in a frail birchbark canoe, listen to the farewells dwindle until the only sound was the dip of paddles and the murmur of the river, and set off at last

The gigantic *canot de maître* or Montreal canoe was the workhorse of fur brigades leaving Lachine each spring for the arduous return journey to the Lakehead. *"Running the Rapids," Frances Anne Hopkins fonds, Library and Archives Canada, accession number 1989-401-2, C-002774*

on the ghostly trail of those adventurers who had gone before him into the vast, silent wilderness.

And so the next step in my search for Simon Fraser was to put the heady pleasures of Montreal behind me as the newly hired young clerk had done, and with the same big red sun sliding between a layer of cloud and the dark western horizon, to set off up the Ottawa River bound for the West.

6

A REGALE FOR SAINT ANNE

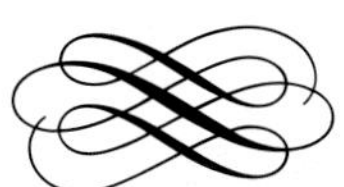

Dusk settled on the nation's capital as I ambled beside the great river Simon Fraser had travelled so long ago, a lad about to turn sixteen, bound for the far northwest and a role he could not have imagined in shaping a province—and a country—still waiting to be born.

In search of the landing where Fraser would have stepped ashore on that very first journey, I walked upstream. On the lazy current, silent as a ghost on the dark water, a rowing shell scudded past. The white shirts of the crew glimmered in the twilight. Pale oar blades dipped, rose, feathered to reduce drag, swivelled and dipped again, a tireless rhythm set to a precise number of strokes a minute.

Coming upriver, taking advantage of the calm deep water, Fraser's voyageurs would have synchronized their strokes in precisely the same way to maximize power and efficiency. Their paddles were short by comparison to modern rowing gear, seldom longer than chin height, except for the bowsman and the steersman who had a longer reach to the water. Carved from light woods like spruce and cedar, the narrow blades were often painted with bright colours or personal devices that identified the owner. Like a hockey player's stick, the paddle was a prized, highly customized personal possession.

The canoe it powered was a marvel of technology. Thin, light birchbark was stitched with *watape* (split spruce root) onto a frame of cedar ribs with ash gunwales and thwarts, and the seams waterproofed with spruce gum. A Montreal canoe like those carrying Fraser up the Ottawa was about twelve metres long but weighed only about ninety kilograms—astonishingly light for a craft that would carry from eight

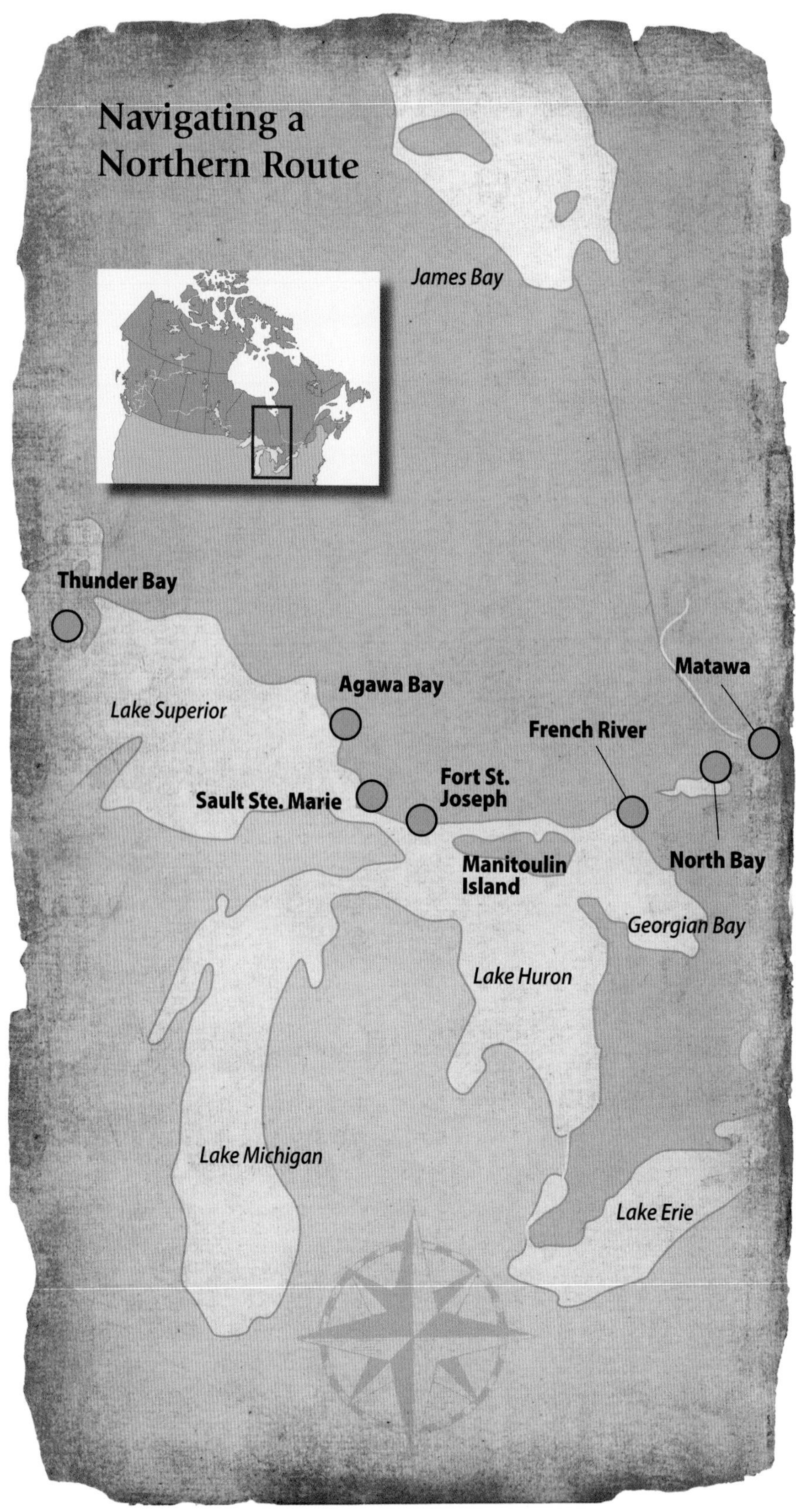
Navigating a Northern Route
James Bay
Thunder Bay
Matawa
Agawa Bay
Lake Superior
French River
Fort St. Joseph
Sault Ste. Marie
North Bay
Manitoulin Island
Georgian Bay
Lake Huron
Lake Michigan
Lake Erie

A full-sized birchbark canoe of the kind that carried Simon Fraser west is a prized exhibit at the museum in Williamstown, Ontario, where many prominent fur traders settled. *Rachele Labreque*/Vancouver Sun

to sixteen crew and up to four thousand kilograms of passengers or freight.

The best crews of voyageurs moved their craft along at a clip that would test even today's Olympic athletes; their paddles entered the water up to sixty times a minute. I watched the modern rowing shell dwindle in the distance as the oarsmen maintained their steady, hypnotic rhythm. Some things, I thought, never change.

Most things do. During those first weeks of May 1792, when Fraser's birchbark craft passed the bluffs—now straddled by Ottawa and its sprawling suburbs and satellites—the skyline consisted only of treetops above the steep riverbanks, their branches graced with the intense green of newly unfolded spring leaves, the whispering canopy of the primeval hardwood forest catching the last slant of light from the setting sun.

For me, the rays from that same sun flared against the glass faces of office towers and government buildings, the windows of the imposing US Embassy and the twin silver spires of Notre Dame Cathedral, the city's oldest church—although it wasn't built until Simon Fraser was in his mid-seventies.

The history of the Ottawa Valley, extending west from the St. Lawrence, has a longer pedigree than the city that adopted its name. The Ottawa River and its beautiful tributary the Mattawa, which rises in Trout Lake near Lake Nipissing at what is now North Bay, had been a highway for Algonquin Indians for millennia.

Moving cargo by canoe demanded the strength and stamina of Olympic athletes but it also had moments of haunting beauty. *"Canoe Manned by Voyageurs Passing a Waterfall," Frances Anne Hopkins fonds, Library and Archives Canada, accession number 1989-401-1, C-002771*

The first European to explore it was the enigmatic Étienne Brûlé, first of the legendary coureurs de bois, sometime before 1615. That was the year he emerged from *Pays d'en Haut,* the trackless bush of the unknown upcountry, to lead Samuel Champlain to Lake Huron.

An illiterate who had gone into the outback as a teenager not much older than Simon Fraser, Brûlé had an astonishing ability to learn aboriginal languages. He later abandoned the European colonies to live exclusively among the Indians. Before he was slain at the age of forty-two, Brûlé had been west as far as Sault Ste. Marie, the narrow isthmus separating Lake Huron from Lake Superior.

By the late eighteenth century, Brûlé's route—up the Ottawa and Mattawa rivers and then down French River to the Great Lakes—was the main passage for the canoes of the spring brigades to the northwest.

These Montreal canoes, *les canots de maître* in the terminology of the time, were only an arm's length shorter than the twelve-metre yachts that compete for the America's Cup. They carried close to three thousand kilograms of freight, six paddlers, a steersman and a bow paddle, several passengers—in this case the clerks and traders—rations, equipment and the crew's personal supplies.

The clearance between the gunwales and the waterline of a fully loaded Montreal canoe would be about the width of a large man's palm. Alexander Mackenzie, waiting in Fort Chipewyan to begin his own voyage west, would later write in his memoirs of the trek:

"On seeing one of these slender vessels thus laden, heaped up and sunk with her gunwale within six inches of the water, [an observer] would think his fate inevitable in such a boat; but the Canadians are so expert, that few accidents happen."

These hardy men rose before dawn, having slept rolled into a blanket under a sheet of bark, or if they had seniority, under an upturned canoe. They paddled up to eighteen hours a day against the current, and like hockey players pacing their shifts, they paused every hour to rest for fifteen minutes and smoke one of the ubiquitous clay pipes that were their equivalent of our disposable paper cups or throwaway plastic razors. Just as we measure the day by coffee breaks, they measured their voyages in pipes, each leg equal to about six kilometres of paddling in smooth water. On average, the voyageurs covered about forty kilometres a day.

For such travellers, young Simon included, the wilderness really began at Ste-Anne-de-Bellevue, now a pleasant bedroom community of Montreal but then a tiny outpost an easy day's paddle beyond Lachine. The small, windowless stone church at the narrows where canoes turned west up the Ottawa River was the last of civilization—as they conceived it, at least—that they would see for the next six months. And as North West Company fur trader Alexander Henry wrote in a colourful 1809 account of his own first expedition to the west thirty years before Simon's, the saint to whom the little church is dedicated is the "patroness of the Canadians in all their travels by water."

This was the point at which the voyageurs considered themselves to be leaving civilization and entering the wilderness. It was where they made final repairs to canoes. There was still time to send an express canoe back to Lachine for any vital equipment they'd forgotten. Then each crew would place an offering in the alms box in Saint Anne's name, say a prayer beseeching her blessing, hear a mass and receive a benediction from the priest asking their safe return from the dangerous and arduous journey ahead.

"The line which marks off the frontier and the farmstead, the wilderness from the baseline, the hinterland from the metropolis, runs through every Canadian psyche," concluded historian William Lewis Morton almost half a century ago.

Today—in a world where humans have the ability to penetrate to every corner of the planet, satellites can photograph every square metre of its surface in enough detail to reveal a tennis ball and space-based mobile communications systems can transmit and receive anyone's instantaneous messages from anywhere—wilderness is perceived as being both under threat and in urgent need of protection.

Philosophers and environmentalists argue that wilderness is our source of spiritual renewal. Industrialists see it as a repository of valuable natural resources. Ecologists worry that increasing erosion and fragmentation may mean extinction for many wild species from grizzly bears to butterflies. And political and ideological conflicts rage everywhere over how much should be set aside in parks and wildlife reserves—13 percent, 49 percent, none?—which are off-limits to developers.

Two hundred years ago, wilderness was perceived in different terms. It was a vast, menacing presence from which human beings required protection. Wilderness was an obstacle that needed clearing. It was "waste" land that wanted domestication. The people who lived in it were "savages" and "primitives" in similar need of civilization. That, of course, was the perception of urbanized Europeans and Asians.

To aboriginal people who occupied and exploited the Canadian landscape before and during the early phases of colonization, the concept of wilderness that motivated these newcomers was entirely alien. Indeed, the word "wilderness" doesn't even appear in the Cree and Chipewyan vocabularies collected by Alexander Mackenzie during his travels in the far northwest.

Those who ventured forth from London, Paris, New York or Montreal defined wilderness in terms of isolation and privation. To those who lived there and had done since time immemorial, it was not "wilderness," it was home. It was not threatening but comforting, a source of sustenance. It provided food, shelter, medicines, and materials for tools, weapons, clothing and transportation.

If the landscape threw up occasional dangers in the form of wild animals or the cyclical absence of game, forest fires, blizzards or intertribal conflict, it's important to remember that danger, too, is a relative perception. Who in Simon Fraser's time could say the dangers of New Caledonia were more or less significant than the perils of poverty, invasion, famine, fire, hurricane or pestilence that afflicted a "civilized" world then convulsed by the Napoleonic Wars?

In some ways, these differences in world view endure right into the present. They manifest themselves in frequent conflicts between First Nations and the dominant culture over natural resource development and land use. Often the issue proves to be not so much whether resources in undeveloped areas should be exploited but the two parties' different attitudes to their relationship with the land itself and the extent to which it should be exploited.

The crucial two centuries of the fur trade that made Canada and launched British Columbia—a period in which Europeans and aboriginal peoples lived together in the "wilderness"—provided an interface for these world views that endures today. It is no coincidence, observed the world-renowned naturalist and writer Fred Bodsworth, that Canada's national emblems are the beaver and the maple leaf, each a symbol both for what is wild and for an industry.

"Nor," Bodsworth is quoted as saying, "is it coincidence that there are more paintings of wilderness lakes, spruce bogs, and pine trees on Canadian walls than in any other nation on Earth. We may scoff, we may deny, but the wilderness mystique is still a strong element in the Canadian ethos."

Before the voyageurs left on the journey from which each year some did not return, there was one more important ritual. Each canoe received a ration of rum, thirty-six litres to each canoe, four litres to each paddler, to be consumed during the voyage.

"Nor is it less according to custom," Henry noted with wry understatement, "to drink the whole of this liquor upon the spot." The saint and the priest were no sooner dismissed, he said, than a scene of intoxication began in which his men indulged themselves in "singing, fighting and the display of savage gesture and conceit."

The voyageurs were a rough, tough and rowdy bunch. I took note of how, at an age when most men have just begun to shave, Simon Fraser nevertheless earned sufficient respect to later command. This small fact, I concluded, provides an important insight into his character.

Just before first light the next morning the paddlers would rise, huddle around a large kettle in which either dried peas or corn had been simmering with half a kilo of pork fat, and eat a breakfast of greasy mush. The evening meal would be the same. So would meals for the rest of the trip, unless they could be supplemented with berries, eggs, fish or game along the way. Then, presumably sweating off evil hangovers, the spring brigade canoes would start up the Ottawa.

A brigade consisted of ten canoes. Three brigades made a squadron. Sometimes as many as three squadrons would make the journey. However many there were on Fraser's first trip, his brigade was bound nonstop for Grand Portage at the far end of Lake Superior.

There the *engagés* hired for the paddling season in Montreal—somewhat derisively dubbed *mangeurs de lard* (pork eaters) for their store-bought travelling rations of salt meat—would rendezvous with *les hivernants*, the men of the north.

The latter, most of whom lived off the land and travelled with rations of dry fish and pemmican, would have wintered with the Indians. As soon as the northern rivers broke up, they would themselves be departing in their smaller *canots du nord*—about half the size of the mighty Montreal canoe—for Grand Portage. The farthest of them journeyed from the Athabasca district in what is now the Northwest Territories.

As Fraser's expedition approached what is now Ottawa, a wisp of smoke might have shimmered on the horizon from the campfire of an Algonquin traveller or from the clay chimney of some isolated Loyalist cabin—but more likely not. Fraser was passing through still largely uninhabited country.

Today, surrounded by the country's fourth-largest metropolitan area, the river valley is but a manicured remnant of that wilderness. Some of Canada's most striking urban architecture crowns its banks. As I walked in the footsteps of Simon Fraser, the thrum of traffic (more than a hundred thousand vehicles a day cross the two bridges flanking my path) muffled the timeless murmur of the river on which he'd travelled.

Tulip Festival was underway. Lawns on the far side of the Alexandra Bridge blazed with bright primary colours, a tiny patch of the natural world's expressionist rebellion erupting between the Gothic revivalism of Canada's Parliament Buildings and the tubular steel and glass modernism of the National Gallery. Farther upstream, the modified art deco of the Supreme Court of Canada flanked the stainless steel utilitarianism of the National Library and Archives. Behind me were the stunning, curvilinear terraces of aboriginal architect Douglas Cardinal's Canadian Museum of Civilization, with fossilized creatures that predated all humanity embedded in its stone walls, the whole structure intended to evoke that ancient postglacial landscape that greeted the first humans. Cardinal's design is so original that it defies categorization.

As I walked beside the river, ruminating on my quest and the differences—and similarities—between Fraser's world and my own, a soft, humid breeze carried shouted fragments from boisterous teenagers waiting for an outdoor rock concert. They were interrupted by the faint squeal from a guitarist testing his whammy bar. Now that was a difference. Or was it? Fraser's brigades enjoyed announcing their arrival with Highland bagpipes. In many a remote northern community, the jig and the reel can still be seen at community dances, and Celtic rhythms and tonality still resonate through our popular music.

I knew from weather warnings on TV that the breeze wafting noises from the Tulip Festival came all the way from Louisiana. The river of air slithers counterpoint to the south-flowing Mississippi, Wabash and Ohio rivers, then spills across Lakes

Fur brigade crews rose at first light for a communal breakfast of greasy mush made from dried peas simmered with half a kilogram of pork fat. *"Breakfast at Sunrise," Alfred Jacob Miller fonds, Library and Archives Canada, accession number 1946-131-1, C-000424*

Erie and Ontario. Arriving here it slams into colder, denser Canadian air to spawn storm cells, sudden downpours and even funnel clouds of the kind I associated with visits to Oklahoma. It's one more reminder of how the continent is woven together in ways that haven't changed since Fraser's day and will certainly outlast our own delusions of permanence.

From dark woodlands to walls of artificial light; from bark wickiups to post-modernist temples of authority; from unsettled wilderness to a population of more than a million; from three colonial provinces so new that the borders hadn't yet been fixed to a sovereign country of ten provinces and three territories touching all three northern oceans, all taking shape within the single lifetime of the man I was tracking: what seems so permanent in the present seldom proves changeless.

Change was certainly in the air in that spring of 1792 as Fraser headed west.

Across the sea in France, Louis XVI was under arrest and would soon be on trial for his life. War was imminent between republican France and European monarchies alarmed by revolution. The growing vortex threatened to suck in the British.

Upper Canada had been carved out of the wilderness to the southwest of Montreal just five months earlier to accommodate Loyalist refugees from the American Revolution. It would be another year before a capital would be established at the muddy clearing called York, four hundred kilometres to the southwest on Lake Ontario.

To young Simon, if he even knew about them, these developments would have seemed almost surreal, so distant and obscure that he was unlikely to spend time dwelling on where they might lead. He had other things to worry about, including his new job as a clerk apprenticed to the North West Company.

Clerks were not the lackeys forever stereotyped by Bob Cratchitt in Charles Dickens's *A Christmas Carol.* Contracted to salaried positions for anywhere up to seven years, they had positions of substantial authority as official business agents for the North West Company. Trading post administration, inventory control, record keeping, quartermaster duties of doling out the rum rations, powder and shot, trading for furs under the direction of higher authorities, even acting as a physician for the inevitable wounds, injuries and illnesses, were all the new responsibilities of the teenaged Fraser.

But from the growing thunder of *La Grande Chaudière* (the big boiler)—a cataract that even fur traders to whom it was a major pain in the neck would pause to admire for its beauty—my walk told me I could be certain of where Simon's attention was focussed.

"The body of water falls 25 feet over cragged, excavated rocks in a most wild, romantic manner," noted Mackenzie in his vivid account of the route from Montreal to the Great Lakes.

Just downstream from the falls, I stopped on the Pont du Portage to admire the capital's architecture, identifying significant buildings by consulting the ingenious

Alexander Mackenzie commented on the wild beauty of *La Grande Chaudière*—the big boiler—although the falls forced a crucial portage at what is now Ottawa. *From* Picturesque Canada: The Country as it Was and Is, *c. 1882*

miniature bronze skyline set up at one end of the bridge for just that purpose. Somewhere close by, the young clerk's heavily laden canoe had come ashore. Down among the rustling trees by the river, remnants of the old portage around the falls can still be seen. And there are the ruins of more recent endeavours.

I crossed a bridge to Victoria Island, a wedge of hard rock in the middle of the river, and stopped to investigate the stone shell of the long-abandoned Ottawa Carbide Mill. Historical plaques informed me that Thomas "Carbide" Wilson was one of those inventive geniuses who registered more than sixty patents, from the arc light to superphosphate, a revolutionary new fertilizer. In 1892, exactly a hundred years after Simon Fraser passed by, keeping his handwritten accounts by candle and campfire light, Wilson learned how to make acetylene gas from calcium carbide and water and discovered that if he mixed the gas with oxygen, it burned hot enough to cut steel. Canadian industrialist Thomas Ahearn used hydro power generated at Chaudière Falls to run Ottawa's first electric railway in 1891; the cars were even heated. Ahearn later invented another technological boon that would soon transform Canadian life, the electric stove.

But I had really come to contemplate the portage that Fraser faced, hoping it would give me further insights into who he was. He'd have known what lay ahead, as I did, by reading the huge foam and bubbles that whirled and eddied downstream on the tea-coloured current. Assuming his senses were more attuned than my own city-dulled perceptions, he'd also have felt the vibration of the falls long before he saw them.

The cauldron is much subdued today from what it was in the time of the voyageurs. The current was diverted into artificial side channels to drive Victorian water mills, a hydroelectric generating station robs energy and a weir slows the force of the river. For all that, the falls still shake the ground where white water boils over the limestone ledges in a thunderous torrent. It's no Hell's Gate, which Fraser would later confront, but for an inexperienced teenager on his first voyage, the falls must have been an intimidating signal of the natural perils that lay ahead.

Ahead lay the Portage de la Mauvaise Musique on the French River, for example, where according to Mackenzie, writing about his first trip from Montreal to the Great Lakes in 1784, "many men have been crushed to death by the canoes, and others have received irrecoverable injuries."

Daniel Harmon, travelling west by the same route in 1800, took note while travelling down the same river that "for almost every rapid we have passed since leaving Montreal, we have seen a number of crosses erected. At one I counted no less than 30."

The son of a tavern keeper, Harmon was born in 1778 in Bennington, Vermont. His father fought in the revolutionary militia that slaughtered the Loyalists in the battle where Simon Fraser's father fought, was captured and died his gruesome prison death. Harmon joined the North West Company in 1796, taking a post as warehouse clerk before transferring to the northwest trade. In one of those ironies of fate, he was later sent to run Fort St. James, founded by Fraser in 1806 in what is now northern BC.

I knew from my reading in such contemporary accounts that voyageurs had to cope with thirty-six portages around dangerous rapids between Lachine and the open paddling of Lake Huron and Lake Superior, and these vast inland seas with their frigid waters and sudden storms offered other hazards.

I knew that there were two portage landing points at Chaudière, one right beneath the falls, the other farther downstream but used only during severe flooding. I'd walked beside both, but I surmised that whenever possible, faced with any extra carrying, Fraser's brigade crew would always opt for the briefest portage. At 643 paces by Mackenzie's count, this first trail was the shortest of the three at Chaudière Falls. It was also the most vexing.

"The rock is so steep and difficult of access, that it requires 12 men to take the canoe out of the water: it is then carried by six men, two at each end on the same side and two under the opposite gunwale," says Mackenzie, to whom all these

Moving canoes, gear and tonnes of trade cargo over portages was difficult, dangerous work and men could be injured or crushed to death. *"Extremely wearisome journeys at the portages," Peter Rindisbacher, Library and Archives Canada, accession number 1988-250-21, C-001922*

portages were so significant that he gives the exact number of paces for each one he cites. In this case, the next two were 700 and 740 paces respectively, for a total of more than two kilometres.

This meant that the cargo of each canoe—more than three tonnes if it was typical—would have to be unloaded, carried to the embarkation point and carefully stowed again a total of three times. The cargo was generally packed into individual bales or barrels, sixty-four in the usual load, along with sundry sacks, bundles and pieces of equipment. When portaging, voyageurs normally carried two forty-kilogram bales of freight at a time, although some would carry three.

Loading and unloading would be directed by the brigade's guide, who generally exercised the same powers as a ship's captain. A clerk like young Fraser would be responsible for keeping inventory of the valuable trade goods without which the trip would be a financial disaster, rations that would sustain the crew for the next six to eight weeks (sacks of ship's biscuits and dried peas, barrels of salt pork and any rum that remained after the frolic at Ste-Anne-de-Bellevue) and the survival gear (an axe, a big roll of birchbark, spruce root twine and gum for repairs, oilskins to protect the cargo in bad weather, ropes for lining through the shallows, knives and fishing lines).

When they weren't loading and unloading for irksome portages such as those at Chaudière Falls, voyageurs paddled their heavily laden canoes for sixteen to eighteen hours a day, maintaining their paddling rhythm of forty to sixty strokes a minute. To put that in perspective, at forty strokes a minute they would lift the paddle, weighing about half a kilogram, 43,200 times over eighteen hours, the equivalent of lifting twenty-five tonnes—in addition to carrying freight over portages. After that work day, the men would snatch five or six hours of sleep, often soaking wet from rain, a portage, a spill or a swamping, and then rise before dawn and do it all over again.

I thought about that as I dossed down in my comfortable hotel bed, queen-sized no less, but not for long.

The next morning I rose early, and with the sun behind me, pulled out for the west following the Ottawa River through the settlements of the Scottish Loyalists, the Irish immigrants—relatives of my wife came in 1819—and those who came later.

I had close to fifteen hundred kilometres to travel to Grand Portage. Past Lac des Chats Sauvages, named not for some sinister feline but for raccoons, past the limestone deposits at Calumet where voyageurs picked up soft white stone to carve pipes for smoking, through the narrow, crooked streets of Fort Coulonge and past the three kids swimming on a school day—playing hooky, I'd guess from their guilty flight when I stopped to take a photograph.

Everywhere there were signs of technological development that most of the voyageurs could not have dreamed. Once fearsome rapids drowned by hydro dams;

Canadian Forces Base Petawawa with three kids sporting retro Mohawks outside the fence and warriors behind it training with space-age weapons; the Chalk River nuclear research facility where Canada has just flirted with its own Chernobyl—a fuel core meltdown narrowly averted during a serious coolant loss that safety regulators have since concluded could have led to a "significant release" of radioactive material that would likely have reached the public; just up the highway at Rolphton, the demonstration reactor that operated as Canada's first atomic power plant for twenty-five years up to 1987.

At Deep River, however, I found a technological connection that reached right back to Simon Fraser's era. I pulled over to visit the Canadian Clock Museum. The connection? Time itself.

In the early eighteenth century, navigators encountered a baffling problem. They could accurately determine latitude, but to determine longitude they had to have an accurate chronometer that told them the time at Greenwich in Britain. The timekeeping technology of the day—pendulum-driven clocks—wasn't up to the task, and certainly not for a pitching, rolling vessel under sail in often wet and rapidly changing environments.

For an expanding maritime empire like Britain's, the issue had enormous political, military and economic implications. The British parliament actually put up a prize equivalent to almost five million dollars for whoever solved the problem.

A British carpenter named John Harrison took up the challenge and solved it by developing an ingenious clock that not only met the criteria for the contest but was so good that Capt. James Cook used it on his voyages of exploration. He returned with effusive praise.

But Harrison ran into a committee of envious scientists who refused to give him credit, and he finally had to appeal to King George III and Parliament to get partial compensation. The old inventor died four days after Simon Fraser was born.

At the converted church that houses the clock collections, I visited with Allan Symons, a nuclear scientist from nearby Chalk River. He spent twenty-seven years doing heavy water research, "deuterium isotope exchange and a little work on tritium." Then he retired in 1999 and used his own extensive library and a personal collection of more than six hundred clocks dating back to Fraser's time to create the core of a horological museum.

A fascinating place it is, too. Symons introduced me to mantel clocks, buffet clocks, sugar-shaker clocks, grandfather clocks, Westclox Moonbeams, atomic clocks, a world-view clock that simultaneously displayed the hour in every time zone on the planet and a whole building that's a sundial. He even has a clock that displays time in binary code with paired columns for hours, minutes and seconds. I concluded you'd need a degree in higher mathematics to figure out when to pick up the kids at school.

"A huge chunk of my pension cheques goes into the upkeep every month," he told me. "It's a madness, I suppose. But I'm single, never married. Most people invest most of their money in their families—well, I figure you can't take it with you, so this is my chance to give something back to Canada. Tomorrow is winding day. . . ." He looked at me, I thought, a little too hopefully.

Six hundred clocks would take considerable winding. I gave my regrets, and beat a retreat to resume my westward quest in the wake of Simon Fraser.

7

WEST OF AGAWA ROCK

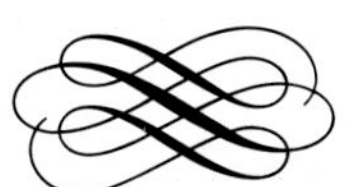

When I left the Ottawa Valley behind and turned west up the Mattawa River, I was still thinking about time and how it defines us and makes us distinctively different from the people of Fraser's frontier, who didn't carry digital wristwatches or listen to the radio. The voyageurs told time when they had to by observing the position of the sun and the length of the shadows. In 1792 a journey took as long as it took, though travellers had a general sense that they'd better get where they were going before freeze-up. Unlike them, I had deadlines to meet and a long haul ahead.

I followed the route that would take Fraser's spring brigade to the La Vase Portages, a high point on the upper river that separates the 140,000 square-kilometre basin of the Ottawa from the basin of Lake Nipissing, which drains westward into the Great Lakes.

From North Bay, Fraser's canoes would make their way west across Lake Nipissing, into the French River and then downstream across Lake Huron to Sault St. Marie and finally along the hazardous north shore of Lake Superior to the great rendezvous at Grand Portage.

Time is relative. Back up the road I'd passed the national nuclear research facilities where eternities of existence are measured in the nanosecond lifetimes of subatomic particles. Now I passed through a landscape where experience is measured in geological epochs, eras and eons.

Once the Mattawa Forks was a place where the Cree, Huron and Algonquian

The sheer face of Agawa Rock with its unusual geology and a mysterious array of pictographs made a striking landmark for fur traders travelling the north shore of Lake Superior. *Ontario Parks*

peoples met each summer to trade, renew treaties and socialize. Today it's a grassy picnic site with a gorgeous view.

I walked up into the town with its sturdy brick architecture that evokes Montreal's old quarter, found a coffee and went back to the river to drink it, looking over the once strategically and culturally important confluence that's now a place where people stop for picnic lunches of potato salad, cold chicken and coleslaw.

The water slid past, dark as obsidian except for the ripples where the currents from two rivers collided.

Toward Mattawa, I'd begun to notice dramatic changes in the landscape. The scenery, at least, had changed little since Fraser's time. The peoples of what anthropologists call the Shield Archaic culture, who lived here for millennia before the first European explorer came through, believed the land itself was alive, the earth populated by the spirits who actively inhabited the region's distinctive glacier-sculpted landforms.

Perhaps there's something to these ancestral memories. The Mattawa River flows down an active geological fault. The fracture line slices through rocks in the Canadian Shield that are anywhere from six hundred million to more than four billion years old, and the movement of the underlying plates triggers frequent small—in geological terms—earthquakes.

Check the map maintained by the Geological Survey of Canada, and this region turns out to be one of Canada's seismic hotspots. It's nothing like the gigantic forces at work off the West Coast but it's certainly not static, with temblors often rumbling through the bedrock.

Once, during the great melt at the end of the last ice age about ten thousand years ago but while the ice sheets were still thick enough to depress the Earth's crust, immense volumes of water pent up in the Great Lakes blasted eastward to the Atlantic Ocean through these valleys.

The huge river that ran through the region for six thousand years carried a torrent of boulders, pebbles, gravel and sand that pulverized and eroded underlying rock. It left the thick layers of silt that provided ideal growing conditions in the valley bottoms. Some scientists think many of the plants and animals that reclaimed Canada after the glaciers began their own long, slow journey of recolonization in this little valley.

On the Mattawa, Fraser's brigade faced eleven more portages over the next sixty-five kilometres—about a third of all the portages on this section of his journey crammed into this one small stretch of river. The worst would be at La Vase Portages, a tedious series of boggy potholes separated by ridges of harder rock. But once over that, the voyageurs finally reached the height of land and crossed into the French River system that flows westward to Lake Huron. Then they would be paddling swiftly downstream, some compensation for the dreary unloading, carrying packs, reloading and then doing it all over again.

From North Bay on the eastern end of Lake Nipissing, the Trans-Canada Highway with its steady flow of semis and eighteen-wheelers promised to take me past Sudbury and its smelters. The world's biggest producer of nickel, Inco Ltd., still exploits the deposit left more than a billion years ago when a ten-kilometre-wide meteorite created the Sudbury Basin with a blast equivalent to ten billion Hiroshima-sized atomic bombs. The voyageurs passed by without an inkling of these vast metal deposits.

I wanted to see the historic French River, the last leg Fraser would cover before entering the big waters of Georgian Bay and turning west to Sault Ste. Marie, so I turned south on the secondary roads. I stopped for lunch at Callander, a charming little place that achieved fame—and later notoriety—on the night of May 28, 1934. That was the night small-town doctor Allan Dafoe successfully delivered five baby girls: Annette, Emilie, Yvonne, Cecile and Marie. The Dionnes were the first known quintuplets to survive.

They were a medical miracle. They were cute. They became an overnight media

Once on the Great Lakes, fur brigades faced no portages but long days of open water and dramatic shorelines in the westering sun. *"Canoeing All Our Yesterday's History," PNG Merlin Archive*

sensation. Hence Callander's sudden fame. But the Dionne children were later taken from their parents by the province, put in a special hospital run by Dafoe and exploited as a tourist attraction—visitors to Quintland paid their money to watch through a one-way mirror while the kids played in their nursery. Hence Callander's notoriety as Ontario's human zoo exhibit.

At Lulu's Café, just down the road from Dafoe's old house, I ducked in for a quick bowl of unbelievably good crab and corn chowder while I consulted my maps, thinking while I ate about Fraser's voyageurs eating their mixture of lard and corn mush.

I pushed on—and got lost. It was raining hard when I pulled into a fishing camp and asked directions from Denise Leduc, whose husband was born and raised on the French River and whose family "has been here since who knows when."

Then I parked my car, shrugged into my high-tech rain gear and hiked downstream through a glacier-carved landscape of gorges and naked outcrops of bedrock that provide habitat for rare plants and animals such as the Mississauga rattlesnake. In an age of jumbo jets and air-conditioned cars that whip us through the countryside on multi-lane super highways, it's hard to imagine the historical significance of this stretch of river, now set aside as a corridor park and used mostly by recreational canoeists.

It had been a travel route for the Ojibwa, the Algonquins and the Hurons for time out of mind before the arrival of the first coureurs de bois, the vanguard of thousands of voyageur canoes. They would carry westward the tonnes of trade goods that would reshape aboriginal economies and would return eastward with the torrent of furs that would transform the economies of Montreal and Canada.

The rock was slick where it was bare and slippery where it was covered by wet lichens, a challenge even for my prized three-hundred-dollar no-skid boots. After a long winter without use, the trail was almost invisible in the groundcover except for an occasional splash of yellow paint to mark the way. I moved with great care.

Below what I could find of the trail, the drop into the river was exceedingly steep.

I discovered that travelling from the margins of the continent to its interior is like a voyage backward through the seasons. I'd been admiring tulip fields in Ottawa, but here in the Canadian Shield I found myself in a sparse late winter landscape of rattling branches and the newest of shoots, everything still waiting for the full burst of spring.

Under an overhang in an escarpment that spilled huge boulders, I paused and listened to the falls at Recollet. The wind in the trees rustled like the moccasins of voyageurs making the portage. Brûlé, Champlain, Radisson, Groseilliers, the La Vérendryes, Mackenzie, Thompson and Fraser had all passed here too.

If the place seemed suffused with spirits, perhaps it wasn't surprising. Ahead of me on the brigade route westward along the north coast of Lake Huron, lay Manitoulin Island. In Fraser's time this was the place where Manitou—the Great Spirit—was believed to live.

I got there late in the day, descending first to Great La Cloche Island through a jumble of eerie granite outcrops, gigantic sheets of exposed bedrock and layers of limestone. I stopped briefly at the bridge to Manitoulin Island, which crosses the narrows through which the fur brigades passed for more than a hundred years.

A chance to visit the home of the Great Spirit doesn't come often. I pushed on past the village of Sheguinadah, then Wikwemikong, Manitowaning, Tehkummah. Once this island was set aside as a refuge for the Odawa and Ojibwa peoples who occupied it. The plan was for people on the mainland to abandon their traditional hunting grounds and settle here. Eventually farmers and commercial fishermen demanded access. In 1862, the year Fraser died, so did the dream of Manitoulin. Most of the island was surrendered to the Crown—but the people of Wikwemikong refused to sign the treaty, and to this day, the eastern side of the island is unceded aboriginal land.

I had just found a headland where I could look over this historic landscape when a dense fog rolled in. It was disappointing to sit in the clammy gloom while daylight slipped away. Suddenly a wind stirred. It shifted around, whispering down Manitowaning Bay like the breath of the Manitou, slipped under the fog and lifted it just high enough for the whole stunning vista of islands and the shining lake of the Hurons to come into view.

When I got back to the mainland, it was 11 p.m. A cold wind blew off the lake as I pulled into Blind River. Fraser would have overnighted here, safe in the lee of the island, so I did too.

The next morning, with whitecaps dusting the lake under darkening skies, I set out for Fort St. Joseph. The short-lived but important military base wasn't there when Fraser first passed on his way west—it was built in 1796—but it later proved a key to preventing an American takeover of the western fur-trade routes to the Athabasca region.

Manitou, the Great Spirit, lived among the tribes that camped on the scattered islands of Lake Huron passed by fur brigades heading west. *"Encampment among the islands of Lake Huron," Paul Kane, With Permission of Royal Ontario Museum © ROM*

I turned south to St. Joseph's Island, following my maps through thirty-seven kilometres of maple forest. Split-rail fences of the kind Fraser would have cut as a boy snaked beside the gravel road. Eventually I arrived at the out-of-the-way national historic site.

It was too early in the season. The gates were locked, so I decided to walk in. It would be about an hour's slog, but at least it was on a road. Just past the point where it was farther to go back than to go on, it began to rain so heavily that the water poured off my hat brim in a steady stream.

The seams of my Gore-Tex jacket began to leak. My pockets filled with water. The rain turned to sleet, dimpling the dark ponds where beavers had been at work. I emerged to the sound of surf as an icy wind splattered the semifrozen rain against my face and onto the carpet of wild strawberries around stone outlines of building foundations.

Only the shell of an old chimney stood high enough to provide some shelter from the elements.

The Americans burned the abandoned fort in 1814, but not before Capt. Charles Roberts, anticipating the War of 1812, had mustered local fur traders and Indians unhappy about bloody incursions into the Ohio Valley following the revolution.

Birchbark canoes are prominent in this 1869 portrayal of a First Nations settlement at Sault Ste. Marie, Ontario, an important waypoint for fur brigades. *William Armstrong, Library and Archives Canada, accession number 1970-188-2230, C-040328*

He led four hundred of them to the Straits of Mackinac linking Lake Huron to Lake Michigan, launching the daring pre-emptive strike that captured Fort Michilimakinac, first built in 1686 as a choke point controlling traffic between the Great Lakes.

Roberts's lightning raid gave the British control of the upper Mississippi and ensured that the river routes from the western end of Lake Superior to the interior remained open to Montreal traders.

By the time I made it back to my car, I was so bedraggled that two other guys thinking of hiking out to the fort took one look at me and got back in their truck. As I turned up the heater, I contemplated Fraser's men trying to make the most of things with little more than an upturned canoe to keep off the rain and an open fire to ward off the chill.

There was one benefit to all this. On the way out I passed a roadside stand and bought a couple of litres of high-quality maple syrup before heading for Sault Ste. Marie where voyageurs' canoes—and, once locks were constructed, seagoing ships—passed over to Lake Superior.

At "The Soo" I wanted to see the house of Charles Ermatinger, born in Montreal the same year as Simon Fraser. He, too, had gone from being a clerk to becoming a partner in the North West Company. He had married Mananowe, the daughter of an Ojibwa chief, and raised thirteen children there before retiring with his family to Quebec.

First I went to pay my respects at the shrine to another kind of explorer. Sault Ste. Marie is the hometown of Roberta Bondar, the first Canadian woman in space. So I stopped in at the Canadian Bushplane Heritage Centre to look at its display of astronaut memorabilia. There were family photos, an amusing note from "Ming the Merciless" written by her sister Barbara—Bondar always got to play Flash Gordon as a kid, and Sis got to be the evil nemesis—badges, a commemorative bust of the kind popular in the eighteenth century and even a suit of the special underwear she wore while in orbit.

After Punch Dickins flew down the Mackenzie River to Aklavik in 1929, covering in two days the 3,200 kilometres that had taken Alexander Mackenzie 102 days, the bush plane emerged as the birchbark canoe of the twentieth century for prospectors, trappers, scientists and the RCMP.

In my time I've flown in battered Beech-18s, Beavers, Otters, Cansos, DC-3s, the Norseman, even a Grumman Goose, so walking through the giant hangar looking at specimens of the planes that opened up the North—in the same way the birchbark canoe had opened up the West—was a nostalgic hour.

How do you describe a bush plane, anyway? The same way you might describe a Montreal canoe. It's versatile, durable, easy to fix and cheap to run, and with the right undercarriage—fat wheels, pontoons or skis—it can land just about anywhere, from a gravel bar to an ice floe. It can carry everything from dogs and fish to specialized equipment, passengers, the mail, a winter's rations, a sick kid or a sack of Christmas presents.

So it was amusing to look over the museum's poker-faced exhibition of the worst bush plane ever built, the Buhl CA-6 Air Sedan. When the prototype flew in October 1935, it was almost a complete failure. It handled so badly that the test pilots both insisted on wearing parachutes, but the altitude it achieved was so low they wouldn't have opened in time. Some, the exhibit dryly observed, claimed the plane was so bad that it set aviation back twenty years.

"The worst damn airplane I ever flew," pilot Douglas Cameron of Kenora is quoted as saying in the exhibit. "It was a ground hugger and you had to fight to break it loose to get off the water . . . . Anyone I ever saw told me it was a pig."

If there's one bush plane to make any pilot forget about the Buhl, however, it's the Beaver, rated one of Canada's ten most important engineering achievements of the twentieth century. The first one flew in 1947, the year I was born, and there are still some in active service.

But I had a long way to go, so I reluctantly turned away from CF-OBS, a Beaver built in 1948 and still in flying condition, went back out past Roberta Bondar's utilitarian underwear and pushed off for Thunder Bay along the north shore of Gichi Gamiing, the great lake of the Ojibwa, so big it makes its own weather.

To us it's Lake Superior. Its dramatic coastlines, haunting coves, rugged hillsides and what resemble maritime vistas make it worth a visit in its own right.

To the voyageurs, it was one more obstacle. For the rest of their journey, they had an open run. The water was deep, so there was no more lining canoes through shallows; there were no more portages and no more rapids to run. Instead, there were sandy beaches where they could camp.

Not that the big lake was without risks. At Agawa Bay, where Fraser's brigade almost certainly put up for the night on the white sand beach, he was now two thousand perilous kilometres from Lachine, Candice Djukic explained. It was her first day on the job at a new government interpretive centre, and things were slow (I was visitor number three). She had plenty of time to tell me how thermal differences between sun-baked rock and the cold lake could result in fast-developing fogs and sudden fast-moving squalls along the craggy shorelines.

The lake could blow up suddenly, Djukic said, with intense storms that spawned water spouts and combers so huge they could easily swamp a heavily laden canoe trying to make way with only fifteen centimetres of clearance above the waterline.

The Ojibwa, she said, claimed the sudden roiling of the water was caused by Misshepezhieu—the Great Lynx—lashing his tail beneath the surface. With a warning about the dangers of rogue waves, she directed me to Agawa Rock, a site where I could see some mysterious pictographs, the first of which had likely been here for two thousand years before Fraser first went past.

I've been in some eerie places in my travels, and this one rated with the best.

Surf breaks over the slippery ledge at the foot of Agawa Rock that visitors wishing to observe pictographs must chance. Sudden storms on Lake Superior were a threat to heavily laden canoes. *Ontario Parks*

This pictograph at Agawa Rock is thought to portray Misshepezhieu—the Great Lynx—a supernatural being whose lashing tail causes violent storms on Lake Superior. *Ontario Parks*

To get to the site, I had to clamber close to half a kilometre, first down a narrow cleft that I later learned was 2.5 billion years old, created when molten rock flooded into pressure fractures and then eroded away over many millennia.

Well, that is the geologists' explanation. The Ojibwa say it happened when a family lost a baby and noticed the tracks of Misshepezhieu. They called on their protector spirits, the thunderbirds, who blasted lightning bolts into the cave where the Great Lynx was hiding. The fog that plagued the voyageurs belonged in Ojibwa eyes to the thunderbirds who used it to cloak themselves when they set out to hunt evil spirits. You know they've found them when thunder rumbles and lightning flickers out over the lake.

Keeping an eye out for Misshepezhieu and his tricks, I edged out along a narrow, treacherous ledge. The swell sucked and slopped below. That surge and the slickness and curve of the rock meant that if one of those rogue waves pulled you off the ledge, you'd never get out.

Ropes had been thoughtfully attached to iron pegs and left dangling into the water so that anyone who fell in had a way to haul themselves up—but these were not reassuring.

Then up on the sheer face of the cliff face—with shafts of sunlight occasionally breaking through a troubled sky, lancing deep into the clear waters and reflecting off huge slabs of rock jumbled below the surface—I saw why the young woman had sent me here.

I saw what looked like four canoes, serpents, a mysterious creature with stegosaurus-like spurs down its spine and great crescent horns, what seemed to be a rider on a horse and the dunce L.F.R. who left his initials in 1937 and a few of his more recent acolytes in the tribe of the stupids.

On the way back up, I spotted a memorial plaque to Selwyn Dewdney, the remarkable writer, artist, anthropologist and father of poet Christopher Dewdney. Selwyn paddled his canoe into some of what were then remote regions of the Canadian Shield and recorded more than 290 of these rock paintings before his death. His ashes were scattered at Agawa Rock.

These images, I learned later, probably dated from Fraser's time or somewhat before. According to the official account provided by the government, early in the 1800s an Ojibwa named Shingwaukonce told how a leader named Myeengun led a war party across Gichi Gamiing from north to south—a formidable prospect even with a modern boat—and the paintings recount his exploits.

That journey has been dated to about 1660, when Jesuit missionaries were active in the region and there was war with the Iroquois. The mysterious horned beast, it turns out, is a representation of Misshepezhieu, who, I gather, chose to still the waters for Myeengun and not lash them into a frenzy with his tail.

From there I drove to Michipicoten River, most westerly of the French outposts in 1632 and a stopping point for the Montreal brigades because it was the start of a canoe route that linked Lake Superior to James Bay. Then it went on to Nipigon River, where Jesuit priest Claude Allouez celebrated the first mass west of Sault Ste. Marie on May 29, 1667.

In sight of Sleeping Giant Provincial Park, I stopped to visit one of the oldest known sites of human habitation in Canada, the terraces below a steep rock bluff. More than fifty years ago, archeologists found distinctive evidence there of an archaic hunting culture that migrated here from the Great Plains about nine thousand years ago, a reminder that in one context, Fraser's trek to the west is a blip of modern history.

The Sleeping Giant is Nanabosho, turned to stone by the Manitou for his presumption in using supernatural powers to swamp a canoe, drowning the two white men who were coming to search for the silver treasure he had hidden. The long, narrow peninsula looks vaguely like a vast human form at rest in the lake; it may derive its name from a legend, but it's also the landmark that told the Montreal canoe brigade that the long journey west was almost done.

I imagined the pace of paddle strokes picking up as the voyageurs looked forward to a regale (extra rations of food and rum) and maybe freshly baked bread when they reached Grand Portage, which lies just southwest of the peninsula—anything other than the lard-flavoured mush on which they'd subsisted for almost two months must have seemed a wonderful prospect.

If they'd made good time, they might even have a few weeks of ease before the men of the north arrived with their furs and preparations began for the long return.

Just then a shaft of sunlight broke through clouds that were as dark as gun metal along the undersides. The lake before Thunder Bay gleamed turquoise and silver where Misshepezhieu stirred, tossing waves across the reefs and up the rocky shoreline. Perhaps it had greeted Simon Fraser in the same way as he arrived at the halfway point of his great journey of adventure.

Simon Fraser

8

HARD WORK IN A HARD LAND

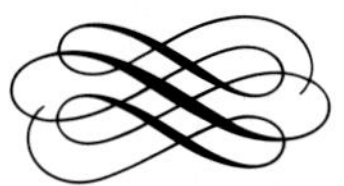

Across from a weary red brick walk-up in a modest residential suburb of Thunder Bay, potholes in the street still full of muddy water from the previous night's rain, I found the place where Simon Fraser received the fateful instructions that led him across the Rockies.

It was here during the annual rendezvous in the summer of 1805 that he was asked to undertake what the North West Company called a "discoverie"—a voyage of exploration—into what is now northern British Columbia and, if possible, to establish trade there.

Alexander Mackenzie, suddenly a fierce competitor in the new XY Company he'd launched after a dispute with North West Company magnate Simon McTavish, had already been through the mountains.

Now Mackenzie's old company felt the cost of its long supply lines biting deeply into its profits and was back on the scent. It was pursuing a two-track policy, simultaneously negotiating with the Hudson's Bay Company for transit privileges through a northern port at Churchill and also trying to find another viable route to the western ocean. John Finlay had conducted a reconnaissance on the Finlay and Parsnip rivers in 1797. David Thompson and Duncan McGillivray had tried unsuccessfully to find a river to the Pacific from Rocky Mountain House southwest of present-day Edmonton in 1800 and 1801.

Fraser was to switch the focus back to the north. By then a thirteen-year veteran of the Athabasca trade, he doubtless saw a chance to make his name—or perhaps

Forts at the Lakehead were abandoned, moved and replaced but the palisades surrounding this replica of Fort William at Thunder Bay resemble those that greeted Simon Fraser. *Stephen Hume*

The reproduction of Fort William, about 15 km from the site of the original establishment in Thunder Bay, Ontario, can draw 100,000 visitors or more a year. *Government of Ontario*

he received a proposal he dared not turn down—in any event, he took on the task. For its part, the company engaged twenty experienced men for his crew and provided equipment and supplies. He must have left immediately; he had close to four thousand kilometres to travel before temperatures plunged, rivers froze, trees shattered in subzero cold and the eternally drifting snows arrived.

At first, I had trouble finding the former site of old Fort William, once an outpost of comfortable accommodation, elegant dining and shops that retailed luxury items to North West Company employees. It also had warehouses filled with wholesale trade goods for the interior.

The whole place was intended to awe as much as to provide security and to expedite freight. It was the eighteenth-century version of market positioning, corporate branding and product recognition in a fickle and fiercely competitive business that today's marketing brains behind Wal-Mart and Microsoft would appreciate. The trade message was clear. If the North West Company didn't have it, you probably didn't need it.

But two centuries after its heyday, I found the original site wasn't marked on any of my maps, I saw no directions to it from the main routes in Thunder Bay and, unlike Fraser's canoe brigade, I wasn't travelling with a guide who'd been this way before.

Finally I found somebody who knew what I was talking about when I asked about the old fort, not the spectacular tourist reconstruction fifteen kilometres out of town on the Kaministiquia River and certainly not the even earlier site at Grand Portage, Minnesota, about fifty kilometres to the south.

John Rossi took a moment from pumping gas in a down-at-the-heels neighbourhood on Thunder Bay's east side to direct me through a maze of side street cul-de-sacs and the weird doglegs that urban planners create when they carve up old communities to accommodate new expressways. First he pointed out the folly of moving the restored fort so far from its original neighbourhood.

"This is a dying core because there's no business," he told me, waving a hand to include the storefront across the street where a water-swollen piece of particle board covered the front window.

Where Fraser saw only a dozen buildings when he walked the main quadrangle within the defensive palisades, Thunder Bay is now a major industrial port. More than two billion dollars a year in wood and paper products cross its docks. The grain-handling terminal, gateway to Canada's western bread basket, is one of the world's largest. A population of more than 120,000 makes it the twelfth-biggest city in Ontario.

Yet the most recent census confirmed difficult times. The city's population had declined 4.1 percent from the previous count. When I pulled the economic stats, I discovered that the largest employers were the municipal government, the province, the regional health authority, the university and the two school boards, in that order. Maybe my guide had a point.

"There's a few malls, but it's not enough," Rossi said. "Fort William, can you imagine if they'd built that downtown, the impact on the city—it would have built the downtown up." Indeed, the heritage park draws a hundred thousand or more visitors a year.

Then he directed me across a bridge with instructions to go right on McIntosh to McNaughton and look for the obelisk. It proved a bit more interesting than that. Every street seemed to begin with "Mc." I missed a turn and wound up cruising McTavish, McGillivray, McKenzie, McLaughlin, McMurray, McPherson, McDonald and McBain before I found my way back, tried again and got myself onto McIntosh.

At the end of this quiet residential street I found what had once been the epicentre of North America's richest business, the corporate colossus of its day, where bold entrepreneurs with a good idea, courage and self-confidence could become rich—or descend into bankruptcy with one misjudged paddle stroke.

This was where the barons of the fur trade met to talk business strategy with the wintering partners. They dined on fine china and drank from crystal at tables laid with white linen. The archetype came out of the Scottish clan system, with the company's directors behaving like tartan chieftains. It was also designed to impress upon employees—and clients—the wealth and power that would surely flow their way from the company's commercial success.

The site was marked by a red granite pillar with a beaver sculpted in bas-relief. The obelisk sat on a crumbling concrete pedestal that was itself set up on a raised flower bed in which there were no flowers. The bare ground was surrounded by three naked flag poles and a manhole cover. A steel fence enclosed the weedy backdrop of a Canadian Pacific Railway humpyard where locomotives noisily shunted grain cars and flatbeds loaded with bright yellow equipment.

All those "Mcs" who left their names on the streets would doubtless have approved of the industrial sound effects. They themselves were nothing if not industrious.

Old Fort William once evoked urbanity in the midst of a vast wilderness. It was "the great emporium for the Interior," said early nineteenth-century observer Robert Cox, whom I found cited in Thunder Bay historian Jean Morrison's exhaustively researched and entertaining book *Superior Rendezvous-place: Fort William in the Canadian Fur Trade.*

"The assortment of merchandise which amazed Cox in 1817 amazes still," Morrison writes. "Just one cassette destined for the west in 1816 held rolls of ferreting silk and ribbons of many colours, papers of pins, playing cards, shaving boxes, common razors, beads, brass 'jews-harps,' sets of violin strings, fine scissors, silk hat covers, tooth brushes, Windsor soap, rolls of blacking, nutmegs, jockey hats and coloured thread."

An inscription proclaims that the lonely and—it seemed to me—rather neglected pillar was erected by the Thunder Bay Historical Society in 1914 "to commemorate the locality made famous by the pioneer fur traders of the North West," the first of whom had built a fort near here on the Kaministiquia River in 1678. The federal government finally got around to installing another cursory National Historic Sites and Monuments plaque in 1981.

In fact this wasn't where Simon Fraser would have landed on his first voyage west in 1792. The early forts built around this site by coureurs de bois and used as an important staging point for exploration of the river systems to the west—Jacques de Noyon in 1688 became the first European to use an ancient Ojibwa trail to climb past the formidable Kakabeka Falls on the Kaministiquia and continue over into the Rainy River watershed—had long been abandoned by the time Fraser came.

Fraser landed at Grand Portage, where the North West Company had moved in 1780, to take advantage of an easier route. It meant a longer carry around falls on the Pigeon River but avoided the brutally steep portage at Kakabeka.

Whatever journals Fraser kept on that trip—if he kept any at all—have been lost or destroyed or languish unnoticed in some collection. Confusion arises from the fact, as historian W. Kaye Lamb points out, that four Simon Frasers were engaged in the fur trade at the time. One document confirms he was in the Athabasca district in 1799, however, that he was made a partner in 1801 on the basis of his work there and that he was at Fort Liard in 1802 or 1803.

Fraser's corporate achievements were recognized in Athabasca, and he was

The most remote trading posts became beehives of activity when trappers arrived to exchange furs for guns, ammunition, bolts of cloth and luxuries like tea and tobacco. *Hudson's Bay Archives N39120*

Birchbark canoes similar to those used by Simon Fraser on his expedition to the Rockies and beyond are still manufactured. These are in storage at Fort William. *Stephen Hume*

given the weighty task of following up Mackenzie's work there. It's conjecture, but considering the length of apprenticeships, it seems reasonable to surmise that he gained his expertise in the Peace River region.

In the absence of Fraser documents, to get a sense of what he and the Montreal brigade would have experienced arriving at "the great carrying place" in 1792, I had to consult Mackenzie, writing in 1798.

By the time Mackenzie's book went to his London publisher for publication in 1801, the North West Company was already preparing to abandon Grand Portage and return to the Kaministiquia River with an even grander establishment that would become Fort William.

The American Revolution meant a new boundary west of the Great Lakes would fall just north of Grand Portage. Canny Montreal merchants, many of them Loyalist refugees with painful memories, had no wish to be picked clean once again by vengeful Yankee customs duties.

When Fraser came ashore on his first journey west, however, the new fort was still just an idea.

Company representatives always arrived looking their best as a matter of policy. Somewhere along the shoreline the canoes certainly put in. The men would have boiled water, washed away the grime of travel, shaved with their straight razors and trimmed each others' hair. Then each would have pulled out the second shirt he'd kept clean since Montreal and tied a colourful voyageur's sash around his waist.

A clerk like Fraser put on his best clothes—a knee-length coat, a linen shirt, probably a ruffled cravat, knee breeches, stockings, boots and a beaver hat—probably a tricorne or cocked hat of the kind popular during the revolutionary period, but for a young man, perhaps one of the top hats just coming into vogue that would dominate men's head fashion throughout the nineteenth century.

The image of a teenager who barely shaved arriving at a wilderness outpost—while wearing a top hat and a frilly shirt, and being carried ashore from a birchbark canoe by men twice his age—may seem peculiar, but this was all about image. The company expected Fraser to play a role that projected its importance and authority.

At Grand Portage, Fraser's brigades came ashore at the foot of a bay and landed in a clearing that Mackenzie describes as a natural amphitheatre surrounded by hills. The fort's cedar palisades were flanked by hay meadows for the permanent garrison's cattle.

Almost overnight the population would explode from a few hundred to more than a thousand. North West Company employees from Montreal, Indian guides and interpreters, free traders from the American territories, buckskin-clad Métis hunters, wintering partners and clerks from the north all mingled to drink, converse and argue in a rich polyglot of French, Gaelic, clipped British accents, Scottish burrs, Yankee twangs and numerous aboriginal languages and dialects.

Men arriving from the north would be treated to a regale on arrival: a ration of rum, bread, pork, butter and tobacco after a year of living on fish and game, pemmican and berries eked out with some flour, sugar and tea.

While the north men lived in tents during the rendezvous, men from the Montreal brigades slept in the open or sheltered under their big canoes if it rained. When it came to the company's owners and managers, there was a strictly observed class structure.

Inside the fort, the shingled houses were off limits to the hired help but "calculated for every convenience of trade, as well as to accommodate the proprietors and clerks during their short residence there." So even fuzzy-cheeked, teenaged Simon enjoyed the privilege of a bed, a roof over his head and fine dining by comparison to the fare offered during the voyage.

The proprietors, clerks, guides and interpreters took their formal dinners in the great hall, which could seat several hundred, at places carefully assigned according to rank. They would feast, writes Mackenzie, on freshly baked bread, salt pork, beef, hams, fish, venison, butter, peas, Indian corn, potatoes, tea, spirits, wine and—a real treat—fresh milk, "for which purpose several milch cows are constantly kept."

The men who paddled the canoes and hauled the bales of freight got just their standard fare. They ate Indian corn with the outer husks removed by boiling it in a strong alkali solution to produce what the Americans called hominy, then mixed with melted suet and a little salt.

"It makes a wholesome, palatable food," writes Mackenzie.

And the social hierarchy appears to have been accepted and even endorsed.

"Though they are sometimes assembled to the number of 1,200 men, indulging themselves in the free use of liquor, and quarrelling with each other, they always show the greatest respect to their employers, who are comparatively few in numbers, and beyond the aid of any legal power to enforce due obedience," Mackenzie notes. "In short, a degree of subordination can only be maintained by the good opinion these men entertain of their employers."

If the annual rendezvous was a time for brigade crews to blow off steam and for the north men to engage in the socializing they'd missed for a full year, the point of the meeting was still business.

Senior partners would talk strategy. Replacements for those leaving service at the northern trading posts would be recruited, and junior clerks such as Simon Fraser, bound for the north, would be assigned to the partner they'd serve for the next five to seven years.

After witnessing the rather sad state of the original historic site, I visited Fort William Historical Park to get a sense of what Fraser must have experienced. I wasn't disappointed, whatever its location. The reconstruction is both compelling and convincing, from the Ojibwa village outside the palisades—where I heard native Indians give a lecture on how to build a wigwam—to the Indian trade house where I was instructed in how the credit system worked.

At the canoe factory, I examined the marvels of engineering that are real birchbark canoes, built on site in the traditional way. And equally important, I got a demonstration at the fur press where I learned how to squash beaver pelts into a waterproof forty-kilogram bale.

From Grand Portage in 1792, Fraser's crew was contracted to carry eight bales of trade goods to the north men's camp at the top of the portage. This meant a hike of almost fifteen kilometres past the falls on the Pigeon River. Then they hiked back with eight bales of fur. If they undertook to carry more, they got a bonus—one Spanish dollar for each extra bale. A shortage of coin in the colonies by the mid-eighteenth century made the Spanish silver dollar the principal measure of exchange in North America.

Then Fraser and the men chosen to winter in the north would walk the portage themselves and set out for Athabasca in one of the smaller, lighter and much faster *canots du nord.* The big Montreal freighters returned to Lachine with their load of furs.

My search for Simon Fraser next took me due west past Fort Frances with its

First Nations hunters like this one wearing snowshoes and a blanket coat kept fur-trade posts supplied with fresh game and pemmican. *Cornelius Krieghoff, McCord Museum M9671009*

pulp mill and a huge log dump, past Huronian Lake and the continental divide where the rivers begin flowing north to Hudson Bay, then down the Rainy River where the canoes turned into Lake of the Woods with its maze of 14,542 islands.

I travelled past old Fort St. Charles on the other side of the lake. Near here Jean-Baptiste La Vérendrye and twenty other voyageurs were ambushed and decapitated in 1736 by a war party out to avenge the traffic in Dakota Indians enslaved by other tribes and sold to the colonial French. The slave trade, it turns out, was not an exclusively American or European evil.

At Kenora I dropped in on a scholarly conference of the Centre for Rupert's Land Studies and got directions from an enthusiastic David Malaher to historic Rat Portage. This was the crossing that put voyageurs on the Winnipeg River, and many considered it the point at which they crossed into the West.

I was glad I'd asked; Malaher explained that there were actually three Rat Portages.

"The east route, that was used by native people who lived along that shore. They had few supplies to carry and no need to travel west to make the crossing," he said. "The west route at Rat Portage, that was the money route, that's where the fur and trade goods went across. There was another portage. We'll call it Rat Portage centre. That was the express route. That's where the VIPs, mail and messengers would cross."

When I went to look at the famous site, I found the narrow neck of land where the man who would found BC had crossed. It now lay buried beneath a public works yard and the right-of-way for the CPR mainline.

The yard had a big sign restricting access to City of Kenora personnel, but the gate was open and nobody was around to ask what the heck I thought I was doing. So I walked across to the Winnipeg River and washed my hands in the waters of the West before continuing my journey.

Simon Fraser

9

IN THE SHAPE-SHIFTER'S FOOTPRINTS

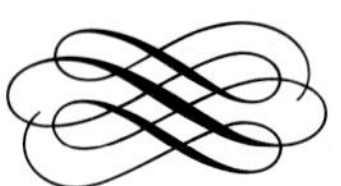

I crossed into Manitoba, leaving the Trans-Canada Highway and turning with the Winnipeg River through Whiteshell Provincial Park. The land was marshy, and I saw plenty of evidence of beavers at work. In Fraser's day aboriginal people would paddle their canoes into the swampy lake margins, as they had from time immemorial, and harvest wild rice with bark winnowing trays and beating sticks. Sometimes they gleaned up to two hundred kilograms a day.

From here I'd have to slant northwest across Manitoba, skirting four-hundred-kilometre-long Lake Winnipeg, the remnant of an even bigger freshwater sea—Lake Agassiz—fed by melting ice sheets. From 11,700 to 9,000 years ago, at times it covered most of the province.

Before going north, however, I wanted to stop at Bannock Point and visit one of the most ancient sites in a Canada that tends to think its history dates from Cartier, Champlain and Cook.

The fur brigades would have swept right past, but a short hike back in the forest from a winding secondary road is a collection of boulder mosaics laid down by unknown people so far in the past that their origins are a mystery, although the site remains sacred to many aboriginal people.

Anthropologists aren't sure of the cultural significance of these figures. They outline turtles, snakes, humans and abstract geometric patterns. Most intriguing, they appear to occur in a great arc that radiates outward from this point through

Ancient ancestors of Manitoba's First Nations laid down mysterious boulder mosaics at Bannock Point. These offering-adorned trees within a stone circle indicate the site is still used for spiritual purposes. *Stephen Hume*

At Bannock Point, east of Winnipeg, the boulder mosaics outline turtles, snakes, human beings and abstract geometric patterns. They were disseminated as far as Nebraska and Alberta. *Manitoba Culture, Heritage, Tourism and Sport*

Minnesota, the Dakotas, Iowa, Nebraska, Montana and Alberta. But the farther they occur from the tablerock at Bannock Point, the cruder they become, which suggests that this is the point of origin.

It was late afternoon. In this strange landscape of lichen-covered pre-Cambrian bedrock and scrub trees struggling for a purchase in the thin topsoil, it was easy to become disoriented. I reminded myself to stay on the trail worn over millennia by thousands of feet.

I tried to use distinctive rocks and trees as landmarks, but with the sun hanging on the western horizon and the shadows lengthening, I soon found it difficult to distinguish what had seemed obvious. For a time I lost track of where I was and gave a sigh of relief when I spotted the orange surveyor's tape I'd tied to a branch where the trail entered the site.

This place, I realized, made my challenges in searching for Simon Fraser seem trivial. It was as old as anything on the planet. It had seen the Ordovician seas that covered Manitoba five hundred million years ago, it knew the Devonian and the Cretaceous seas, it had seen ice ages come and go, life forms wax and wane, the mass extinctions in which life itself had almost vanished and then rebounded. Even Lake Agassiz's long reign was a blip on this time scale.

As I walked among the haunting mosaics, some so large you'd need to be in a hot air balloon to fully perceive them outside the imagination, I thought about the small plaque out by the road. It warned that there are no fixed interpretations for the figures found here.

"Anishinabe and other first nations believe they were left long ago for the benefit of all people that might visit to receive their teachings and healing," it said. "There are many levels of understanding and therefore many ways to interpret the teachings. With each visit, they take on greater significance."

I thought about Wee-sa-kay-jac, the shape-shifter, the mischief maker, who travelled the Canadian Shield with a pack on his back filled with songs. His footprints are said to be everywhere. Also everywhere were the midges, punkies, gnats, no-see-ums and the forty species of mosquitoes, blackflies, horseflies, deer flies and bullheads that draw blood when they bite. I was grateful for my can of bug repellent.

At the heart of the complex I found a great circle. At its centre stood a small cluster of trees that rippled and shimmered with colour. I realized I was looking at many-hued ribbons, bits of faded and deteriorating cloth, bundles of feathers and twists of tobacco. These were offerings.

This holy place was already ancient when Simon Fraser passed by, and two centuries later it was still in use, suffused with meanings that run deeper than the overlay of imported faiths that travelled west with the priests of Europe.

With those ideas to ponder, I drove northwest under Grandmother Moon, past the nuclear laboratories at Pinawa, down the lower reaches of the Winnipeg River—its fearsome rapids tamed now by six dams—past the long-vanished site of

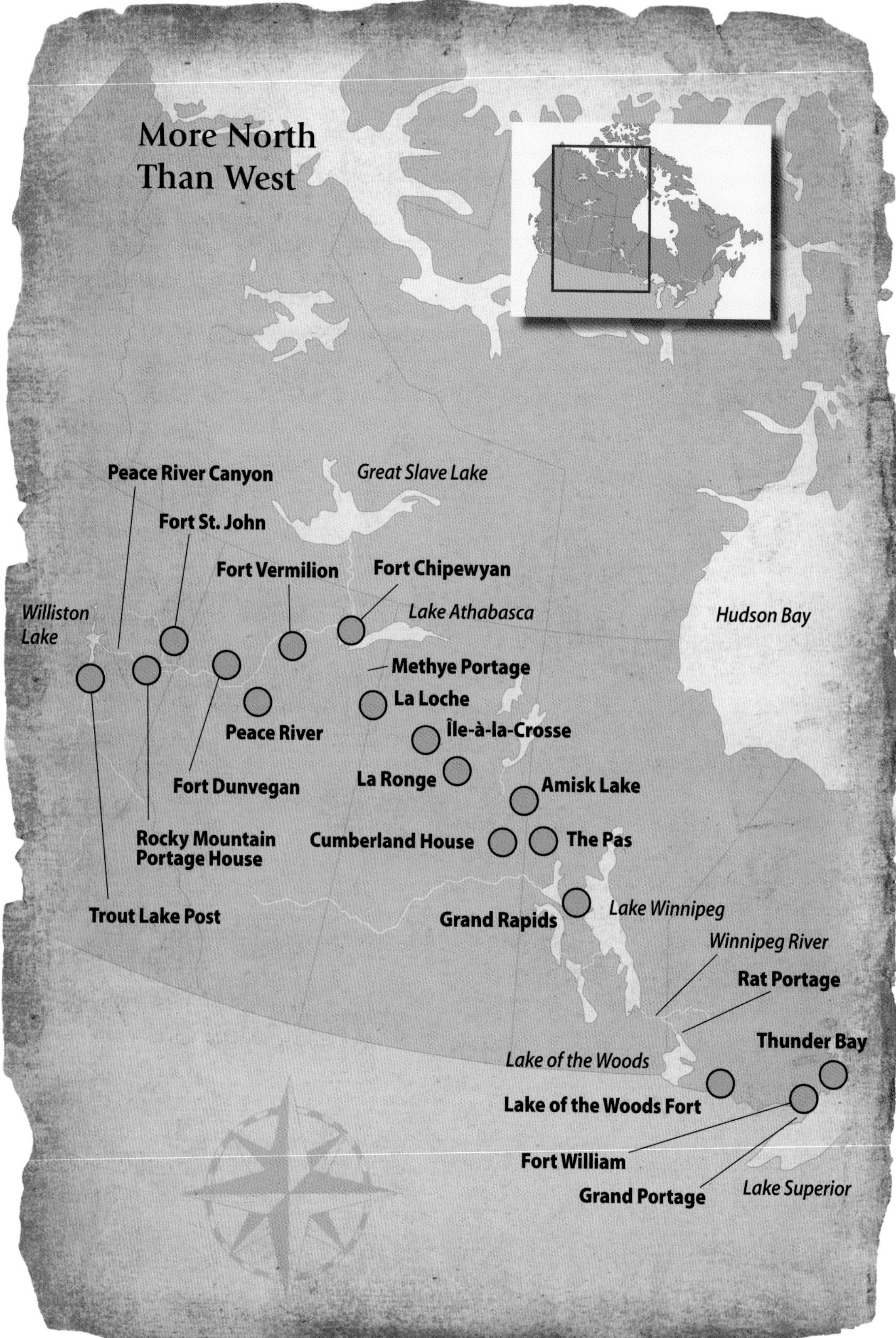
More North
Than West
Peace River Canyon
Great Slave Lake
Fort St. John
Fort Vermilion
Fort Chipewyan
Williston Lake
Lake Athabasca
Hudson Bay
Methye Portage
La Loche
Peace River
Île-à-la-Crosse
La Ronge
Fort Dunvegan
Amisk Lake
Rocky Mountain Portage House
Cumberland House
The Pas
Trout Lake Post
Grand Rapids
Lake Winnipeg
Winnipeg River
Rat Portage
Thunder Bay
Lake of the Woods
Lake of the Woods Fort
Fort William
Grand Portage
Lake Superior

the North West Company's Fort Bas de la Rivière, where Fraser would have paused, through the dispersed settlement of Fort Alexander to the sudden blue expanse of Lake Winnipeg.

The next day, crossing the 53rd parallel, my trip meter ticked past 4,371 kilometres.

At Grand Rapids, Cedar Lake spills through the narrows into Lake Winnipeg. I stopped to watch squadrons of white pelicans sailing serenely below the hydroelectric dam that now exploits the fall of water that gave the place its name.

The rapids compelled Fraser's brigades to line their canoes for two leagues—more than ten kilometres in today's measurement—before embarking for The Pas and the mouth of the Cree's Kisiskatchewani Sipi, the swift-flowing Saskatchewan River first visited by Henry Kelsey more than a century earlier.

At Cumberland House, the inland post founded by Samuel Hearne, the brigades turned sharply north up the Bigstone River to the rapid-filled Sturgeon-weir River. It led to Amisk Lake. Even today this is still mostly roadless wilderness. To get there I had to backtrack into Manitoba and head even farther north to the mining town of Flin Flon, eight hundred kilometres northwest of Winnipeg.

Flin Flon is the only place I've been that's named after a character in a science fiction novel. In J.E. Preston-Muddock's 1905 book *The Sunless City,* Josiah Flintabbatey Flonatin descends through a bottomless lake, finds a golden city at the planet's centre and eventually escapes through a gold-encrusted hole in the Earth's crust.

A group of prospectors found a copy in a cabin in the bush in 1914 and passed it around during the long, dark winter months. The next season they found a hole—

Josiah Flintabbatey Flonatin, character in a science fiction novel that entertained some prospectors one dreary winter, bestowed an abbreviated form of his name on the mining and smelting town of Flin Flon, Manitoba. *Jonathan Naylor*/Vancouver Sun

and a showing of gold ore—so one of them proposed naming their claim Flin Flon for the character who'd entertained them all winter.

The truth turned out to be as wild as the novel. The prospectors had staked claims on one of the richest copper deposits ever found. Today, stacks and head-frames from the Hudson Bay Mining and Smelting Company's mines and smelter are visible long before you arrive in the moonscape of blasted rock that surrounds the town.

Drifts and mine shafts honeycomb the rock below Flin Flon, and 360 metres underground, in what might be a high-tech scenario from *The Sunless City,* a bio-secure lab occupies an unused part of the mine. It conducts genetically contained research on more than five hundred plant species, from rare orchids to trees whose bark contains potent anticancer agents.

But I was in search of the old frontier, not the new one, so I crossed the border into Saskatchewan. At the village of Creighton, I looked up Dennis Strom, the regional economic development officer who also happens to be an archeologist and fur-trade historian.

Strom was only too happy to direct me to the Sturgeon-weir River and a little-known North West Company fort on Amisk Lake's Warehouse Bay, which was the distribution point for all the northern routes.

"The fort was about 12 miles from the Sturgeon-weir, which the Nor'Westers called La Maligne because it had so many shallows and rapids," he said. "Take the trail through the bush and you'll come to Limestone Point where the voyageurs would stop for a rest after coming up the river."

That meant negotiating about fifty kilometres of slippery road that was gravel in name only. It was raining heavily when I arrived, but by now I was as used to getting soaked as the voyageurs must have been, so I hiked down the ancient trail to Limestone Point.

My guide had told me that if I listened hard enough, I'd hear the paddles of Fraser's brigade canoes, but the drumming of the rain on the leaves was loud and drowned everything except the cry of a solitary loon. It was too wet even to eat my sandwich, so I headed next for Frog Portage, a crucial transfer point into the 300,000-square-kilometre drainage of the Churchill River system, which flows 1,600 kilometres from west to east across northern Saskatchewan and Manitoba.

It was here that the North West Company traders successfully intercepted Chipewyan canoes bound for Cumberland House. They paid a bit less for the furs, thus increasing their own profit margins, but saved the Indians many days of tedious travel.

Just past Frog Portage, Strom told me, I'd find a reconditioned mining road that would take me cross-country to La Ronge, my next stop. It would save me a six-hour drive south to Prince Albert and back north again.

"It's a narrow road," he warned. "If you meet traffic, you pull way over or you'll get a rock the size of a softball through your windshield and you'll cry."

I found the road, all right, but it soon became clear that "reconditioned" is a relative term. It dwindled to a muddy, sloppy, pot-holed track, and by the time I realized I'd gone too far, it was too narrow to turn around.

Then it really began to rain. Sheets of muddy water obscured the windshield of my rented Impala. The street tires had little traction, and I kept slithering toward the soft shoulders, and beyond them, deep ditches filled with water pouring out of beaver ponds. I put the car in low and slowed to a crawl. Great—I had about a hundred kilometres before me and no way to go back.

Ahead I saw flashing lights. It was a Saskatchewan highways department four-by-four—off the road and mired axle-deep in the mud. I wound down my window to ask if they wanted a ride, but the crew waved me off. They had another four-by-four coming to pull them out, one said, and if I slid off the road I'd likely be on my own until things dried out.

Three hours later I had inched my way to La Ronge, a settlement of 2,700—half the population aboriginal—that straggles down the shore of the lake bearing the same name.

The next leg of my journey, and Fraser's, would take me to Île-à-la-Crosse, where James Douglas, another fur trader who shaped BC's future, served his apprenticeship. It meant another 175-kilometre trek down a remote unpaved road with no services or habitation, so I stepped into Robertson's Trading Post to pick up emergency supplies.

Before I collected my cans of tuna, bars of chocolate and bug juice, I took a nostalgic look around the kind of all-purpose frontier store—buy rations for your bush camp, replace broken gear, trade some furs, pick up the usual groceries, you name it—that's vanishing from the Canadian landscape.

Simon Fraser would have recognized Robertson's in an instant, but I hadn't been in a store quite like it since buying powdered eggs, canned bacon and a good skinning knife at Weaver & Devore Trading Ltd. in Yellowknife more than thirty years ago.

I admired a smoke-tanned moosehide jacket with elaborate Cree beadwork ($900), decorated moosehide gloves ($200) and hand-sewn moccasins ($80). I goggled at the albino wolverine trapped by Paul Adam in 1987 and the thirty-eight-kilogram lake trout caught by Philip John Blacklake the same year.

But much as I wanted to linger, I had a long way to travel. As I penetrated deeper into the northern bush, even AM radio signals faded into static until the dial flashed "none" whenever I pushed the seek button.

I arrived at Île-à-la-Crosse with the sun low in the western sky and drove into the village where Europeans and aboriginals have lived together in harmony for over two hundred years. The first trading post was established here by Louis Primeau the year before Simon Fraser was born. By the time Fraser passed through for the

The rough and ready Trading Post at La Ronge, Saskatchewan, is a thriving contemporary descendant from the fur-trade era and still supplies bush rations for hunters, trappers and anglers. *Canadian Press*

first time, it had become an important provisioning and staging depot for the Athabasca trade.

The place has another resonant bit of history, and I went up to the old cemetery above the lake to find it. There, after searching among gravestones with famous fur-trade names like Fiddler and one just marked "Trapper," I found the marker for the Reverend Sister Marguerite Marie, born Sara Riel, who died at the age of thirty-four on December 27, 1883.

Louis Riel's sister had come here in 1871 with the Grey Nuns to serve in the school, dispensary and convent, perhaps because there was an old family connection with the place—Louis Riel Sr., the visionary firebrand's father, was born here.

A young man raking the lawn told me where to find the footings in the grass that were all that remained of the old trading post: go down the lane past the helicopter pad at the forestry headquarters, go down to the beach and look for the big spruce.

Boats were pulled up much as Fraser's canoe would have been in 1792, but now they were aluminum and not birchbark, and four-wheeled all-terrain vehicles were parked nearby. I looked across the breathtaking vista of the lake that the brigades had crossed on their way north to Buffalo Narrows and La Loche, my next destination.

At La Loche, another 165 kilometres north, a huge red sun balanced on the northwestern horizon. If I were Simon Fraser, I'd be settling in for the night and hoping for a decent sleep in preparation for the next morning's assault on Methye Portage.

At the north end of Lac la Loche, sandy ground rises to the height of land beyond which all rivers drain toward the Mackenzie River rather than Lake Winnipeg and Hudson Bay. Early travellers called it Portage la Loche.

This twenty-kilometre marathon follows an ancient aboriginal trail and culminates in a dangerously steep descent to the Clearwater River. It was first crossed by Peter Pond in 1778 when Fraser was a toddler.

Explorers had sought a Northwest Passage for three hundred years before Fraser—well, this was it, not a secret ocean channel but a cruel slog by foot. Beyond this continental divide, the canoes were in the Clearwater River, a tributary of the Athabasca. Canoemen could paddle with the current all the way across what is now northern Alberta to Athabasca Lake, the depot at Fort Chipewyan—resupply point for all the northwestern trading posts—and if they so desired, on down the Mackenzie to the Arctic Ocean.

Onward lay the rich and untapped lands of the western watersheds, and still farther, the unknown potential beyond the Rockies. Through the maze of their snowy passes lay the country for which Simon Fraser was bound.

Few of the great explorers and fur traders who crossed the divide separating the North from the Prairies could have been unaware of the significance of Methye Portage.

It seems that almost all who crossed paused at the summit to marvel at the stunning vista that abruptly unfolded before them.

"The eye looks down on the course of the little river, by some called the Swan River, and by others the Clear-Water and Pelican River, beautifully meandering for upwards of 30 miles," wrote Alexander Mackenzie in 1801. "I beheld my people, diminished as it were, to half their size, employed in pitching their tents in a charming meadow, and among the canoes which, being turned upon their sides, presented their reddened bottoms in contrast with the surrounding verdure. At the same time, the process of gumming them produced numerous small spires of smoke, which, as they rose, enlivened the scene, and at length blended with the larger columns that ascended from the fires where suppers were preparing."

Up on top of Methye Portage lay Rendezvous Lake. There brigades from the distant Mackenzie trading district—some of the posts as far to the north again as La Loche was from Fort William—would meet crews from the south and exchange their furs for trade items.

For me, however, the road had briefly come to an end. Short of dragging a canoe down the portage by myself and paddling the Clearwater solo—an intimidating thought at the best of times—there was no way west into Alberta. I would now have to turn south and drive almost to Edmonton before heading north again to the Peace River district where Fraser would prepare for his dramatic venture across the mountains into New Caledonia.

On the way south, the dark underbrush glistened with the green sparks of animals' eyes catching the headlights. The clouds parted somewhere between Buffalo

Rendezvous Lake lay on the Methye Portage, portal to the Athabasca District. Traders met there to exchange trade merchandise for furs bound for Fort William. *Peter Rindisbacher, Library and Archives Canada, 1988-250-19, C-001920*

Narrows and the turnoff to Île-à-la-Crosse, and a full moon illuminated the whole immense landscape. I stopped my car, killed the engine, turned off the lights and climbed to the top of a little knoll.

As far as my eye could see, from horizon to horizon, there was not one light. The stars were brilliant, and the Milky Way made a glowing river in the black sky. All around me the night thrummed with the chorus of spring frogs, and somewhere in the distance coyotes or wolves were howling. This much, I could say for certain, I shared with Simon Fraser.

Simon Fraser

10

BOMBS, BISON AND BLACK GOLD

My road south proved long and wearying from Lac la Loche and Methye Portage, where Simon Fraser's brigade had passed over into the fabled Athabasca territory and clear paddling to what is now British Columbia.

No accommodation was available anywhere along the route. The one small motel at Île-à-la-Crosse was filled with construction crews, and the fishing lodges and lakeside resorts along the way either had not yet opened for the season or were sporting No Vacancy signs.

Fraser himself would have been travelling for about a month now, sleeping out, enduring the rain and eating his dreary rations. He was probably thinking fond thoughts of arrival at Fort Chipewyan with its library, a warm bed, a convivial drink, conversation and a commissary among the other comforts.

I could have used a bed myself, but I drove on through the clear, moonlit Saskatchewan night, slowing for the frequent patches of ground fog hanging over hollows where the road dipped into muskegs and creek bottoms. It was well past midnight, and I was the only traveller.

All along the road I saw the gleam of animal eyes reflecting my headlights: the fluorescent green of deer freezing in the underbrush, the sharp white glint where a badger waddled down the shoulder, the streak where an oversized weasel or maybe a pine marten humped across the road. I counted a red fox, a wolf and eight skinny

The trail of Simon Fraser led down many twisting backcountry roads, like this one in the arid rain shadow that falls on the British Columbia Interior near Pavilion. *Bill Keay/ Vancouver Sun*

bears grazing on new shoots in the ditches, their dark pelts looking even blacker than the shadows cast by the moon.

After crossing the Alberta border at Cold Lake, I decided I could drive no farther, but it looked as though I'd be sleeping in my car. Every hotel and motel seemed to have a No Vacancy sign or no sign at all. I stopped at an all-night convenience store and fried chicken stand—what Fraser's voyageurs would have given for one of these along their route!—and asked the cashier if he knew of anything. A miracle. He directed me to a nondescript establishment that he thought might have a room. If I went to the back door and asked whoever was cleaning up the bar, they might let me in.

He was right. But a few hours later, I practically levitated out of bed to a sleep-shattering roar. I rushed to the window. Overhead four CF-18 fighter jets flew in a tight formation and then peeled off one by one and climbed away, the thunder of their afterburners rattling the windows.

The war planes explained the scarcity of accommodation. Operation Maple Flag—the annual top-gun war games for fighter pilots over the huge Cold Lake Air Weapons Range was underway. Ten countries, including Canada and the United States, had sent their best fliers to compete in mock dogfights and aerial missions.

In Simon Fraser's time, the favoured weapon was the musket, so inaccurate at fifty paces that most soldiers didn't aim, just pointed and fired massed volleys. Among the coureurs de bois and Fraser's stealthy native Indian companions, the silent, deadly tomahawk ranked a close second as the weapon of choice.

Now here I was, blearily watching warriors practice with weapons so powerful and sophisticated that a single pilot with a fully armed CF-18 could have destroyed a whole army arrayed for battle during the American Revolutionary War that had claimed Fraser's father.

And how could Fraser have imagined that the tomahawk of my time—tested right here at Cold Lake and later deployed to destroy the armies of Saddam Hussein in faraway Iraq—was a self-guided missile that could fly thousands of miles in a few hours and carry a warhead capable of obliterating a whole city?

The air weapons range, more than 1.2 million hectares straddling the borders of Alberta and Saskatchewan, is immense—as big as 14,600 farms like the one Fraser's father had homesteaded in upstate New York.

In 1805, as the fur trader passed to the north on his dash for the Rockies before winter arrived, Britain's cold war with Napoleon had flared into open conflict, although the distances were so immense, and information travelled so slowly, that it's doubtful many in the far west paid much attention.

The Russians were allies then. They would be enemies again in the Crimea before Fraser died, then they'd become allies, then enemies in World War I, then allies in World War II, then enemies again through the Cold War.

The Americans, who had been enemies when Fraser was a child and had dispossessed his family, would soon be enemies yet again, attacking Canada in 1812 while Britain was distracted with Napoleon's campaigns in Europe. Then they'd be allies for two world wars, the Korean War and NATO's military incursion into Afghanistan.

This place, where Canadian-made weapons of mass destruction are tested—the guidance systems for cruise missiles, for example—was the creature of my own generation's Cold War, created as the Soviets and Americans rattled their nuclear sabres at one another and bristled with ballistic missiles.

Early fur traders took note of the bitumen seeps that eventually led to a rush for black gold beneath farmers' fields like the one hosting this pump jack in northern Alberta. *Andrew Penner*

But in 1805, as Fraser headed west, the Americans and their ambitions were viewed with deep suspicion, particularly since they clearly had designs on the territory beyond the Rockies. One of the North West Company's strategic objectives was to block such expansion and secure any fur resources for their investors in Montreal.

Business and the complicated politics of empire were entangled then as they are today. That is one thing that our time and Simon Fraser's still have in common.

Sleep proved impossible as the supersonic jets roared overhead, so I wearily set out again, this time heading north to Fort McMurray in Alberta.

When Fraser first crossed the Methye Portage, the industry in which he worked was the biggest in North America. He couldn't have imagined it at the time, but he was passing through a treasure trove of resources that would eventually make the fur trade look like a tiny blip in the history of commerce.

Beneath his feet was the biggest known reserve of oil in the world. Nobody cared much about petroleum in 1805. Coal had just emerged as the energy source of choice for Europe's Industrial Revolution; oil as we know it was an oddity and wouldn't become a commercial resource for another forty years.

Yet Fraser's fur traders were passing oil sands deposits that cover more than 140,000 square kilometres and contain as much as 2.5 trillion barrels, more than four times the known reserves in all the Middle East. Estimating recoverable reserves and their value is speculative, of course. Assuming just for fun, however, that all the oil could be recovered and prices were a round-figure hundred dollars a barrel, this resource would gross $250 trillion.

In Fraser's time the fur traders travelled the Clearwater River—past what are now Fort McMurray and Fort MacKay—on their way to Fort Chipewyan. Even then, with no inkling of the magnitude of what lay beneath their feet, they knew there was definitely something there.

Cree traders first reported that a black pitch they used to waterproof canoes oozed from the banks of a western river when they travelled to Hudson Bay in 1719. Pond, who later served as a mentor to Alexander Mackenzie before being forced to leave the fur trade because of his violent ways, marked sites where he'd seen tar deposits on a map he made of the Athabasca region.

Mackenzie's journal makes a specific reference. He was travelling down the Clearwater to what he called the Elk River; we now call it the Athabasca. It flowed north to what he called Lake of the Hills, our present-day Lake Athabasca.

"At about twenty-four miles from the fork, are some bituminous fountains, into which a pole of twenty feet long may be inserted without the least resistance," he wrote. "The bitumen is in a fluid state, and when mixed with gum, or the resinous substance collected from the spruce fir, serves to gum the canoes. In its heated state it emits a smell like that of sea-coal. The banks of the river, which are very elevated, discover veins of the same bituminous quality."

Alexander Mackenzie noted herds of bison along the Peace River. They proved a vital food source for isolated posts at the precarious fringe of the fur trade. *Frederick Arthur Verner, "The Stampede," 1883, oil on canvas, Collection of Glenbow Museum, Calgary, Canada, 55.28*

Verner

Today Alberta's oil sands represent one of Canada's biggest megaprojects. Trucks the size of a suburban house haul the bitumen-rich sands from vast open-pit mines to high-tech production facilities that transform it into high quality synthetic crude.

The Alberta government's energy department says oil sands producers move enough overburden and ore every two days to fill Toronto's Skydome or New York's Yankee Stadium.

One paper published by the Canadian Energy Research Institute in Calgary estimates that proven reserves in Alberta's oil sands, which now produce about a million barrels a day, will contribute $541 billion to Canada's gross domestic product over the next ten years, put $93 billion into government coffers and support 293,000 jobs across the country.

It's predicted that by 2015, production from these deposits will account for 70 percent of Canada's total oil output, dominating the economic landscape of the province and the country in much the same way the fur trade did in Fraser's time.

But while charting the changes in the landscapes through which Fraser travelled was one of my objectives, staring into the world's biggest hole in the ground had limited fascination. I pushed on toward the Peace River district. Another red-hot oil and gas play was underway around Fort St. John, once a fur-trade hotbed in its own right, but I wanted to see bison, as essential to the health of remote forts as the supermarket is to oil patch workers and their families.

The bison, main source of food for the hunting cultures of the Great Plains, was also a staple for fur brigades emerging from the rugged Canadian Shield into the high plains of northern Alberta and British Columbia east of the Rockies.

In 1793 Mackenzie travelled up the Peace River. In the vicinity of the Kiskatinaw River, a tributary crossed today by the Alaska Highway between Dawson Creek and Fort St. John, he recorded in his journal a conversation with a Beaver Indian who said he could remember back sixty winters. The bison, an elder told him—it's not clear from the narrative if he means the same man—had begun to show up in the region within his own lifetime.

But Mackenzie observed "vast herds" in the "magnificent theatre of nature" created by groves of rustling trees interspersed with golden-hued grasslands. The same park-like vista still characterizes much of the valley of the Peace River, although farm fields now encroach upon the plateau above the river, and many of the rich alluvial flats beside the watercourse are cultivated.

"At this time the buffaloes were attended by their young ones who were frisking about them," Mackenzie wrote. "The whole country displayed an exuberant verdure . . . equally enlivened with the elk and the buffalo, who were feeding in great numbers, and unmolested by the hunter. . . in every direction the elk and the buffalo are seen in possession of the hills and plains.

"On the high grounds, which were on the opposite side of the river, we saw a buffalo tearing up and down with a great fury, but could not discern the cause of his impetuous motions; my hunters conjectured that he had been wounded with an arrow by some of the natives."

A few days later, during a reconnaissance up the riverbank, he wrote, "We found a beaten path and before we had walked a mile, fell in with a herd of buffaloes, with their young ones: but I would not suffer the Indians to fire on them, from an apprehension that the report of their fowling pieces would alarm the natives that might be in the neighbourhood; for we were at this time so near the mountains, as to justify our expectation of seeing some of them.

"We, however, sent our dog after the herd, and a calf was soon secured by him. While the young men were skinning the animal, we heard two reports of fire arms from the canoe, which we answered, as it was a signal for my return; we then heard another and immediately hastened down the hill with our veal."

The same panorama must have greeted Simon Fraser on his first ventures up the Peace in the subsequent decade or so.

In 1800, it's estimated, as many as sixty million bison roamed the great plains, sustaining western Canada's Sioux, Ojibwa, Gros Ventre, Assiniboines, Cree, Blackfoot, Dene and Métis. Even the Kutenai far to the south would cross the mountain passes to hunt bison.

Yet within Simon Fraser's lifetime these great herds would dwindle to near extinction. Guns increased the killing efficiency of plains tribes. Soon they were joined by settlers who hunted the bison for food. Then they were slaughtered commercially for their hides; the meat was left on the plains to rot.

By 1840, when Fraser had long retired to a farm in the Eastern Townships of Ontario, the bison herd had declined by twenty million animals. By 1885, the plains bison had been wiped out in its former range and only a small remnant herd survived in Yellowstone National Park.

The larger, more solitary wood bison, a subspecies found in the remote prairies of the Slave, Peace and Athabasca river deltas, survived in greater numbers. In 1922 the federal government set aside Canada's largest national park to ensure its protection in northern Alberta.

Today one can still see bison in the Peace River area, but they are raised commercially.

The XY Bison Ranch near Fort St. John, for example, was selected as one of BC's ten best ranching operations in 2002. It raised the shaggy beasts in their natural habitat on the south-facing Peace River hills that once sustained the great herds seen by Mackenzie and Fraser when they passed through on the respective journeys west.

Simon Fraser

11

A HARD PUSH TO FORT MISERY

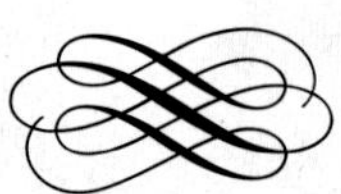

We lean into a new bend in the Pack River, where a gravel bar crowds the channel to the inside and a mineral-stained rock face looms ahead. The Teflon-coated bottom of Clint Desrosiers's jetboat carves a near-perfect arc on dark water.

Whisked in relative comfort up the river that would prove the key to the entrepreneurial foundations of the future British Columbia, I recalled Fraser's account of his struggle ascending this ancient waterway. He was weary, wet and frustrated. Some of his men were mutinous, and his battered canoes were in a perilous state as he journeyed to the spot from which an undreamed province would be forged. It would be an amazing alloy of newcomers from Europe and Asia and of the indigenous peoples who already occupied the landscape. None of them could have imagined the magnitude of the changes that would follow the North West Company's expansion beyond the Rockies.

True, Europeans were already off the coast, yet the founding of a continuously occupied trading post in the remote Interior Plateau was a moment of genesis, an originating event, the first tremor in a series of interlocked economic shifts that would ultimately transform cultures, societies, families and world views, in some cases with cataclysmic effect—and not only for aboriginal nations.

And yet the new would not, could not, simply erase the old—it never does—but would instead absorb it and be absorbed, alter it and be altered, so that in many ways the BC we inhabit today remains a place where both past and present coexist.

The province is a palimpsest. A new text is continuously inscribed upon older narratives that, if not easily discernible, are nonetheless part of our shared story. Fraser and his two hundred-year-old troubles on the Pack River sprang easily to my mind.

His own historical account of travel on the river actually begins—in mid-sentence, at that—with his second trip, six months after he'd founded the trading fort he called Trout Lake Post on what we now call McLeod Lake.

The explorer left a three-man garrison there during the winter of 1805–1806 to trade for furs that he described as the best he'd ever seen. He returned to Fort Dunvegan in what is now Alberta to marshal supplies, organize a crew and collect the gear necessary for a more ambitious expedition to the west as soon as the ice went out in the spring.

Travelling up and down the Parsnip and the Pack that fall had been deceptively easy. He'd had the benefit of lower water and the gentler currents at the end of

Logs bound for mills at Mackenzie, BC, cross the Parsnip River as Clint Desrosiers pilots Stephen Hume and Heledd Mayse upstream in his Teflon-bottomed jetboat. *Mark Van Manen/*Vancouver Sun

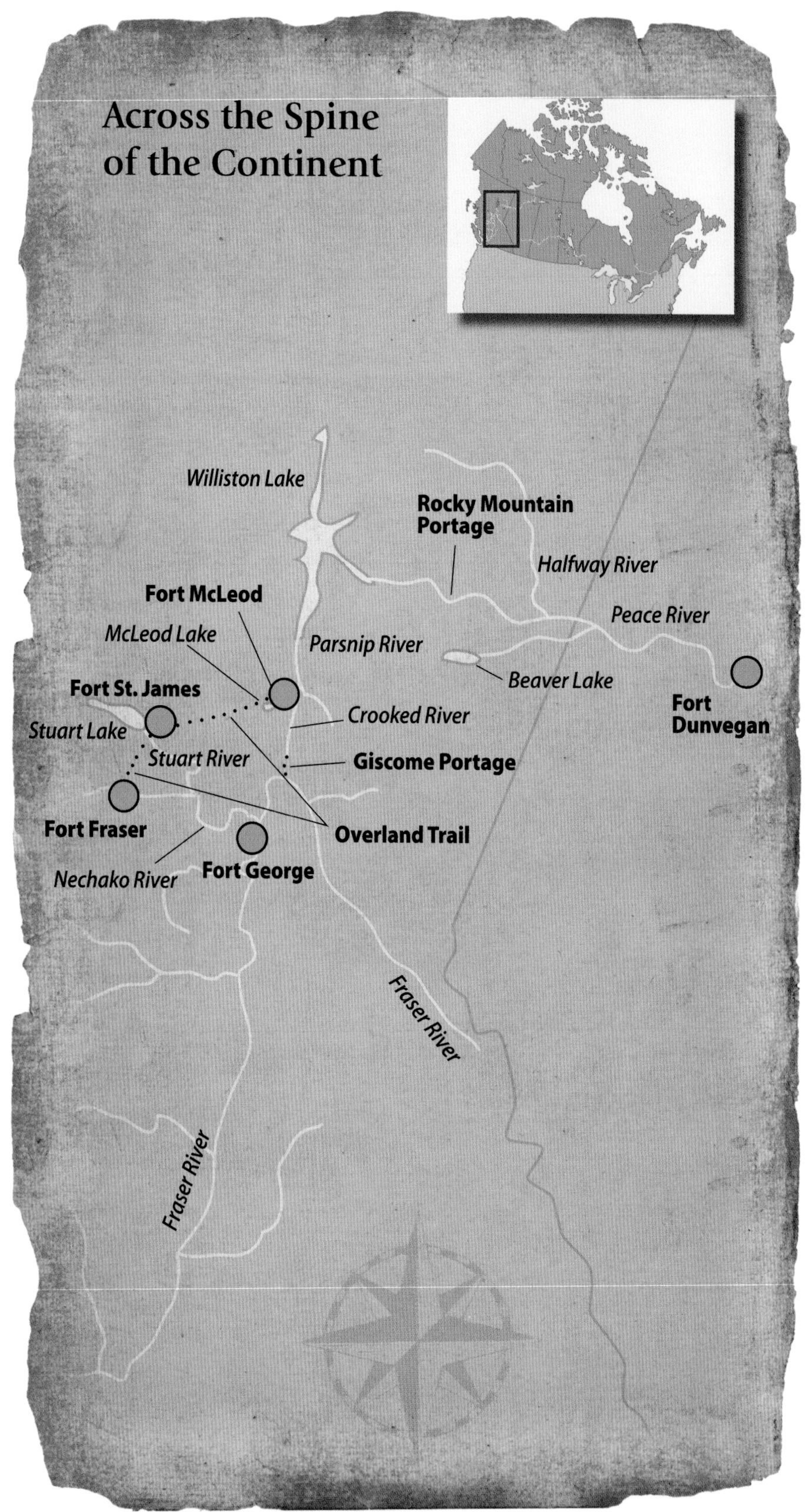
Across the Spine of the Continent
Williston Lake
Rocky Mountain Portage
Halfway River
Fort McLeod
Peace River
McLeod Lake
Parsnip River
Beaver Lake
Fort St. James
Fort Dunvegan
Crooked River
Stuart Lake
Stuart River
Giscome Portage
Fort Fraser
Overland Trail
Nechako River
Fort George
Fraser River
Fraser River

summer. The following spring he had the freshet to contend with, as we did. As the high country snowpack melted, muddy torrents came thundering out of the Rocky Mountain Trench.

Desrosiers explained that the high water we were riding was nothing compared to Fraser's day.

"I think we have global warming here," he said. "The environment is changing dramatically. When I was a kid, the snow was twenty feet deep—right up to the eaves. Now the snow pack is five feet—and gone real fast. But you can imagine what it must have been like for those guys in Simon Fraser's day. The runoff from twenty feet of snow must have been something else."

Unlike North West Company voyageurs propelled upstream by muscle-power alone, however, I was riding in what Desrosiers calls "the Cadillac," a high-tech marvel constructed to his personal specifications. The light but rigid aluminum hull skimmed swiftly through water no deeper than the thickness of your average Tom Wolfe novel. Its bottom armour of low-friction materials enabled it to skid right over bars and even logs hidden beneath the surface. A folding canopy kept off the rain, and commercial-free satellite radio boomed country rock over the sound system.

The Mackenzie-based outfitter had the $45,000 craft specially built so he could run clients of his company, Rocky Mountain Trench Adventures, up the wild rivers of the Peace River watershed. Tourists come from everywhere to admire the towering geography above the submerged canyons of the Peace Reach on Williston Reservoir, to observe grizzlies and mountain goats in the Omineca Range or to fish for trout weighing up to ten kilograms. And while I can be a cranky purist about the virtues of a silent canoe in the outback, this time I'm grateful for the deafening power of a V-6 engine.

The Pack River is not big in comparison to the mighty Peace or the violent Fraser, but the current proved strong enough at high water that I was glad I'd abandoned my plan to paddle up this final leg of Simon Fraser's journey to New Caledonia.

Fraser had six wiry voyageurs for each canoe, and it was still a brutal slog even by their hardy standards. My crew consisted of me and my teenage daughter, Hel, already an experienced expedition paddler who had gamely volunteered to help out.

Desrosiers asked one question when I broached the idea of canoeing up from Hudson Hope at the foot of the Williston Reservoir to McLeod Lake. "How much time have you got?"

Point taken. The reservoir behind W.A.C. Bennett Dam is huge—the province's largest body of fresh water, more like an inland sea than a lake—and now that we were bucking the strong current on the Pack, I saw what the experienced outfitter was gently hinting at.

The river can appear deceptively tranquil, but boils and back eddies will suddenly slam a boat sideways. Dark, foam-streaked water seethes around partial logjams hidden around sharp bends. Here and there, collapsing banks had toppled still-rooted trees toward the water. From the jetboat they are hardly noticeable, but for a canoeist—I know from bitter experience—sweepers like these could make a pleasant float decidedly unpleasant.

As someone who has shot rapids on the Nahanni River, travelled the Liard and the Peel, experienced the heart-stopping shock of a spill into the ice-cold Mackenzie and paddled through everything from the rugged Canadian Shield to the prairie badlands, I've learned the value of caution during spring runoff, even on apparently easy water.

A sudden eddy can swing an unwary paddler beneath low-hanging branches that brush him into meltwater so cold his survival time is measured in minutes. A tree dragged down by the current can snap back to the surface with enough force to break a canoe in half. The undertow at an unexpected logjam can crush a hull, or worse, suck a spilled canoeist under a jagged tangle to drown.

So I'd decided to restrict my own exploring to the gentler waters around the site of the long-vanished first fort—washed away, some say, in a flood in 1823 and later relocated on higher ground.

Josie Tylee, who lives in the Tse'Khene settlement that coalesced around the trading post Fraser founded at McLeod Lake, said that from time immemorial this river route served as "the people's highway" between breakup in April and freeze-up after late November.

Today about a third of the band's nearly four hundred members live in the village. The forward-looking community pins hopes for an economic base on logging

Clear-cuts in forests laid waste by a vast pine beetle infestation around Mackenzie, BC, leave a patchwork of devastation in the boreal forest near the confluence of the Parsnip and Pack rivers. *Mark Van Manen/*Vancouver Sun

its Treaty Eight lands, although the mountain pine beetle infestation raging across the Interior Plateau—more evidence of global warming—is now a cause of growing alarm. Almost everywhere I looked, I saw telltale red swaths of dead and dying trees.

But there's also hope of capturing a piece of the boom sparked by American demand for Canadian oil and gas. The previous year the band had signed a long-term agreement with Duke Energy, which already had a transmission station in the vicinity. And newly elected Chief Alec Chingee saw possibilities in a growing urban appetite for wilderness recreation and cultural sightseeing.

"We might want to look at tourism in this area big time," he said. "Why can't we use the historic trails and waterways? We can tie them into the historic site here. If we could take tourists and show them how people travelled here two hundred years ago, I think there would be real potential. We're the first fort west of the Rockies and north of San Francisco."

As former chief Harley Chingee reminded me, "That highway [from Prince George to Chetwynd] was only built fifty years ago. Before that it was all rivers and trails."

"Yes, all the way from Summit Lake [just northeast of Prince George] to Fort Ware [on the upper Finlay River] there was nothing but bush. I remember that," Josie Tylee told me. She was born in 1937 and had only two years of formal schooling, but she knows how to dry meat, dry and smoke fish, dry berries, skin a moose and tan the hide, make moccasins and shoot a grizzly bear if she must.

"There was no motors," she said. "People used to go by paddle or pushing with a pole. People used to work so hard then but they were happy, they lived off the land. When we were young people we had to work hard just to survive. That's my education—a hard life. But I'm still here. No complaints."

Repeated entries in Fraser's journal as he battled the icy, unexpectedly strong current show how durable one had to be to survive on that frontier. The weather was bitter. He was soaked by rainstorms. Men were sick and exhausted. It was still snowing on the mountains. His canoes were in a sorry state.

Even the one sturdy craft that had carried him all the way from the Great Lakes rendezvous the previous summer was on its last legs. Those he'd obtained locally were poorly constructed from inferior materials. His clerk John Stuart, the party's skilled canoe-builder—already emerging as Fraser's able second-in-command and later to play a crucial role himself in the birth of a new province—had apparently been too busy setting up a new base at the foot of the Peace River canyon near Hudson's Hope to oversee the local construction of new vessels.

So, as the party made its way upriver to McLeod Lake, even Stuart was hampered by a canoe that leaked constantly, was difficult to paddle and seemed in perpetual danger of capsizing.

"It is the worst made that I ever saw and is more like a trough than a canoe," Fraser noted in his journal on Wednesday, May 21, 1806. "I am surprised how Mr.

Cheryl Steele, who runs the oldest store in British Columbia, moved to McLeod Lake from Burnaby in 1981, never left and says she never will. *Mark Van Manen/ Vancouver Sun*

[James] McDougall [the other clerk], who was present, would allow such a one to be made."

Things got so bad that, on the second day out, Fraser ordered the canoe taken apart and rebuilt before continuing. Soon he stopped again to have the seams of all the canoes resealed with spruce pitch. Then a canoe had to be patched after a submerged snag tore a gaping hole. Then more repairs. More holes. More leaking seams. This was not exactly the easy reconnaissance he'd made the previous October.

But the Trout Lake post he founded in 1805 (his men called it Fort Misery) still does business two hundred years later. This bestows upon the McLeod Lake General Store the distinction of being the oldest continuous commercial venture in all of BC.

Cheryl Steele came to the store from the Lower Mainland about twenty-five years ago—"a Vancouver girl, born at Vancouver General"—and stayed to raise her two sons, Trevor, twenty-nine, Todd, twenty-seven, "and my nephew, Jason Steele, he came for two weeks and never left—he's been with me for fifteen years now."

The store, just across the lake from the site of the original fort, is housed in one of the old Hudson's Bay Company log structures that superceded the originals long after its merger with the North West Company in 1821. It was moved over from the historic site when the highway pushed north more than half a century ago. Today it's the kind of small-town store that offers a little bit of everything and nothing of what you can learn to do without.

"When I first came here I used to take furs," Steele told me. "It's changed . . . yeah, it's changed. Not too many trap anymore. A few old ones do, but I'm losing my old ones, one by one."

She said it's pretty slow in the winter but that business can be surprisingly brisk during the summer months, when tourists and anglers visit the three lakes

Against a striking Peace River sky, rolled hay bales are scattered across northern prairie fields that in Simon Fraser's time were roamed by herds of bison, elk and deer. *Mark Van Manen*/Vancouver Sun

in the vicinity and Alaska-bound traffic takes Highway 97 through the Pine Pass to Chetwynd and then up Highway 29 to Hudson's Hope and Fort St. John.

It was to Fort St. John, surrounded by the clamour of a frenzied oil and gas play, that I'd followed the elusive Simon Fraser's track down from northern Alberta, stopping along the way to talk with Dallas Wood at the museum in Peace River.

He explained the ephemeral nature of so many of the forts—there were seventeen on the Peace between Lake Athabasca and Hudson's Hope—the scant records and the fact the documentary record that so enamours historians might itself be misleading.

"There might have been other [earlier] trips [across the Rockies] that we have no records about," he mused while a noisy elementary class on a school field trip swirled around us. "There were all these free traders, they didn't want to keep records—in many cases they were illegal, and the companies were not very happy about their being here.

"There were vast distances over dangerous terrain. We tend to forget that many of these men did not return. Their graves are all along these rivers. They died. They drowned in rapids. They were killed in accidents or by enemies," Wood said. "It does dismay and depress me as a Canadian historian how little is known about these incredible people. This museum, for example, has to do more when we expand. We have to do much more on Simon Fraser and David Thompson. It's irritating to see the hoopla over [American explorers] Lewis and Clark."

In 1793 Fraser travelled west; in 1805 he was a full partner of sufficient stature to be entrusted with the formidable task of crossing the Rockies, expanding the North West Company's business there and finding a strategic trade route to the

Pacific. As historian W. Kaye Lamb points out, Fraser is nearly absent from the verifiable documentary record between these two dates.

One clear reference to Fraser before 1800 is a pay schedule for the Athabaska District for the year 1799. I found it included in an idiosyncratic compilation of documents entitled *Les Bourgeois de la Compagnie du Nord-Ouest: Récits de Voyages, Lettres et Rapports Inédits Relatifs au Nord-Ouest Canadien* by L.R. Masson. First published in 1889, it's obscure enough that when it was reprinted in 1960, only 750 copies were made. I found one in a university library that, judging from the lending record stamps in the back cover, had only been borrowed eight times in the last forty-five years.

For all the dry brevity of that payroll list, one detail jumped out to suggest why it might have been considered worthy of inclusion.

Fraser is listed as a clerk reporting to John Finlay. Was this the same Finlay who had come west with Alexander Mackenzie and then crossed the Rockies himself, exploring both the Parsnip and Finlay rivers in 1797, just four years after Mackenzie returned from his famous journey to the Pacific?

As is often the case in these scant early records, there are confusing contradictions.

Some historians—Father Adrian Gabriel Morice, Margaret Ormsby and W. Kaye Lamb—say the exploration was done by "a certain" James Finlay, about whom there's a dearth of information. But R.M. Patterson, who wrote *Finlay's River,* a comprehensive history of the watershed, after exploring it himself and consulting Hudson's Bay Company journals, says it was John Finlay who made the sortie to the river that now bears his name.

Patterson cites "the Journal of John Finlay" that was included as part of a working draft found at Cumberland House for Samuel Black's official report on his subsequent 1824 exploration. The journal's authenticity, Patterson says, was vouched for by Chief Factor James McDougall, who served as clerk at Trout Lake Post under Fraser.

Gordon Bowes, who compiled eighty-one eyewitness accounts for *Peace River Chronicles,* credits John rather than James. So does Elizabeth Brown Losey in her history of the fur-trade forts.

Some historians make the case that as early as 1794, John Finlay was in command at Rocky Mountain Fort (not to be confused with Fraser's Rocky Mountain Portage House near Hudson's Hope), located upstream from present-day Fort St. John at the confluence of the Moberly and Peace rivers. If so, it's likely that Finlay staged his western explorations from there.

But like so many other trading posts, Rocky Mountain Fort lapsed into mystery. Its palisades rotted away, and its location was forgotten for 169 years until Simon Fraser University archeologist Knut Fladmark led a dig that uncovered its relics.

The lonely tombstone of Davitt and Peter Fisher, who died in 1904 and 1905 aged 8 and 11, peeps forlornly from tall grass in the cemetery at what was once Fort McLeod, founded in 1805 by Simon Fraser. *Mark Van Manen*/Vancouver Sun

In fact at least five known trading posts in the vicinity give Fort St. John a claim on being the first European settlement in what is now BC—although Yuquot on the west coast of Vancouver Island might challenge. John Meares built a trading post there in 1788, and Don Pedro Alberni's Catalonian soldiers garrisoned a Spanish fort at Friendly Cove in 1790.

All these establishments, including those around the present Fort St. John, were eventually abandoned, some forever. After one gruesome event in which the clerk and four voyageurs were ambushed and shot to death at St. John's Fort in 1823, the Hudson's Bay Company closed all its forts between McLeod Lake and Fort Dunvegan. Fort Nelson, also founded in 1805, was likewise closed for many years after the clerk, his wife and children and four other North West Company employees were slain in January 1813, and the outpost burned to the ground.

No doubt during those long winters while serving under Finlay, Fraser listened intently to stories about the route through the mountains and the unknown country far to the west of what the plains tribes called "the Backbone of the World."

In the early fall of 1805, making haste for the mountain passes before the snows came, Fraser must have stopped at many of these forts on his way south from the comforts of Fort Chipewyan and the extensive library that made it the Athens of the North, according to its proud founder, Roderick Mackenzie.

"That's the sort of thing a historian would really like to know about," Wood told me. "It's hard to imagine coming from somewhere like England to here with the incredibly long winters. What would you do? You'd be cut off from the outside world. You'd be lucky to get your mail once a year. This is something a modern person used to instant communication finds difficult to understand."

So Fraser would have paused at Fort Vermilion, at now-vanished Fort Forks where the Smoky River flows into the Peace, at Fort Dunvegan and at Rocky Mountain Fort on the Moberly, which would close when he established the Rocky Mountain Portage House across from present-day Hudson's Hope, just below the mouth of the awesome Peace River canyon.

Simon Fraser

12

AT THE DROWNED CANYON

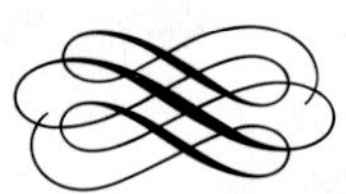

In Fort St. John I visited the museum and archives and lucked into Wim Kok, a teacher at Northern Lights College with an interest in fur-trade history. He had stopped by to pick up his daughter Leslie from her summer job, and on the spur of the moment, tossed her the car keys and gave up his afternoon.

Kok guided me down winding dirt roads and across farm fields to show me where some of the forts had stood. Equally interesting were his insights into the parallels between the economic events of Fraser's era and the present.

The fur trade, Kok said, was the eighteenth century's version of globalization. Social impacts were similar, right down to multinational corporate mergers and a drive to improve financial efficiency by closing small-margin operations—with similar angry protests of betrayal from those suffering the local consequences.

Furthermore, the North West Company's transportation network plugged small and self-contained regional economies into a huge world market, creating local wealth that enabled previously marginalized groups to access the manufactured goods of the Industrial Revolution. Not so different, he argued, from Fort St. John today.

"The boom here really started when the Alliance pipeline tied this region to the northeastern United States. We went from a small regional market with limited pipeline capacity into this vast North American market with large delivery capacity," Kok said. "That, of course, is also when BC gas prices took off. Once you have that link between a potential supply and a market demand, the forces for change are enormous."

Once Fraser crossed the mountains to New Caledonia and permanently connected the fur supply to the huge European market, those same forces went into motion two hundred years ago.

"I think the awareness of the enormity of Fraser's accomplishment is very little," Kok said as we strolled on the bluffs above the site of long-forgotten Fort des Epinettes, established at the mouth of the Beaton River in 1806 to service the Beaver Indians when Rocky Mountain Fort was closed. "In BC, perhaps a bit more awareness—there's a river and a university named after him—but elsewhere in Canada? No."

The air was sweet with the scent of saskatoons, wild onions peeped through grass still slick with dew and we paused in our discussion of history while Kok took measure of the darkening sky.

"If it rains, we'll really be in trouble," he said, nodding at the dirt track and my rented Impala. "This will turn into Peace River gumbo—slicker than a string of snot in a bucket of eels."

I dropped him off at home, regretfully bid him and bustling Fort St. John farewell and headed west on Highway 29. I followed Fraser's route west up the

The park-like benches of the Peace River, seen here from the air, teemed with bison, elk and deer when Alexander Mackenzie and Simon Fraser passed through. *Mark Van Manen/Vancouver Sun*

Fertile farmlands and park-like settings that awed Alexander Mackenzie in the Peace River Valley will vanish beneath the reservoir if plans for another major hydroelectric dam proceed. *Ian Lindsay/*Vancouver Sun

Peace River valley, through the lovely country that will soon join the realms of the drowned if plans to develop the Site C hydro facility are approved. I was bound for Hudson's Hope, a friendly community of about eleven hundred, located right where the great river carves through the Rocky Mountain wall from west to east.

Here I got directions from Melodie Godsman, "curator, floor sweeper, bill payer, whatever" at the local museum. She led me out to the steep riverbank and pointed out where her brother Steve lives across the river on or near the site once occupied by the now-vanished Rocky Mountain Portage House. He settled there after a career-ending injury in the oil patch eighteen years ago. The chains parted on a truck carrying drill pipe and he was clipped by one of the pipe racks. Twelve ribs snapped off his spine and his pelvis shattered, leaving him, in the dry accounting of actuaries and insurance adjudicators, "83 percent disabled."

"Just like Simon Fraser," his sister said proudly of her brother's lifestyle. "He's got no power, no municipal water, no services at all—but he's quite happy. He lives there with his dogs and canoes across."

He might not be so happy, she said, if plans to develop the Site C dam go ahead. While her father and her grandfather both worked building the dams on the

Steve Godsman, disabled by a catastrophic oil patch injury, lives with his pets in a small cabin not far from where Simon Fraser established Rocky Mountain Portage House but worries that plans for a new dam on the Peace River will flood him out. *Mark Van Manen/* Vancouver Sun

Peace, "even the BC Hydro employees—and that's about 60 percent of the people in Hudson's Hope—are not too thrilled. I don't think it's worth drowning this beautiful valley for the revenue they're going to get. But it's been so long in the works that everybody's kind of fatalistic.

"My brother's going to be washed out along with the Rocky Mountain Portage House," she said. "He's not too happy about that. No, he's not too happy."

I went over to visit him, hitching a ride with his mother, Evie Edinger, who was taking her son some groceries in her four-wheel-drive truck.

"When they brought me to the hospital they told me, 'Don't hold out any hope.' Two hours later they told me he's maybe going to make it but it's going to be bad. Now he's out here. He's come back just by strength of will," she said.

Godsman is a bearded, wiry man whose rolling gait hints at the extent of his injuries. He showed me the remnants of the old ferry landing from before there was a bridge across the Peace, introduced me to his nine dogs and pointed out the levels to which water was predicted to rise behind a Site C dam.

"All the reasons for not building it in the first place are still there. It's the best farmland in the Peace and its just going to turn into a big mudhole like Williston Reservoir."

When Simon Fraser built his staging post where Steve Godsman now lives, he already had a good idea of what to expect on his way west. Mackenzie had been up the river in 1793, Finlay had made his foray in 1797 and David Thompson had been probing the eastern slopes of the Rockies.

Mackenzie never knew what lay ahead of him and thus attempted to bring his canoes around the initial white water in the canyon. He left an account of five terrifying days attempting to lead his party through the gorge before he abandoned the idea.

First there was the current itself, blasting over a succession of rapids, cascades and falls with a "resistless impetuosity" that repeatedly damaged and threatened to sweep away the frail bark canoes.

Then there was a constant rain of debris, shaken loose by the immense force of the river from the high canyon walls "from whence huge fragments sometimes tumble down, and falling from such an height, dash into small stones" that threatened to brain anyone unfortunate enough to be in the wrong place.

Mackenzie's men were spent, the vital canoes were battered, they'd come within a hair of losing one canoe and the supplies it carried. Then, when he scouted upstream, he discovered the canyon walls narrowed to forty-five metres and the river squirted through like the jet from a high-pressure fire hose.

"It was really awful to behold with what infinite force the water drives against the rocks . . . tossed in high, foaming half-formed billows, as far as the eye could follow it," he noted in his expedition journal.

Mackenzie wisely decided to retreat. He ordered his men to prepare to portage over the adjacent mountain, sent scouts to find out where the rapids ended, and when they returned, raised his men's flagging spirits with a meal of wild rice sweetened with sugar and a ration of rum.

Where the fur traders saw a fearsome impediment to their business, the engineers of a later age saw industrial potential waiting to be tapped. Damming the canyon likely never occurred to Fraser or Mackenzie. In the first place, there was no technology capable of such an undertaking, and in the second, the premise would have seemed lunatic.

Michael Faraday was only fourteen when Fraser portaged around the same

Simon Fraser was forced to portage over nearby Bull Head Mountain but dams later drowned the Peace River Canyon beneath the largest body of fresh water in British Columbia. *Mark Van Manen*/Vancouver Sun

canyon. Not for another twenty-one years would the scientist discover electromagnetism, the principle used to generate hydroelectric energy—and it's doubtful whether the explorer had even heard of electricity as we understand it.

Today the canyon that came so close to ending Mackenzie's trek to the Pacific Ocean is the source of an enterprise that dwarfs even the fur trade.

The Peace River Dam and, a bit farther upstream, the W.A.C. Bennett Dam, collect runoff from a single drainage system the size of the province of New Brunswick. Or to put it in the concrete terms preferred by hydro engineers, the 150-metre deep Williston Reservoir holds enough water to fill a hundred bathtubs for every person on earth.

What would Fraser, relying on the light of a campfire to write his journal entries, have made of a prediction that a century after his death virtually everyone in North America would have access to instant light at any time of day or night? Or that people could write on a self-illuminated tablet without pen, ink or paper and then transmit information almost instantaneously from sender to recipient? Or that the Peace River canyon itself would be harnessed and would supply energy to a grid connecting the entire western half of a then-dark continent, about fifty million customers?

The scale of the Bennett dam is mind-boggling in its own right, even for people used to twentieth-century megaprojects. The artificial lake behind it, which drowns the upper Peace and large sections of the Finlay and Parsnip rivers, is the largest body of fresh water in BC.

Between 1964 and 1968, during construction of the earth-fill structure at the Bennett dam site, five kilometres of conveyor belts moved ninety-one million tonnes of glacial till from an ice-age moraine, enough to fill a ninety-tonne truck every thirty seconds. That, says BC Hydro, is enough to construct a wall four metres high and three metres wide from Vancouver to Halifax.

The powerhouse below the dam is the largest in the world, and its turbines are housed in a cavernous underground room the size of three football fields.

Yet when Fraser passed by on the Bullhead Mountain portage, the electric light bulb wouldn't be invented for another seventy-four years, and not until he'd been dead and buried for several decades would the first electric street lights be turned on in Victoria, the new capital of a new province in a new country.

From Hudson's Hope, I'd pressed on to Mackenzie, a forestry town—dominated by the mills of Abitibi and Pope and Talbot—that shows off the world's biggest tree crusher on the main boulevard. It was where I'd arranged to charter Desrosiers's boat for a run up the Pack.

We embarked at the point where Alexander Mackenzie landed in June 1793; a lonely cairn in a stand of lodgepole pine above Williston Reservoir commemorated the event. All around us the leaves of the poplars and trembling aspen spun silver in the breeze.

In the flooded landscape transformed by the Williston Reservoir, Stephen Hume clambers a snag to look for the inundated mouth of the Pack River, Simon Fraser's route to New Caledonia. *Mark Van Manen/Vancouver Sun*

Out on the lake, we paused to exchange pleasantries with Ed Bappert, unmistakable in his bright orange suit, who pulled his boom boat alongside to swap gossip. He's been twenty-seven years a log sorter. Then Desrosiers opened up his engines and got his boat planing, and we headed up the submerged Parsnip looking for the wide bay that now comprised the mouth of the Pack. We'd know it, he said, by the cluster of snags, weathered to a soft silvery colour and topped by an osprey nest.

Sure enough, the snags made a surreal landmark where they jutted from the vast expanse of water, a telltale of the flooded forest beneath the surface that signalled where the Pack curved down toward what used to be its confluence with the Parsnip.

In Mackenzie's day, the Pack was a small tributary of the much larger river. Fraser commented sardonically in one of his journals that "the great man" must have been taking a nap when he passed, because he missed it. Today it's the unruffled arm of a lake, and I'd have missed it, too, without the expert guide.

We hurtled beneath a bridge linking a long causeway that the logging trucks from the Interior Plateau crossed like clockwork ahead of their boiling plumes of dust. While hundreds of swallows swooped and dived to feed on an insect hatch, we watched the trucks dwindle into dots. The lake narrowed to a river channel, and a telltale current got stronger as we rose toward Tudyah Lake before continuing on to McLeod Lake.

It took Fraser and his voyageurs seventeen gruelling days to paddle upstream from Hudson's Hope to where he would found the new fort. For me, shouting to be heard above the blare of the engine, a trip up the Pack and back to the river's now-drowned confluence with the Parsnip would be a day's outing—with time

Bears attacked several of Simon Fraser's crews and can still be a problem. Trapper Mack Tylee, 75, mauled near McLeod Lake by a grizzly bear Sept. 3, 2000, still needed assistance from wife Josie years later. *Mark Van Manen*/Vancouver Sun

out for a pleasant lunch on the sandwiches we'd bought that morning at Sweden's Bakery in Mackenzie.

Where Fraser put in hours that often ran from three in the morning until eight at night, we had time to watch the ospreys feed their nestlings, examine some recent moose tracks just filling with water and note the fresh bear scat on a sandbar—a reminder that, just as in his time, this was still grizzly country.

Fraser had kept a sharp eye out for the huge bears, and so did I. Josie Tylee's husband, Mack, seventy-five, agreed that was a good idea when I stopped to visit at McLeod Lake. He still hasn't recovered from a mauling he received on September 3, 2000.

Mack spent forty years on the trapline, a living link to the fur trade of old, and knew the bush as well as anyone. He'd been out for a Sunday drive with Josie. He stepped out of the truck for a moment and startled a young male feeding on berries.

"I heard him screaming," Josie recalled. "I went to see what was happening. The grizzly bear just come out and started running at me. So I ran back to the truck, I was so scared. I thought he was going to get me, too, that bear."

She called to Mack. When he didn't reply, she drove frantically for help. The bear was gone when she got back. She thought for sure her husband was dying.

"He was so badly damaged, we thought he was not going to make it," she said. "They flew him to hospital. He was in a coma for a month and he spent three months in hospital in Vancouver. But he's a tough guy. He's a strong, strong person. He's a changed person, too. But to me he's a good husband, a good father, a good provider. He's a trapper. It's still good. When I tell these stories I remember all the good things we have done together."

So when I saw that fresh bear scat on the gravel bar, I was happy to climb back in the boat and continue up the Pack, under the bridge on Carp Lake Road, past the slough behind the fort that marks an old river channel and into McLeod Lake.

Stephen Hume and Heledd Mayse cross McLeod Lake by canoe to land as Simon Fraser did when he founded the now-vanished North West Company fort that became the first permanent European settlement in British Columbia. *Mark Van Manen/*Vancouver Sun

Swift and informative as it was, there was still something vaguely unsatisfying about the high-tech trip. The next day, walking through the bee-loud cemetery at the historic site, contemplating the common fate that awaits all shapers of history and listening to the nickering of a couple of ponies hobbled in the meadow at the old fort, I went back across the river and borrowed a canoe from Cheryl Steele's son, Todd. He agreed to bring his own power boat downstream and retrieve it so I wouldn't have to paddle all the way to Mackenzie or struggle with the strong current on the way back.

I put in below the oldest store in BC, and with my daughter Hel, paddled the same waters as the fur brigades, across the lake to the place where it all began.

We paused in the reeds near the spot where Simon Fraser most likely stepped ashore two centuries ago, then turned toward the river. The current caught us, turned the bow and pulled us downstream, slipping without a sound past the lines of Tse'Khene anglers fishing from the bridge, past the slough and its eagle tree, around the bend, leaving behind the sound of traffic and sliding silently through the curtain of time into the heart of a country where only wind and water speak in their old, old language, the same tongue heard by paddlers two hundred years ago.

"The past is never dead. It isn't even past." Nobel Prize-winning writer William Faulkner made this observation more than half a century ago, and I'd begun to see its truth.

The strand of BC's future history that was begun at Fort McLeod is spliced into First Nations' stories first told during the last ice age, perhaps earlier. It is part of a narrative braided from the experiences of Quebec and Ontario, from the dreams of ordinary men and women, from the exploits of famed explorers, from the uncelebrated lives of nameless Métis voyageurs whose sweat made the fur-trade routes possible, from the struggle for global supremacy among four great empires and from the birth pangs of a fragile new republic destined to become the most powerful state the world has yet seen.

As we picked our way into the chutes of the Pack River—downstream from the oldest continuously operating commercial establishment in BC, Washington, Oregon and the whole slope west of the Rockies and north of Spain's California missions—I looked into the cold, dark current and thought then how it resembled Fraser's life.

So much was obscured in the sweep of time and forgetfulness, with the scant documentary history of Fraser's accomplishments showing here and there like a few exposed sandbars in the narrative, the other contours and complexities of his life hidden like shoals beneath a constantly shifting surface on which, when you look, you see only reflections of yourself looking back.

Simon Fraser

13

FORTS BEYOND THE ROCKIES

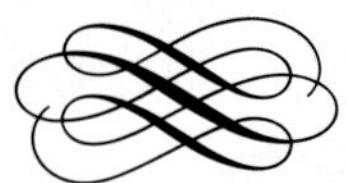

In the darkest winter months of 1806, long before its rapids were drowned behind hydro dams, the wild river that now winds sedately beneath the bluffs downstream from the once-terrifying Peace River canyon was silenced by ice more than a metre thick. Only here and there—where some peculiar upwelling of the powerful current prevented freezing—did the slick, black shimmer of open water punctuate the silent eternity of white.

Simon Fraser had successfully struggled past the nightmarish canyon in the fall of 1805. He had turned his battered canoes south up the swift Parsnip River and then followed the Pack River to McLeod Lake, where he'd founded a trading post. But by Christmas, back on the eastern slopes of the Rocky Mountains, he was hostage to the seasons. His immediate world was reduced to slow motion, as though time itself had become viscous and then stalled, like the river that first turned to slushy frazil, then packed solid, then shattered along the shoreline as pressure ridges heaved blocks of ice up onto dry ground.

Winter was a time of hardship and hunger. As winter tightened its grip, Fraser was out in the open, trekking to a meeting with his colleagues at Fort Dunvegan, twelve days journey to the northeast in what is now Alberta, to discuss the next steps in his venture beyond the mountains.

The new year dawned over a landscape muffled in deep snow, and the men at Rocky Mountain Portage House—located in a long-vanished clearing across the river from where Hudson's Hope now looks over the valley—faced two weeks of

Fur traders like Simon Fraser hired professional hunters to supply them with fish and game but voyageurs also hunted and fished when possible. *Voyageur or "coureur du bois" with rifle and axe, Frederic Remington, Glenbow Archives NA-1406-55*

difficult travel to the next fort downstream. It took even longer to journey upstream to the little outpost at McLeod Lake. Travellers had to carry more than forty kilograms of rations in addition to their winter gear.

Communication with the North West Company nerve centre at Fort William had ended as couriers waited for ice to leave the waterways. Dispatches on the progress of his present venture, to be forwarded with returning voyageurs on Lake Superior, would reach the partners in Montreal just as the rivers froze for yet another winter.

Largely unknown to Fraser and his companions, the Napoleonic War had now gone global. And as Fraser trudged toward his meeting at Fort Dunvegan, Meriwether Lewis and William Clark prepared to abandon rain-soaked Fort Clatsop, their temporary winter quarters at the mouth of the Columbia River.

Snow fell steadily here at Hudson's Hope, where Fraser sought to secure his company's gateway to riches beyond the Rockies. It muffled the distant thunder of the canyon and its impassable rapids, buried the upturned bark canoes, piled up on the rooftops and drifted shoulder deep against the walls. The explorers welcomed snow as insulation that kept the cabins snug—so long as the drafty fireplaces with

This map of New Caledonia, much of it still blank, appeared in missionary and linguist Father Adrian Gabriel Morice's 1904 history of the region. *History of the Interior of Northern British Columbia Formerly New Caledonia [1660 to 1880], William Briggs, Toronto*

their chimneys fashioned from mud and green sticks had an ample supply of wood to burn. Cutting firewood, cord after cord of it, remained one of the crucial jobs at every northern fort, along with hunting.

Hunters were essential to provide the high volumes of calorie-rich fish and game required for survival. Native Indians were contracted as hunters, and Fraser's men hunted whenever the opportunity arose. While the company sought furs, it also encouraged its Indian clients to trade dried fish, pemmican—a high-calorie mix of meat, fat and dried berries—and jerky, or strips of wind- and sun-dried meat.

The cold was intense on the upper Peace River in that winter of 1806, so bitter that at Rocky Mountain Portage House the North West Company garrison made special note of it.

Around them, as I know from my own winters in the Arctic, trees froze and cracked like gunshots. On clear nights, smoke from the chimneys rose straight into a black sky that blazed with stars. Human flesh froze solid in less than a minute if exposed to the wind.

A man named Farcier was laid up with frostbitten toes in mid-January. Two men named La Londe and Grandbois came in from a hunt having starved for five days. In another incident, Lalleur fell through the ice and lost his blanket, kettle and axe, forcing two freezing men to share one dry blanket.

The situation was grim enough that, frozen toes or not, Farcier was soon back foraging for fish at Moberly Lake—he caught one whitefish and returned to report he'd not eaten for three days.

Fraser was still away. He had left just before Christmas in 1805, travelling down the frozen Peace to consult with the experienced senior men from the company's Athabasca department at Fort Dunvegan.

The auburn-haired, snub-nosed trader's journals show frustration but little dismay. He was tough. He'd survived the Loyalist expulsions that followed the American Revolution and was already a seasoned frontiersman. He'd spent almost half his life on the shadowy fringes of European expansion across the continent. Now he was preparing to push the operations into the unknown country that would become New Caledonia and eventually BC, a deeply risky financial venture for the company and certainly dangerous for the men he proposed to lead there.

Business interests and the forces of geopolitics drove the enterprise. France and postrevolutionary America had found a congruence that posed a serious threat to British interests in North America. Now Fraser and the North West Company raced to extend their economic domination of the fur trade west of the Rockies and thus secure future claims to sovereignty in the face of American expansion westward. This wasn't nationalistic patriotism, it was fear of future American protectionism and crushing tariffs on cross-border movement of goods.

While Fraser was at Dunvegan planning the next spring's operations, he left John Stuart in charge at Rocky Mountain Portage House and facing troubles other than the brutal cold. Discontent was brewing. Game was scarce. There was fear of starvation, which Stuart's journal entry for February 8 says laconically "very probably may happen."

Stuart's journal notes that on January 3, 1806, he sent two men up to McLeod Lake, which had a garrison of three men with La Malice in command.

Three weeks later James McDougall, Fraser's second in command, left Rocky Mountain Portage House on a vital reconnaissance mission. In 1805, he had ventured west from McLeod Lake, following a small river system and then travelling overland on an Indian trail. He got to what is now known as Carrier Lake, about twenty-five kilometres east of present-day Fort St. James at the eastern end of Stuart Lake.

McDougall's mission in early 1806 was to find the big lake farther west. His party carried light trade goods—axes, knives, beads—for the McLeod Lake post, and McDougall planned to push on immediately for the west, where the Tse'Khene people told him there was a powerful tribe called the Carriers. Fraser wanted contact, intelligence about navigable routes to the Pacific and furs.

But on February 19, Stuart's journal notes that after fourteen days of travel,

Carrier children wearing traditional dress dance against the sunset over Stuart Lake during a pageant commemorating Simon Fraser's arrival in 1806. *Bill Keay*/Vancouver Sun

two of the men who had accompanied McDougall were back at Rocky Mountain Portage House.

"To their surprise and distress, [they] found no person at the house [McLeod Lake], which they supposed to have been abandoned 10 days before their arrival but they were not able to follow Lamalice's Road on account of its being filled up with snow," Stuart wrote.

"They tell me that Mr. McDougall immediately took an account of all the property he found there, vis. 320 skins, sundry furs besides a few trading articles and 30 pounds of flour & a little sugar in the bottom of the keg. Luckily for them that found the flour, having just finished all their provisions except about three pounds of meat."

A week later, with McDougall chafing at the delay, La Malice arrived back at Rocky Mountain Portage House. He'd been forced to abandon McLeod Lake, he said, when the two men under his charge went hunting and didn't return for upward of a month.

There's a gap in the documentary record. Apparently Fraser quickly took charge; the post at McLeod Lake was quickly regarrisoned. McDougall reached Stuart Lake to the west and claimed the territory for the North West Company.

While there, McDougall met some of the Carriers. He had given one of them, named Duyunun, a square of red cloth. It was a simple gift but it would prove invaluable to Fraser six months later.

McDougall returned with glowing news. There was a vast lake, fish and game were abundant, there were many Carrier people and—most important for Fraser—he had learned of a river from the lake that was said to drain into a bigger river, which itself flowed south into an even greater river that they thought must be the Columbia.

By now the worst of winter appeared to be over. It was still cold, but game was suddenly abundant. Fraser began pre-positioning supplies above the Peace River canyon.

Then, on April 23, his journal recorded alarming news. Indians who were not Tse'Khene had come down the Finlay River, the north fork of the Peace, to trade. They already possessed iron, trade ornaments—and guns.

This was a shock. Fraser attempted to elicit more information but found them "not much inclined to satisfy our desires, which perhaps is not a little owing to the little knowledge we have of their language for our interpreters are none of the best."

He did learn of an immense river to the west, larger even than the Peace, which was connected to a big lake beyond Stuart Lake and eventually reached the sea.

"They represent it as different from the Columbia, but say it is from that quarter they get most part of their goods and the only place from where they get guns and ammunition," Fraser observed. "They positively affirm that white people came there in the course of the summer, but as they came on discovery that they had little goods. I have seen a pistol brass-mounted with powder and ball which they say they had from them."

Fraser would have had good cause to feel his heart sink. If another exploring expedition had already passed through the region the previous summer, whose was it? The hated Hudson's Bay Company? Worse, American free traders? Russians from Alaska?

No record of any such expedition to the northern Interior has ever been found, historian W. Kaye Lamb points out. Father Adrian Gabriel Morice, who wrote the definitive history of New Caledonia and a two-volume study of the Carrier language, emphatically says there's no record of the mysterious expedition—because there wasn't one.

The immense river Fraser couldn't identify was the Skeena, Morice says, and the Indians the trader met had been dealing with the Tsimshians who served as middlemen after obtaining goods from ships visiting the north coast.

"Had he [Fraser] been better acquainted with the ways of the Dene nation," Morice wrote, "he would have known that its members call whites anybody who conforms to the whites. Those [people called whites] who traded occasionally at Bear Lake were only Tsimshians from the coast."

But in the spring of 1806, Fraser knew none of this. He must have worried that his opportunity was slipping away, perhaps to some unknown expedition's benefit. His journal takes on a fretful tone. Delays seemed interminable in launching his own expedition to the west and Stuart Lake.

His canoes were in bad shape and needed repair, but the inexperienced men sent to gather birchbark to build new ones had ruined the bark. More had to be obtained, causing further delay. Some of his men were insubordinate. La Malice, who had abandoned the McLeod Lake post, showed up with a woman for whom he'd paid three hundred livres (about $1,600 today) and was adamant that she should accompany him despite Fraser's orders to the contrary.

Fraser gives little evidence of being a misogynist—no more than most men of his era, at least—but he was aware that constant bickering over women was the source of a great deal of discontent among the voyageurs. Furthermore, since First Nations women were the object of this unrest, there was always a potential for tense and even violent relations with local people.

"It is a lamentable fact that almost every difficulty we have had with Indians throughout the country may be traced to our interference with their women or their intrigues with the women of the forts," noted George Simpson, governor of the Hudson's Bay Company after the merger with the North West Company in 1821. "In short, nine murders out of 10 committed on whites by Indians have arisen through women."

But Fraser needed every experienced hand he could muster and finally relented. La Malice could bring his woman with him—but with a caveat. "I would grant him permission to take her, but not as his property." Only if she was willing would she go. She was willing.

Fraser wanted urgently to get away early to beat the June high water he knew would follow the big melt in the high country. On May 5, he moved five packs of supplies over the portage around the impassable Peace River canyon in preparation for departure. It seemed his timing was prescient, for the ice suddenly broke and began to move in the river. Then it jammed, "amazing strong and thick," the river rose more than three metres in twenty-four hours and the weather once again turned so cold that Stuart had to abandon his repairs to a canoe.

To complicate things, a large band of Tse'Khene had arrived "in a starving condition . . . poor devils, quite emaciated." They told Fraser they had been attacked by Beaver Indians near Fort Vermilion the previous summer. The Beaver had driven them off their hunting grounds and into the mountains "where they undergo great misery, according to their reports."

Fraser, never one to let an opportunity slip away, set the skilled Tse'Khene women to making *watape,* the spruce-root cord used to lash together canoe frames and stitch hulls. Others were sent to find more birchbark, gather spruce gum for sealing seams or make poles and paddles.

"I am really concerned about the backwardness of the season," Fraser wrote May 10. "The river is yet chock full of ice and people continually crossing upon it. Made up 560 pounds pounded meat, 76 pounds grease and 120 pounds dried meat, into bundles to be sent over the Portage tomorrow. Another pack was made and the small canoe gummed . . . "

Then during the night of Thursday, May 15, the ice in the river went out with a roar. Despite the broken, jostling jumble streaming away on the powerful current, an express canoe was immediately dispatched to Fort Dunvegan with news that the expedition's departure was imminent.

On May 20, 1806, Fraser closed the year's financial accounts for Rocky Mountain Portage House and spent the morning writing business correspondence and personal letters. At 3 p.m. he crossed the river with Stuart and set off over the portage.

The trail his men had hacked almost twenty kilometres through the bush was "amazing bad," he wrote. It was 10 p.m. by the time the two weary men reached the encampment above the canyon. The next morning, on May 21, he rose early to launch his bold expedition into the unknown.

Simon Fraser

14

FIRST ENCOUNTERS

The Carrier band that followed the powerful Chief Kwah was in its Stuart Lake summer camp on July 26, 1806, waiting in the lowlands around the mouth of Beaver Creek in Sowchea Bay, about six kilometres southwest of the present site of Fort St. James.

We know the precise calendar date only because it is mentioned in a copy made in 1878 of a now-missing letter written by Simon Fraser to "the Gentlemen Proprietors of the North West Company" from Stuart Lake in August of the same year.

To the Carrier people—called the *Agelh Ne* (the ones who pack) by their Tse'Khene neighbours, but by themselves the *Dakelh-ne* (the people who travel on water)—it was just another day in the season they named *Danghan.* That was when they gathered roots and bulbs for food, cut birchbark for baskets and roofing material on winter lodges, harvested willow and nettle for the making of rope and fishnets, and awaited the arrival of the salmon.

The soopollalie berries were in season, and women were gathering the staple that fur traders would call russet buffalo berry or soap berry and botanists know as *Shepherdia canadensis.* They would place a birchbark basket under the berry-laden branches that abounded near Beaver Creek and hit them sharply with a stick to shake the fruit loose.

This simple technology yielded a surprising quantity of the berries in a short period of time, notes Nancy Turner, the world-renowned ethnobotanist from the University of Victoria. It helps explain, she writes, why it was one of the most

A pensive Jordie Ann Erickson waits for dancing to begin during a pageant at Fort St. James.
Bill Keay/Vancouver Sun

Great chiefs from as far as the coast, among them Nisho'ot of Port Simpson, Hlengwah and Semedik of Kitwanga, visited Fort St. James in 1928 for the centennial of Hudson's Bay Company Governor George Simpson's visit to New Caledonia. *Image A-04233 courtesy of Royal BC Museum, BC Archives*

widely exploited fruits in what is now British Columbia long before and long after Fraser arrived.

Fresh soopollalie was whipped with water, and the resulting froth, which is similar in texture to beaten egg whites, was eaten as "Indian ice cream" at feasts and festive occasions for families. Dried and formed into cakes, it was preserved as a crucial food source during the long winters when the rivers froze and game was scarce.

But mostly the Carrier band awaited the arrival of the first of three consecutive runs of sockeye that normally arrive in July, August and September after a journey of more than a thousand kilometres up the Fraser River. These fish with distinctive crimson flesh would be split and hung on racks in smoke houses, dried and carefully stored in bales for winter consumption.

Kwah was a master of the salmon fishery. At a small island where the lake flowed into the Stuart River, he had a weir made of wooden stakes and fish traps woven from willow bark and spruce boughs. He was known for meticulous maintenance of his weir and for his uncanny ability to predict the sockeye's arrival.

Simon Fraser, meanwhile, was making his slow way up the Stuart River. By the fur trader's reckoning, he was close to a thousand kilometres by water from Rocky Mountain Portage House, deep in unknown country and surrounded by people from whom he didn't know whether to expect a friendly or a hostile welcome. He didn't know it at the time, but the future of his whole bold enterprise depended upon Kwah.

Bob Grill, superintendent of the federal government's national historic site at Fort St. James, is emphatic: the Carrier chief has been nominated as a person of national historic significance and he deserves that designation.

"Kwah was the most influential person in the fur trade at Stuart Lake. Kwah was fifty-one when he met the fur traders for the first time," Grill told me when I dropped by for a chat in his cluttered office. From here he looks after what is considered the most important collection of original buildings from the fur-trade era in Canada.

"He'd already established himself as a powerful chief. Kwah could have annihilated [Fraser and his companions] but he didn't. What he decided to do was reconcile the interests of his people with those represented by Fraser. He was a great statesman. He must have just been a force."

Accounts of that first meeting between Kwah and Fraser differ in detail, depending upon the source, but it's clear that the future of New Caledonia and what followed hinged upon the moment.

Kwah, who had been born about 1755, was descended from another great chief, Na'kwoel, born in the 1600s. Kwah had come to prominence, not just because of his lineage, but because of his hunting prowess and his success in war against other hostile bands to the south. Indeed, the native Indians encountered by Fraser at the

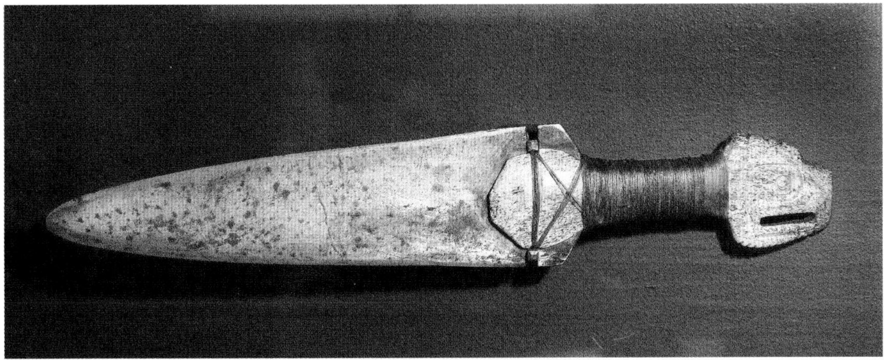

Tradition long held that this dagger was obtained by Kwah at a potlatch in the mid-1770s but research by Royal BC Museum curator Grant Keddie shows it to be of more recent manufacture. *Bill Keay/Vancouver Sun*

confluence of the Stuart and Nechako rivers were likely survivors of a massacre about 1780 for which Kwah had led a devastating retaliatory campaign. His triumphs bought his people a quarter-century of security.

According to Father Adrian Gabriel Morice, writing his *History of the Northern Interior of British Columbia, formerly New Caledonia,* July 26 was a windy day on *Nak'al Bun,* as Kwah called Stuart Lake. The prevailing breeze from the northwest was brisk and, with a nearly fifty-kilometre reach from the Tachie River on the lake's north shore, the waves must have been stacking up into a short, tight chop as they entered the shallows.

Morice says the Carriers who had camped beside the lake across the river mouth from the present-day village of Nak'azdli were surprised by the appearance of two large canoes struggling against the wind as they came out of the lee of the headland that lies between Beaver Creek and Stuart River.

One of their shamans, Duyunun, however, had already met James McDougall, who had given him a square of red cloth and told him that white people would return to build a trading post. Thus Kwah must have known that the strangers were coming.

According to stories passed down to Kwah's great-granddaughter, Lizette Hall, who recorded them in her book *The Carrier, My People* in 1992, the lake was very calm that day as they observed four large bark canoes rounding what is now called Leon's Point.

So—two canoes or four? Windy or calm? And where exactly did the fateful encounter occur, across from the present village or around the point?

Shauna Hesse, a visual artist who works summers as an interpreter at the Fort St. James historic site, chatted with me in the old warehouse. The air around us was redolent with the perfume of smoked moosehide as she told me her own researches pointed pretty clearly to Sowchea Bay as the location of first contact.

"I wanted to do a first contact painting," she said, "so I've been trying to figure out where it actually happened."

She began by examining the landscape with a painter's eye, seeking visual clues in both the written and oral histories that wouldn't have changed over the intervening centuries.

On the day we talked, strolling out of the shadowy warehouse to the boardwalks, the wind was out of the northwest, as Morice's informants told him it was blowing. The vivid blue of the lake was flecked with whitecaps that gleamed and glistened in the sun.

"When Simon Fraser's canoes came out of the river," Hesse said, pointing as we squinted into the bright sunshine, "did they turn across the wind or into the wind? I think they turned into the wind, as any sensible canoeist would do today. And where were the people? Were they along the eastern end of the lake [where the village of Nak'azdli is today] or were they off a bit to the west where that marshy region [at Sowchea Bay] might offer better fishing and hunting for small game just before the salmon arrived?"

Her logic seemed impeccable to me. Regardless of the specific spot where first contact occurred between Fraser and Kwah's band, both versions generally agree on what happened next.

The Carriers heard a kind of singing they had never heard before, and some were concerned that this might be a war party. But Duyunun put on the red cloth given him by McDougall and paddled out to meet the strange canoes. The visitors took Duyunun aboard their big vessels, but when those still ashore saw his canoe floating without him in it, they assumed the worst and took to the bush. Fraser's party, says Hall, landed in a deserted camp. On Duyunun's assurance that the visitors were friendly, people came out of the woods.

The encounter was fraught with misunderstandings from the outset, however, Grill said. First, in what could have been a disastrous breach of protocol, the newcomers mistook the shaman Duyunun for the chief, a profound insult that Kwah chose to overlook.

Second, when gifts of tobacco were offered, the Carriers didn't know what it was, tasted it and threw aside the bitter substance. When some voyageurs demonstrated its use by lighting their clay pipes, there was cause for even greater alarm. The Carriers cremated their dead, and Morice recounts that at the sight of strangers with pale skins breathing smoke, there were fears that they were ghosts from the land of the dead, still full of their cremation fire.

And in a final humorous misunderstanding, when gifts of soap were made to Carrier women, they mistook them for cakes of fat and tried to eat them. The men—Carrier and newcomers alike—then watched in amazement as the women suddenly began to foam at the mouth with soap bubbles.

For Fraser, the problems were more complex than he had expected.

"Right from day one there was a huge misunderstanding about the nature of the deal [with Kwah and the Carriers]," Grill said.

To Fraser and his partners, trade was a purely commercial transaction, an exchange of goods to the business profit of both parties. To the Carrier, trade denoted a special, almost sacred relationship that established and affirmed certain obligations to share in times of need.

So when fur traders withheld items in expectation of payment yet wanted Carriers to share their food in times of famine, it created an immediate source of friction and resentment on both sides.

"The fur traders are trying to be self-sufficient," Grill mused. "They cross the Rockies and discover there are no buffalo, no elk, none of the big game to which they are accustomed. They want furs at a different time than the Carrier are used to trapping. They write about the lazy Carrier—they weren't lazy, they just had different things to do."

To make things worse, the sockeye run was unusually late in 1806, not arriving until September 20, perhaps because of the same late spring and very high water that had delayed Fraser's departure.

Although Kwah and the Carriers hadn't been hostile, they also hadn't been inclined to simply drop their seasonal activities to go hunting and trapping on behalf of the newcomers.

Fraser complained in his first letter that the Carriers were "indolent," fishing was poor, there were no large animals to hunt except caribou "which is too sly for us," and his men were reduced to eating dried carp. Once the Stuart Lake sockeye had arrived, though, it wasn't long before the traders were griping about having to eat salmon every day.

More important, Fraser reminded his superiors in his letter that if his venture west of the Rockies was to be a success, he must be supplied adequately with trade items that the local people wanted. Also, to build and staff more posts, more clerks would have to be recruited.

In fact, unlike some of the bands to the east, Kwah's people were not dependent upon a North West Company monopoly.

"They are independent of us," Fraser worried, "as they get their necessaries from their [Tsimshian] neighbours who trade with the Natives of the sea coast."

Later, in another letter, Fraser reported corroborating evidence. On a journey to the western end of Stuart Lake he encountered people with spoons, metal pots and muskets that they had apparently obtained in trade from the coast via "Cook's River"—probably the Skeena and its tributary, the Babine.

The lack of provisions delayed Fraser sufficiently that he was forced to confront reality: his planned expedition to what he thought was the Columbia could not safely be launched before the onset of another winter. His normally ebullient spirits seemed quite depressed by the time he wrote a quick note to John Stuart, who had been dispatched to investigate reports of yet another major lake to the west.

"I assure you I am tired of living on fish and I feel quite dull and lonesome since you left me," Fraser wrote on September 29. "Nothing goes on to my liking. I hate the place and the Indians."

The traders complained about the isolation, but nobody complained about the lustrous beaver, marten and fisher pelts that sent wealth cascading into the coffers of the North West Company. Thanks to New Caledonia and diversified markets, Fraser's company was able to prosper while the rival Hudson's Bay Company struggled with a financial crisis caused by the Napoleonic Wars blockading its traditional European markets in Germany and Russia.

So it's not surprising that despite nothing going to his liking, Fraser quickly set his men to clearing land, cutting logs and erecting a new trading post at the site where McDougall had emerged from the bush.

Grill, a qualified cabinetmaker, started his career as a labourer working on the restoration of the Fort St. James site that began in 1974.

"I came from Denver," he said. "I heard they were looking for carpenters to help rebuild an old fort. I thought, that's for me. I'd always wanted to move north and when I crossed the Stuart River bridge and saw the lake, I knew I was home. They said, 'Okay, start tomorrow' and I did. I trapped on weekends and learned how to hew logs. Seven years ago, I became superintendent—it's the best job in the world."

Grill said he is still astonished by the architectural genius that built the North

Bob Grill, site superintendent at Fort St. James National Historic Site, himself a trained cabinetmaker, explains the modular construction genius of the early fur trade. *Bill Keay*/Vancouver Sun

West Company fort in 1806 and carried out renovations in 1820, 1850 and 1880.

"These guys built a fort in months—with an axe," he said. "If you go out and look at the dovetail corners, you can't put a credit card in the join. How did they do that? I don't know."

One thing he does know is that the people who erected the structures were brilliant at log construction. Unable to curb his enthusiasm for the subject, he took me for a stroll through the existing buildings—a warehouse and fur store, a cache for dried fish, the men's quarters, the store where trade goods were dispensed, the factor's house—and explained how, from the beginning, they had devised a form of modular construction.

"You get your logs, square them, cut them in ten-foot lengths and you assemble them into walls. It's piece on piece construction; it's like early plywood. You want a building ten by ten or ten by twenty, or twenty by thirty, or twenty by forty; you can expand to whatever you need. You can take them apart and reassemble them. When the lower logs rot, you just take the walls down and put new logs in."

This is how remnants of the 1806 warehouse come to still exist in the present structure two hundred years later, he explained. Each time subsequent factors did renovations or expansions at the fort, they used wood that was still good from earlier structures.

Left: New Caledonia provided luxuriant, lustrous furs like those hanging from the rafters at Fort St. James National Historic Site's restored warehouse, considered the finest surviving architectural example in North America. *Bill Keay/*Vancouver Sun

Right: Fort St. James began as a North West Company fort and ended as a Hudson's Bay Company post but one thing that hasn't changed is the spectacular view down Stuart Lake. *Glenn Baglo/*Vancouver Sun

Later that evening, volunteers in the community were doing their annual ghost walk in which scenes from the past in Fort St. James are brought to life. Leon Erickson and his kids re-enacted the meeting between Fraser and Kwah as a fiery red sun sank toward the northwestern horizon far down Stuart Lake.

It's doubtful either Fraser or Kwah could have dreamed that the rough clearing in the woods where the explorer fretted and the chief weighed his options would become the capital of a rich new trading empire, New Caledonia, from which would rise the great province that came to anchor a new country stretching across the northern half of the continent from sea to shining sea.

Exhibits at Fort St. James National Historic Site strive for authenticity, right down to the clutter of a working fur trader's quarters. *Bill Keay*/Vancouver Sun

15

BOLD MEN, BEAUTIFUL WOMEN

When Simon Fraser and his brigade of Cree interpreters, Scottish clerks, Métis hunters and French-Canadian voyageurs pushed up the Peace River to establish a base beyond the Rocky Mountains, they knew only that they could expect the unexpected.

Fraser and his party were at the farthest end of a tenuous supply line that reached across an entire continent. It passed through territories that were often disputed by warring First Nations and contested by fierce competitors from the Hudson's Bay Company.

They had to be tough, resilient and resourceful men and women—the brigades relied heavily upon women, particularly First Nations women—for the skills needed to survive in unfamiliar and unforgiving country. For all that, their position was never secure.

All who agreed to accompany Fraser knew they were venturing into a vast unknown from which some and possibly all might not return.

Several exploratory probes had already penetrated the mountain wall, most notably Sir Alexander Mackenzie's dash to the Pacific Ocean and back in 1793. John Finlay had followed with explorations of the Peace River's two main branches, the Parsnip and the Finlay, in the summer of 1797. But David Thompson's failure to breach the Rockies from the headwaters of the North Saskatchewan River in 1800 and 1801 were a reminder of the difficulties that lay ahead.

Fraser's intelligence on the West was scant, other than what James McDougall garnered from a short foray. He knew little of the tribes with whom he hoped to establish trade on the far side of the Rockies. What he heard from local people must have raised apprehensions. Conflict already swirled around the little outpost he'd named the Rocky Mountain Portage House, with reports of native Indian raids and counter-raids. At least one of the tribes on the other side of the mountains was said to be numerous and sometimes warlike.

Furthermore, Fraser knew that once on the Pacific slope his interpreters would be dealing with languages, dialects and customs with which they weren't fully conversant. Beaver interpreters would translate into Cree, Cree would translate into French, French would translate into English and then the reply would return by the same tortuous route. That left plenty of opportunity for disastrous misunderstandings on both sides.

One thing Fraser knew for certain. The country into which he'd been instructed to extend the North West Company's trading empire was anything but uninhabited wilderness. Later settlers would claim to have found an empty land in the wake of recurring pandemics—smallpox, influenza, measles, diphtheria, whooping cough and other diseases—all of which proved extraordinarily lethal to populations with little natural immunity.

In the aftermath of devastating epidemics, colonists perceived the landscape as largely deserted but Simon Fraser's journals show he found a land filled with people like this woman and toddler photographed at Fort George.

Image A-06066 courtesy of Royal BC Museum, BC Archives

Compared to the boreal forests, the Pacific slope was a densely populated and socially complex region. It was occupied by people who were members of several large language groups. These divided into numerous "national" groupings that themselves subdivided into tribal groups, clans and extended families that competed, sometimes violently, for control of resources and trade routes, the means to impose political and cultural hegemonies, and the opportunity to broker alliances that furthered their strength and authority.

In the New Caledonia founded by Simon Fraser west of the Rockies, the North West Company's traders initially encountered three powerful tribal groups. Their influence waxed and waned as they acquired new technology and reaped the benefits—and paid the price—of sweeping economic changes that would utterly transform the shape of their societies.

But when Fraser passed beyond Fort Alexandria, where Alexander Mackenzie had decided to turn back on his journey down the Fraser River to the Pacific in 1793, he began encountering new nations.

Using the names applied by their neighbours, through whom he was first introduced to them, Fraser called these peoples the Atnah, the Askettih, the Hacamaugh and the Ackinroe.

Ethnologists would later call them the Shuswap, the Lillooet, the Thompson and the Coast Salish. They prefer to call themselves by their own names—the Secwepemc, the St'at'imc, the Nlaka'pamux and the Sto:lo—although within each of these linguistic and cultural groupings, subunits have their own local names.

But for all the clinical language of ethnologists and the bloodless accounts of scholarly historians—sometimes more interested in marshalling facts into arguments than the often unruly passions of individuals—it's important to remember that the encounters between cultures were also meetings between human beings.

Thus commercial engagements of supply and demand in the global fur market were frequently marked along their interfaces by the emotional entanglements that occur whenever vigorous young men and women are thrown together by circumstance.

Cree women were the most comely "of all the nations which I have seen on this continent," enthused Alexander Mackenzie, who passed through their country before his momentous expedition to the Pacific Ocean in 1793. He was not alone in expressing an appreciation of First Nations femininity. Comments upon the beauty of aboriginal women leap with noteworthy intensity from the pages of fur-trade journals, memoirs and letters.

Englishman Nicholas Garry, accompanying a border survey around the Great Lakes region, rhapsodized over the beauty, intelligence and flashing black eyes of Ojibwa women. It was an opinion shared by North West Company trader Peter Grant, who thought their charm rivalled that of supposedly more civilized and accomplished "belles" back in European society.

Early nineteenth-century artist George Catlin was smitten by "beautiful and voluptuous-looking" Gros Ventre women, but was also partial to "exceedingly pleasing and beautiful" Mandans. Fellow painter Rudolph Kurtz almost swooned after observing some Aricara women bathing in a stream—"so slender yet round, so supple yet firm . . . such grace." During his travels, artist Paul Kane was so taken with a Métis woman named "One that looks at the stars"—she danced with him at a Christmas party at Fort Edmonton—that he later painted her portrait, which now hangs in the Royal Ontario Museum.

The studiously religious Daniel Harmon, a Bennington-born contemporary of Simon Fraser in the New Caledonia fur trade, attended a "famous Ball in the Dining Room" thrown by North West Company magnates during the annual rendezvous at Grand Portage in 1800. He found himself pleasantly surprised by the social skills, dancing abilities—and propriety—of "this Countries Ladies, whom I was surprised could behave themselves so well, and who danced not amiss."

David Thompson, the great geographer of the west, also admired the contours and complexions of women he met on the Flathead River, whom he described as having skins like the "palest new copper after being freshly rubbed," remarking that they were "remarkably well made" beauties.

And trader Alexander Henry's lively accounts of frontier life in Fraser's time indicate that aboriginal women were far from reticent in their appreciation of the eligible young bachelors who arrived in their midst. He describes how one young woman courted him with such ardour and persistence that he married her.

No one should be surprised by the attentiveness of these fur traders to the women they encountered or to the interest of aboriginal women in the exotic strangers, said Adele Boucher, a retired teacher, bison rancher and historian with an interest in the Fraser era.

"When you think of all those people who came through here [in the fur trade], they were all human," Boucher told me when we chatted on the bluffs above the Peace River townsite.

First, the traders were almost all young men in their late teens or early twenties and well in the grip of their testosterone storms. Second, they were employed in a business that could separate them from the society of women for years at a time, immersed in what scholar Adele Perry, in her book *On the Edge of Empire: Gender, Race and the Making of British Columbia, 1849–1871*, has called the homosocial culture of the frontier. Females were more than sex objects; they were a symbolic civilizing force of domesticity.

Another dynamic was also at work. In aboriginal cultures where marriages were often no less diplomatic than those arranged among European elites—a social tool for expanding and securing trade relationships and for arranging kinship ties that served to ease tensions between groups—attachment to a fur trader through a marriage could enhance a chief's prestige, bring economic benefits to a band and give

Many fur traders took wives from among the tribes they dealt with. Artist Paul Kane was so impressed by Cun-Ne-Wa-Bum when she danced with him at Fort Edmonton that he later painted her portrait.
With permission of the Royal Ontario Museum © ROM

a daughter elevated status.

For a trader, who often relied totally upon his aboriginal clients for his own survival, being able to call upon relationships that extended beyond the purely commercial might prove the difference between life and death in a moment of crisis.

"At the average fur-trade post," pointed out Peace River museum curator Dallas Wood, "they sent out a clerk—a kid who could read and write and keep accounts. He knew nothing about how to survive. He had to hire aboriginal people to help him subsist."

An aboriginal or Métis wife, taken in what became known as marriage *à la façon*

Making snowshoes was just one of the technologies crucial to survival in the boreal forest during Simon Fraser's fur-trade era. *Library of Congress Prints & Photographs Division LC-USZ62-133503*

du pays (in the fashion of the country)—according to aboriginal rites—was often a pivotal factor in a trader's success or failure.

Such a wife came with essential survival skills in her repertoire. She knew how to make snowshoes and moccasins. She could butcher a moose. She knew the habits of animals and how to set snares for small game in times of hunger. She knew how to dry meat, smoke fish, make pemmican and preserve berries for the winter months. She could serve as an interpreter, an intermediary between cultures and a negotiator.

And, not the least important, she made a lively home out of a dreary barracks.

Until recently—probably as a lingering consequence of the stratified, race-conscious society of the colonial era that superceded the fur trade, in which upwardly mobile newcomers were intent upon validating their claims to sovereignty over an already-occupied landscape—eyes have been politely averted from these relationships.

But over the last twenty years a new generation of brilliant female historians like Adele Perry and Sylvia Van Kirk has been shining new light upon the phenomenon. Observed through a feminist prism, the neglected study of cross-cultural integration signified by the taking of "country wives" by traders and voyageurs now assumes a major role in understanding the origins of Canada, its values and world views.

"In most other areas of the world, sexual contact between European men and native women has usually been illicit in nature and essentially peripheral to the white man's trading or colonizing ventures," writes Van Kirk in her remarkable book *Many Tender Ties: Women in Fur-Trade Society, 1670–1870.* "In the Canadian West, however, alliances with Indian women were the central social aspect of the fur traders' progress across the country."

To be sure, as American writer Walter O'Meara details in his book *Daughters of the Country: The Women of the Fur Traders and Mountain Men*, some aboriginal women were abused and exploited by callous and brutal men—just as some women in mainstream society suffer similar fates today. Some were simply abandoned by husbands when they retired from the fur trade. Other native women like Charlotte Small, Lisette Duval and Catherine Sinclair, the informally contracted country wives of David Thompson, Daniel Harmon and Charles Ermatinger, stayed with their husbands all their lives. Contrary to one common stereotype, their affectionate husbands stood by them in spite of the bigotry, prejudice and racism of an emerging colonial overclass. In some cases, husbands publicly refused to demean the legitimacy of marriages made under Indian sanction by submitting their wives to a second "Christian" marriage on return to Canada.

"The Nor'Westers' disdain for the formalities of European marriage may have resulted from the strong Scottish influence in the Company," Van Kirk concludes. "In Scotland, at this time, it was possible for a legal marriage to be contracted without the sanction of either civil or religious authorities; all that was necessary was for the couple to express their consent in front of a witness."

Thompson took his wife back to Canada with him and built her a house in Williamstown in the Eastern Townships, not far from where Simon Fraser eventually settled.

The fine house occupied by the Ermatinger family still stands in Sault Ste. Marie. Harmon, who thought a great deal about moral conduct, left an even more enduring legacy. He wrote down his feelings about Lisette Duval:

"Having lived with this woman as my wife . . . Having children by her, I consider that I am under a moral obligation not to dissolve the connexion, if she is willing to continue it. The union which had been formed between us under the providence of God, has not only been cemented by a long and mutual performance of kind offices, but, also, by a more sacred consideration . . .

"How could I spend my days in the civilized world, and leave my beloved children in the wilderness? How could I tear them from a mother's love, and leave her to mourn over their absence to the day of her death? Possessing only the common

First Nations were crucial to the survival and success of the fur trade, supplying food and essential technologies. But everyone depended upon the contributions of hardy, highly skilled women like these two from the Carrier nation working at Fort St. James. *Glenbow Archives NA-1164-3*

feelings of humanity, how could I think of her, in such circumstances, without anguish?"

Some did simply abandon country wives when it suited their convenience. William Connolly left his Cree wife, Susanne Pas-de-nom, and returned to Montreal to marry an attractive society woman, Julia Woolrich. That particular abandonment had an ironic twist. On Connolly's death, a son by his first wife sued for a share of the estate and the court ruled for his entitlement on grounds the first marriage was legitimate. A daughter from the first marriage, Amelia, married Sir James Douglas, and entered society herself as first lady of the colony that would become the province of BC.

Some left wives behind out of compassion rather than ruthlessness. They felt it more humane to leave their country wives in the company of their kinfolk than uproot them to live in an alien and hostile society. Often they continued to provide for them and paid for the education of children born to these country marriages.

"Mackenzie had a son, Andrew, in Fort Vermilion [between Peace River and Fort Chipewyan] who lived to be fifteen or so," Boucher told me. "He also had a daughter with another woman who was a country wife. He took that child to Scotland with him and she was raised by his sisters, her aunts. Maria did come back to Canada and married and there are still descendants."

Simon Fraser, too, apparently had children by a country wife while serving as a clerk in the Athabasca district. A letter he wrote to clerk James McDougall from Fraser Lake in 1806 said that he had no concerns for his children so long as they were under McDougall's protection. In another letter he instructed, "Anything that the Children are in want of and that can be had please give it to them & Charge the same to my acct." But by February of 1807 he was writing to John Stuart to confess, "Yes my friend I have once more entered upon the matrimonial state and you would have a hearty laugh if you heard of our Courtship."

How many country wives Fraser took during his many years in the fur trade isn't clear. It's certain that he was not accompanied by a country wife when he left the business to settle on a farm and woodlot near Cornwall, Ontario, where he married Catherine Macdonell and raised a second (or third) family. His country wives' identities and fates have never been ascertained, so far as I could determine from the available records. In that, they are part of the uncertainty that surrounds much of the explorer's early life and career.

Given the vital role so many women played in the close economic partnership between aboriginal and European cultures upon which fur-trade society relied, Fraser's unknown wives, their children, and the new nation—the Métis—that they represented are also inextricably tangled up in the continuing narrative of Canada and British Columbia.

Simon Fraser

16

A MESSAGE TO THE FUTURE

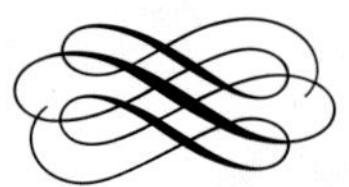

In the flood of letters and emails that followed the first instalment of the *Vancouver Sun's* search for Simon Fraser and the birth of modern British Columbia, one query particularly piqued my interest. It came from a man who'd grown up in Fort St. James but had been working for many years on Vancouver Island. He bore a deep nostalgia for his time there and great fondness for the people and landscapes around Stuart Lake.

Had I heard, he wanted to know, about Simon Fraser's graffiti?

He hadn't seen it himself, but he'd heard as a kid that somewhere near Fort St. James, the fur trader had succumbed to the same yearning that still moves some folk to paint their names on roadside boulders or carve their initials into trees. Fraser was said to have left his autograph as he passed by, just as earlier explorers Samuel Hearne and Alexander Mackenzie had done.

In fact, when I poked around in the loft of the old North West Company warehouse at the Fort St. James National Historic Site, I noted that those who followed Fraser also hadn't hesitated to leave their graffiti.

"Alexander Campbell Murray, Stuart Lake, New Caledonia, British Columbia" was a legendary Hudson's Bay Company fur trader who won the Governor-General's medal for mathematics as a student but chose a life in the wilderness. He rose to prominence at Fort St. James just as Louis Riel was being hung. Donald Todd pencilled his name on the logs in 1892. W.E. Connell did the same on April 4, 1897. William Bunting signed on August 2, 1909. Agnes McKinnon, HBC clerk, added her name just before Christmas in 1942.

The intent couldn't be considered in the same light as the one that motivated Carrier people to paint mysterious symbolic pictograms on rock faces around Fort St. James and that today comprise one of the cultural treasures of BC's northern Interior. But surely all these people, Carriers and newcomers alike, did share that same yearning for graffiti's momentary sense of permanence in a landscape so vast and timeless.

The rock paintings depict guardian spirits, a shaman's animal familiars, supernatural avatars, mythological beings or simply personal iconographies for the dreams that came to seekers in ritual vision quests. Such images are not unique to New Caledonia. They're found across BC from Stuart Lake to the Stein Valley and from the Similkameen to the Gulf Islands, and they are associated with hunting societies from Australia to Africa to prehistoric Europe and Asia.

Rock faces around Stuart Lake abound with pictographs. Many depict animals and may indicate their abundance, others appear to portray supernatural beings. *Heledd Mayse*

The paintings around Fort St. James, however, are among the most dramatic and best preserved examples of such artistic expression to be found anywhere. They should rightly be considered of national significance as part of Canada's cultural heritage. I've never understood why as British Columbians we have not launched a comprehensive program to recognize their significance in our own collective history.

My inquiries about the signature led me to Pat Hampe, one of those community-minded volunteers who chaired the local Friends of the Fort St. James National Historic Site Society. Pat told me that she, too, had heard of the graffiti but hadn't seen it herself. She was pretty flustered the day I called, up to her eyeballs in preparations for the town's two-hundredth birthday party, trying to track down a slew of misplaced computer files and helping to plan for the homecoming dinner and dance that promised to be the keynote of the celebration. Still she generously set aside some time to meet and discuss it with me. Then she called me back. She had a contact who had seen the mysterious signature. Would I like to see it?

The next day my daughter Hel and I made our way to Cam and Anne McCormick's newly built house high on a rocky outcrop overlooking the lake.

The glassy surface of Stuart Lake reflects a summer sky not far from the outlet to the Stuart River where Simon Fraser first encountered Chief Kwah. *Bill Keay/Vancouver Sun*

Cam had first come to Fort St. James in 1954, sitting in the same classrooms as Pat Hampe, who would accompany us on this small expedition of discovery. He'd gone to Simon Fraser University as an undergraduate, completed a master's degree at the University of BC, then gone teaching in far-flung places—Hixon, Prince George, Lake Cowichan, Houston, Kitimat—before returning to Stuart Lake to work as vice-principal and now principal at Sowchea Elementary. He also rents out kayaks to tourists for paddling expeditions down the lake.

"Everybody multitasks here," he told me. "When we came back, we just picked up where we left off. We love the environment, we love going out and enjoying it, but it's the community that keeps you."

What we were looking for was at a remote location down Stuart Lake. In my tight time frame—to my daughter's disappointment—it wasn't close enough for a kayak trip, but Cam said he'd run us down the lake in his Zodiac with its big Mariner outboard.

We launched the inflatable from a beach not far from Our Lady of Good Hope Roman Catholic Church, where Father Adrian Gabriel Morice did much of the prodigious research that went into his seminal history of New Caledonia. The church was built in 1873 by Morice's predecessor, Father Georges Blanchet. Logs for the church were skidded more than six kilometres across the frozen lake by thirty members of his Carrier congregation. At a rate of two logs per day, it took two months of winter skidding to assemble enough to build the church.

It was from here that Morice devised the syllabary that transformed Carrier into a written language, compiled a dictionary, wrote a Carrier grammar text and even published a newspaper in Carrier. All the while, he gathered and recorded stories from Carrier elders.

Zooming down the lake in Cam's boat, I listened carefully while he explained the weather hazards, on the theory that local knowledge generally trumps the meteorology from some computer barn in faraway Vancouver.

"The weather usually comes in from the west and you can see it coming so you have plenty of time to get off the water," he explained. "But if it comes from over there"—he gestured toward the low hills above the lake's south shore—"then it comes in really fast.

"My dad always warned me, if you see a line of cloud over those hills, black on one side, white on the other, get off the lake. It can go from flat calm to metre-high waves in less than twenty minutes."

Luckily for us there was not much wind and only a mild chop as we ran toward Pinchi Bay down a long stretch of sheer cliffs below Pope Mountain—named, I was told with a snort, for Maj. Franklin Pope who got lost on it in 1865 while surveying a never-completed telegraph route for Western Union.

To the Carrier people, the mountain is named Nak'al and has supernatural significance. In Fraser's time, it was believed that a village inside the mountain was

Privately owned Battleship Island, named for its resemblance to a First World War dreadnaught, looms from Stuart Lake near Pinchi Creek. *Hanson Family*

inhabited by a race of little people with extraordinary strength, strong enough to leave a massive rock balanced on the cliff face above the water.

On the way out, Pat pointed out historic landmarks and the homes of old-timers. Behind us was the Russ Baker monument. The bush pilot who founded Pacific Western Airlines first saw Fort St. James flying into Germansen Landing and so liked it that he settled there in 1937, just in time to spend the war flying military units and survey teams into the wilderness.

When three US Air Force B-26 bombers made a forced landing in the mountains, Baker found them and rescued twenty-four airmen. This earned him the US Air Medal in 1942 and later a personal commendation from President Harry Truman. He died in 1958 and was buried where he wanted to be, in a grave blasted from the rock above Stuart Lake.

There was the house of Al Mooney, long-time country doctor about whom everybody seems to have a charming story. Pat's was particularly poignant.

"I was ten months old. I had pneumonia and I was dying," she said. "My parents had had the last rites given to me. Dr. Mooney had just come from a conference and he was in Terrace. He had some samples of this new drug, penicillin, and he drove all the way [about six hundred kilometres] from Terrace and injected me. He saved my life. He saved a lot of people's lives."

Behind me, Cam pointed to Battleship Island, a block of stone that rises suddenly from the lake. It bears an eerie resemblance to one of those World War I cruisers with slab sides and a raked hull. Beside us, cliffs rose hundreds of vertical metres from water that was the dark blue of a gun barrel. It was on these faces that Cam pointed out rock paintings. Some were in places that seemed impossible to reach. Many depicted animals. Some, to my eye, were clearly supernatural beings. Others included—judging from interpretations of paintings I'd seen elsewhere—what I took to be more mundane information: the time of day the painting was

Stephen Hume, Pat Hampe and Cam McCormick (standing) survey rock faces on Stuart Lake in search of Simon Fraser's signature from 1806. *Heledd Mayse*

Among the rock paintings placed around Stuart Lake can be found the weathered, fading signature of Simon Fraser above the date 1806. *Heledd Mayse*

made; how many days the artist had waited for his vision; the simple declaration of ownership of his dream.

The pictographs were surveyed in 1978 and anthropologists think there may be a correlation between the number of animal figures depicted in a painting and the species' abundance, a fact of central importance to the Carrier people who hunted and trapped them. So it's not surprising that there seemed to be a surfeit of fish designs.

We put in for a closer look at a couple of spots. Others we had to observe from the water, the ledges being too slick and precarious. The images were amazing. Most probably date from the nineteenth century, I was told later, but some perhaps from the eighteenth or earlier.

Still I felt a strange sense of connection between these images and those I'd seen on the cliffs above Agawa Bay on Lake Superior and the strangely disorienting, maze-like sacred site in Manitoba that dated from the earliest known human cultures in North America.

We'd been travelling for a good chunk of the morning when Cam put his tiller hard over. There, hidden from general view, was what we'd been looking for. It was weathered and part was rendered faint against the background staining of the rock, but I could clearly make out "Simon," part of "Fraser" and "1806" scrawled across the stone in reddish pigment that was similar but not so intense in hue as that used for the rock paintings.

The writing was the same florid eighteenth-century copperplate script I'd seen on Simon Fraser's correspondence in the archives at Simon Fraser University. To my mind there was little doubt that the same hand had produced the autograph upon this stone.

We drifted quietly, wallowing a bit in the chop as the waves slopped and echoed in the undercuts. It was a contemplative moment for all of us. Fraser had been buried for 144 years—he died on August 18, 1862—and yet here was a message from that young explorer to us. He'd paused to mark his passage for those he must have been confident would come after him. He'd left us his signal to the future, made in the brightness of his youth, declaring that he'd been here at the farthest edge of the known world.

Simon Fraser

17

THE FAINT ROAD WEST

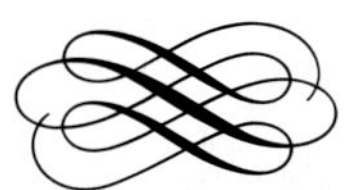

In the pitch-dark hour between the setting of the moon at 3:30 a.m. and the first flush of sunrise along the rim of the Nechako Plateau, the lake that Carrier speakers call *Nak'al Bun* glimmered in the starlight.

Awakened by another all-night trucker growling up through his gears on Highway 27 and unable to get back to sleep, I'd slipped out for a wee-hours stroll along the southeastern shore of what the *British Columbia Gazetteer* dutifully records as Stuart Lake.

This was once the capital of what is now British Columbia, in its day a key administrative centre in a global business enterprise. It sat at the nexus of a vast network of commercial trade routes. Today it's a friendly, bustling little blue-collar community of just over two thousand people about nine hundred kilometres north of Vancouver by road.

Fort St. James is still a relatively prosperous place by provincial standards. Average household income exceeds the provincial average by more than seven thousand dollars, according to census figures posted at BC Statistics, and the incidence of low-income households and individuals is far lower than the rest of BC.

These days Lower Mainlanders tend to think of Fort St. James as the end of the line. Beyond it the pavement gradually peters out. There's a rough back road over Mt. Mackinnon to Fort McLeod and gravel roads to outposts lingering from the Omineca gold rush—Manson's Creek, Germansen's Landing—but even they eventually dwindle away into the northern bush.

From Our Lady of Good Hope Church, built on Stuart Lake in 1873, Oblate missionary Father Adrian Gabriel Morice mapped New Caledonia, recorded its history and devised a written form for the Carrier language.
Bill Keay/Vancouver Sun

On the scale of the geological time by which landscapes evolve, a couple of centuries are inconsequential. As I looked out over the water, listening to the night sounds—a faint breeze making the cottonwoods rustle, the murmur of the lake as it slid away to the northwest—I considered how it must have appeared by night in 1806, the same restless, inky expanse that seemed alive in a way that the ominous black bulk of the mountains did not.

The cliffs below Mt. Pope, then Pinchi, then Tchentsut—rugged outcrops reaching well over a kilometre into the heavens, marching away into the distant Omineca wilderness—formed inscrutable, motionless blocks of shadow. But the lake trembled. A faint luminosity played across its surface as ripples caught and reflected light from a Milky Way that poured across the heavens.

Not far from where I stood, James McDougall, the man the Tse'Khene called *Mutsikanutlo* (Curly) stepped out of a thick stand of spruce that crowded the lake's edge. He and two companions stood gazing down the lake with their arms folded and their guns angled across their chests, writes Lizette Hall, who heard the description of the moment from Carrier elders who knew people alive at the time.

It was April, and travel was still hampered by ice and a late spring. The three men had trekked westward three and a half days from the North West Company's newly established post at McLeod Lake, just under 135 kilometres to the northeast.

Simon Fraser had sent McDougall to reconnoitre and evaluate reports from the Tse'Khene around Hudson's Hope of another powerful and more numerous tribe to the west and of a river that flowed from a great lake to what he thought must be the Columbia.

A trade route to the sea could mean enormous savings for the North West Company, which had to ship its furs and trade goods by canoe over thousands of kilometres of rivers and portages. The expense was damnable. It was labour intensive, every year there were losses of men and cargo in the dangerous rapids and in storms and each year commerce was interrupted for six months of winter freeze-up. A viable shipment route from the far west to the sea would be a major coup for the Nor'Westers in their battle with the Hudson's Bay Company.

McDougall blazed a spruce tree with his axe, claimed the territory for the North West Company on Fraser's behalf, and mistaking one of the Carriers he met for a local chief, made him a present of a square of red cloth.

The exploring party didn't make camp but left immediately to carry news to Fraser confirming that the stories of rich fur country to the west were accurate. A report from McLeod Lake was dispatched with a courier named D'Allaire who almost didn't survive the journey, Fraser notes in his journal on May 14. The river was still choked with ice, and a block fell on D'Allaire's canoe from the steep bank and destroyed it. He was forced to cover the last day's travel on foot.

The exact spot where McDougall first gazed down the lake is lost, but it was somewhere near where I stood. Here Fraser built the fort around which the present community now sprawls. Most of the original fort is gone, although it's believed that some of the two hundred-year-old timbers cut by Fraser's men for the original warehouse were reused in the present building, which dates from the late nineteenth century.

Behind me the town slumbered on. Even the fire crews in the rooms next to mine at the New Caledonia Motel hadn't yet begun to stir. Soon enough they'd be up, clattering down to greet the dawn in their orange jumpsuits, dispersing noisily to the trucks that would distribute them to their far-flung assignments. Once this was an all-male performance, but now the guys' early morning jibes and laughter are interspersed with the lighter sound of female voices.

The time I'd chosen to pick up Fraser's trail had not proved fortuitous. Even as I made my way north, following the route of the old Cariboo Wagon Road built at the command of Governor James Douglas (who once served as a Hudson's Bay Company clerk at Fort St. James), a series of fast-moving storm cells had raced across the tinder dry Interior.

In a matter of days, forty-six forest fires had been ignited, most by lightning. More than forty-three thousand hectares of forest—almost five hundred square kilometres—was ablaze or burnt by the end of July. Two fires straddled Carp Lake to the west of Fort McLeod. They were relatively small compared to the fire at Cat

Canoeists bound for the Nechako River following the same route used by Simon Fraser enter a set of rapids on the Stuart River just downstream from Fort St. James. *Bill Keay*/Vancouver Sun

Mountain to the north, which exploded to three thousand hectares, but they had sideswiped my plan to use the rough back roads to trace McDougall's route into new country with my sixteen-year-old daughter Hel.

I curbed my enthusiasm for bushwhacking and settled to investigate surviving segments of *Nyan Wheti* (the trail across) of the Carrier–Tse'hene that McDougall followed west from Fort McLeod; it then continued on to Babine Lake. F.W. Howay's popular *History of British Columbia: The Making of a Province*, published in 1928, describes the 133-kilometre trail over Bettee Mountain that was later used to move trade goods and furs between Stuart Lake and McLeod Lake.

"A trail—the first highway, so to speak, in British Columbia—was built across the intervening distance. Thereafter, the long, roundabout travel up the Parsnip, down the Bad River and the Fraser, and up the Nechako and Stuart rivers, was happily avoided."

If *Nyan Wheti* was the first road, it was already several thousand years old before Fraser encountered it. While rivers and lakes served as "highways" for the people who had occupied what is now BC since the dawn of human memory, a network of trails linked the watersheds.

An astonishing variety of valuable trade goods passed over these routes. Obsidian, a black volcanic glass, was desirable because it produced the sharpest cutting edges known. Rare sea shells gathered on the west coast of Vancouver Island travelled across the Rockies for use as prehistoric currency and as ornamentation by cultures inhabiting the Great Plains—some are said to have been found as far away as Mexico. Jade from the Fraser River and turquoise from Central America travelled these routes, and perhaps even coins from China.

Some of the routes were called grease trails because they accommodated traffic in the exceptionally valuable oil rendered from the candlefish or oolichan in coastal fisheries from the Fraser to the Nass.

So the trails followed by Alexander Mackenzie to the Pacific in 1793 and by McDougall from Fort McLeod to the Carriers in 1806 were established long before any European walked them.

Fraser and others in the fur trade called all these ancient trails "roads." Even the dreadful, boggy, mosquito-plagued path Mackenzie followed overland to the Pacific is called "the West Road" in journals. In truth these trails bore no resemblance to anything we'd call a road in the twenty-first century. On the other hand, in Fraser's world, the difference between what people called a road on the frontier of his childhood in upstate New York and a grease trail in the bush of BC's north central Interior when he was thirty is a matter of semantic hair-splitting.

I found one surviving pack trail segment west of McLeod Lake. Just like the "roads" I'd seen described in the New England wilderness of 1776, this one was a barely discernible opening in the trees. It wound off into the green gloom of the cool, moist, sub-boreal forest that's protected by the provincial park surrounding Carp Lake, a pothole scoured out by a glacier that left a scattering of drumlins that are now small islands.

The day was hot, and the mosquitoes, bulldogs and blackflies were vicious even at noon. With a dollop of bug juice, I was able to enjoy the extraordinarily beautiful surroundings. Sunlight filtered through the forest canopy and scattered golden shafts among the pines.

The air vibrated with the background noise of insects. Embroidered on the soundscape were the trills of songbirds and the strange, liquid croaks that ravens make. I passed lots of fresh moose sign and numerous scars on trunks where the "quill pigs"—porcupines to city folk—had been gnawing to get at the soft layer beneath the bark.

Even with an occasional deadfall to clamber over, under or around, I could see why Fraser would call this a "road." Over the millennia, human feet had packed the soil into a deep groove. It still made for easy walking—and not just for humans, judging from the large, very recently deposited pile of bear scat that steamed in the middle of the trail.

Early summer is not a good time to surprise momma bear and the cubs, especially if she happens to be a grizzly. I made plenty of noise and beat a cautious retreat. Not without reason. Fraser had several unpleasant encounters with bears in 1806. The first occurred on July 13 when two of his men named La Garde and Barbuellen saw two cubs in a tree and beached their canoe to shoot at them—a big mistake. The sow grizzly took exception and rushed out of the woods. The two men fled the enraged mother bear, and Barbuellen leaped into the river with the bear on his heels.

"As La Garde was advancing another bear suddenly rushed upon him and tore him in a shocking manner," Fraser wrote. "Had not the dogs passed there at the critical moment, he would have been torn to pieces. The bear left him to defend herself against the dogs and during the interval he ran off and jumped into the river, and from thence it was with much difficulty he could walk to the canoe. He received nine or 10 bad wounds and we encamped early to dress them."

The next day Tabah Tha', an Indian hunter accompanying Fraser's expedition, and his wife were walking on the riverbank when they startled a large grizzly bear and her two cubs. When the hunter shot and wounded the bear, she attacked his wife.

"She instantly laid down flat upon the ground and did not stir, in consequence of [which] the bear deserted [her] and ran after her husband, who likewise fortunately escaped unhurt. . . . He was immediately sent back with other Indians in search of the one he wounded, which they then found and killed with seven shots, and brought the meat to the canoe, which made all hands a couple of good meals."

By this time, Fraser had been travelling for nine weeks since leaving the portage above the Peace River Canyon on May 21. Unlike Mackenzie, he'd been battling high water and a powerful current as meltwater flooded off the slopes of the Rockies into the headwaters of the Parsnip.

Fraser's brigade had turned from the Peace into the Parsnip on May 28. Ahead lay an arduous ascent following Mackenzie's route to Arctic Lake, then a short portage over the height of land to Portage Lake. It wasn't long, only about six hundred paces and "one of the finest portages I ever saw," but now the rivers were flowing south and west to the Pacific, not north and east to the Arctic.

I'd had to abandon Fraser's route around Tacheeda Mountain, about halfway between Prince George and McLeod Lake. I had neither the budget to fly over the route nor the time to follow the Parsnip by canoe as it left the roads behind and reached deeper into the trackless bush.

Instead Hel and I turned west to explore the route that Fraser didn't take. Thanks to his reporting, countless others subsequently did.

On the headwaters of the Parsnip, struggling with the current and driftwood that blocked his entry to the lake beyond—he would descend it to the river that now bears his name by way of James Creek, Herrick Creek and the McGregor River—he encountered a man and his family whom he describes only as "the strange Indian."

"The former seems very intelligent and communicative. He gave us a great deal of information concerning this part of the country, and drew us a chart of it, at which he seemed very expert," Fraser noted.

"Had he been at Trout [McLeod] Lake, he said, he would have shown us a more safe and shorter way to the Columbia [the Fraser] by which he said we would have been at the Carriers land ere now."

To the Leidli T'enneh people near what is now Prince George, it was known simply as *Lhedesti* (the shortcut) by which they reached the Tse'Khene to the northwest.

The route—via the Crooked River from McLeod Lake to Summit Lake, then over an easy portage that follows an ancient river channel cut by glacial meltwater nine thousand years ago—was to become the most important commercial link between the Pacific and Arctic watersheds for more than a century.

After the economic importance of the fur trade was eclipsed by the discovery of gold, the portage was "discovered" again in 1863 by a black prospector from Jamaica. John Giscome left his name on the old portage when he wrote a letter to a Victoria newspaper describing the route from the Fraser to Summit Lake. For some years in the early decades of the twentieth century, Giscome Landing at the foot of the portage became a strategic stop for steamboats running the upper Fraser River between what is now Prince George and Tete Jaune Cache in the Rockies.

For many years, right into the last century, pack trains travelled the Yellowhead Pass from the riverboat landing at Tete Jaune Cache and through the roadless Alberta bush providing a direct western land route to Fort Edmonton via Hinton and Edson.

Freight bound north to the Omineca gold camps or early homesteaders in the Peace River district would be offloaded at Giscome Landing and hauled up to Summit Lake. Then it would descend the Crooked River to McLeod Lake, then the Pack and the Parsnip to the Peace. Travellers moved so many rocks out of the shallows to ease canoe passage that it was jokingly referred to as "the wagon road."

In response to a petition from 399 miners, the provincial government paid more than nine thousand dollars to widen the old portage trail into an actual road, although it fell into disuse as the miners moved on in search of new workings.

Later still, trappers Albert Huble and Edward Seebach opened a trading post at the landing, and it acquired the district post office. When World War I brought a road to Summit Lake in 1919, however, the old landing and its portage dwindled into insignificance.

The post has been restored as a heritage site, and the portage is maintained as a recreational trail, so we turned east off the highway and went for a look. The squared log house that Huble built was for Anne Hart, whom he'd met and married in Ontario on his first trip to the outside. She was five months pregnant when she made the trek to New Caledonia, and the house is still sturdy enough to live in. It should be. The couple raised four daughters and three sons in it. Around it, dreaming in sunny meadows behind split-rail fences, the general store and post office with its false front, the warehouse, the blacksmith shop, a trapper's cabin, the barns, sheds and root cellar all look pretty much as they did more than a century ago.

I stopped for apple pie and ice cream and a chat with Zarrah Holvick, who was clerking in the restored trading post, while my daughter foraged for a patchwork quilt among the examples for sale. Then we meandered down to the muddy green expanse of the already huge Fraser. Among the willows we explored the ruins of a riverboat, and then, with rain squalls ghosting across the horizon, set off for its vital confluence with the Nechako River at Prince George.

It was there that Fraser would really drop off the map. On the Nechako, he

Simon Fraser learned of the Crooked River from the Tse'Khene and it later became the most important link between the Pacific and Arctic watersheds. *Heledd Mayse*

John Giscome, a black prospector from Jamaica, left his name on the portage that linked Pacific and Arctic watersheds in 1863, but Simon Fraser knew of the "shortcut" from First Nations fifty-seven years earlier. *Painting courtesy Huble Homestead Historic Site*

would be in uncharted country. Mackenzie makes no mention of it in his account of his dash to the Pacific. Fraser's journal entry for July 11 notes that they reached the mouth of this major northern tributary at sunset. I arrived at dusk, too, and strolled down the strip park along its sandy banks. Somewhere nearby, Fraser made his camp. He seems to have been taken aback by the Nechako's size and by the fact that nowhere was it mentioned in Mackenzie's account, although Fraser expressed certainty that it must be the route to the Carriers that McDougall had reported.

It's difficult today, with cellphones, electronic navigation by satellite triangulation and twenty-four-hour roadside service for a rental car, to imagine how precarious Fraser's position must have felt. The next day, on July 12, they exhausted their supply of pemmican. From then on, they'd have to rely on jerky and what the hunters could shoot. For crews weakened by the arduous journey so far and the scant rations, the Nechako's strength was daunting and relentless.

"The river is entirely overflown, no use can be made of the poles, and the current is too strong to be steered by the paddles and we make more use of the branches [pulling themselves along] than of both," Fraser noted. In all, they covered only fourteen kilometres for the whole day, about a 2.5-hour walk on city streets.

By now Fraser's already-battered canoes were in sorry shape, and there were almost daily stops to make repairs. The wear and tear on his men, even those not attacked by bears, was taking a toll in sickness, injuries and exhaustion. Some of his Tse'Khene guides appeared fearful of going farther into Carrier territory as they approached the Nechako's confluence with the Stuart. Perhaps their failure of nerve came because they knew the stories of the dreadful massacre in the vicinity by a Chilcotin war party, and of the terrible vengeance exacted by the Carriers.

Still Fraser was clearly a leader. Despite the hardships and failing morale, he pulled his crews together for the last push up the Stuart, a beautiful, green, fast-flowing stream. His journal of the adventure ends abruptly with the entry for July 18, when they'd just made camp on a beautiful hilltop. We know that Fraser reached Stuart Lake—from letters written that August to report his mission's success to colleagues at Fort Dunvegan and McLeod Lake—on July 26, 1806.

Almost immediately, using spruce logs cut from the stand where McDougall had first blazed a tree and looked down the stunning panorama of the lake, Simon Fraser set his men to building what would become Fort St. James and the capital of New Caledonia.

Simon Fraser

18

THE CARRIER RIVER OF LIFE

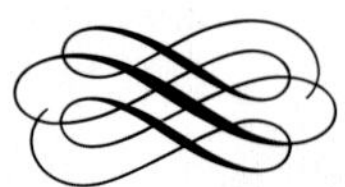

The wonderful thing about looking for a story in a town like Fort St. James is that you ask somebody a question, and they ask somebody else, and the next thing you know you're sitting in Vince Prince's black and red skiff skittering through the Stuart River rapids that bedevilled Simon Fraser two hundred years earlier.

"I'll have to ask you sit down," he said politely as we approached the chute. "We've lost some people in the canyon. We lost a kayaker. And one who fell out of a boat—it was four days before the canyon gave him up and we found him just a quarter of a mile downstream."

Okay, I can take a hint. I sat down. I wouldn't want the last episode of my search to wind up floating face down in a whirlpool. And I wouldn't want to offend my host, who in some ways epitomizes the fusion of cultures in which BC was conceived and born.

The beautiful green sweep of the Stuart was more than just a highway to Carrier people like Vince's ancestors, it was a bountiful source of food and building materials. One archeological survey found that the riverbank is studded with many pits once used as caches for food storage, several thousand of them at one site alone near the river's confluence with the Nechako.

"Dad used to come down here in a thirty-eight-foot dugout," Vince said quietly as we bucked and yawed through the riffles at the tail end of the white water.

Vince held a buttoned-down job for six years as a business consultant in Prince

Vince Prince, who lives on the small island that was his famous ancestor Chief Kwah's fishing territory, turns his skiff south on the historic Stuart River, a highway for the fur brigades and First Nations. *Bill Keay/*Vancouver Sun

George, then returned to his roots and started his own small business.

"I was making fifty-two thousand dollars a year, but hey, I don't like the city," he said. "I started here in 2000. I was trying to get my actual work time down to thirty days a year. I guess by now I've got it down to fifty days. We seem to earn enough. I take it easy. I work on crafts. I do a lot of drums."

Vince—his Carrier name is Atsulh (the dog that knows which way to go)—is one of those who claim direct descent from Chief Kwah. Today he makes his home on Nu Yiz, the island in the outlet of the river where Kwah maintained his ancestral summer camp, the place from which he tended his famed salmon weir.

Like many of the people in Fort St. James, Vince is your classic multitasker. For six years, he's run Nu Yiz Boat Tours, offering sightseeing trips to the pictograph sites on Stuart Lake as well as guided trips down the Stuart River, where there is an abundance of moose, bear, eagles and waterfowl.

But perhaps more important, at least judging from the sudden flash of enthusiasm with which he warms to the subject, he and his companion Treena run a special cultural camp catering in particular to youth considered at risk. For kids with a First Nations background, it provides an opportunity to reconnect with their cultural roots in a tangible way. For other kids it's an opportunity to get beyond

Vince Prince shows off a traditional pit dwelling he built using detailed drawings made by Father Adrian Gabriel Morice to record the technique. *Bill Keay/Vancouver Sun*

Pit houses like this one, built by Vince Prince, provided warm, secure dwellings during the long, bitter winters of the boreal forest. *Bill Keay*/Vancouver Sun

both the romantic illusions and negative stereotypes that so often cloud our ability to see one another clearly.

At the camp there's a traditional winter pit house that he reconstructed using the notes and drawings made by Father Adrian Gabriel Morice, the ethnographer priest who ministered to Fort St. James from Our Lady of Good Hope Church from 1885 to 1905. Vince collects moose, deer and bearskins from other hunters, even going out to pick them up at kill sites in the bush, and keeps them in a freezer so that teenagers can be taught how to stretch, flesh and tan a hide. There's also a working smokehouse, so kids at the cultural camp can catch and process up to fifteen hundred sockeye a year in the traditional manner, then share their catch with elders and families in need.

"We provide probably forty to forty-five families with the fish that we catch, so we work really hard. When kids from one village went home with their fish, the elders had a potlatch so they could give out their salmon," he said. "They learn that being Indian, you have things that you can be proud of, things you know are in your blood."

He said that the camp shows young people—who may have become disconnected from who they are as a people—how there is a continuity that reaches from the distant past to the present and that life in the natural world has a structure as demanding as anything you'll find in corporate culture.

"We say to them, okay, this is who you are back in 1545," said Vince.

"This is the time you pick the berries. You pick in the cool of the morning before the mosquitoes are out. If you wait until the evening, they'll eat you alive. You go in the morning because the birds are trying to beat you to it." He chuckled. "Then you go check net.

"'You mean we have to pull net before breakfast?' they ask. 'Sorry,' we say, 'that's the way it's done.' But you know, when you're out there ten minutes after sunrise picking fish out of the nets, when they bring fifty and sixty salmon home—that's some experience."

Our trip down the river was not just to give me a sense of what Simon Fraser saw on his final push toward what would become the capital of New Caledonia. It was also to remind me of the authenticity behind the cultural camp, what it seeks to achieve and the threat that "progress" continues to pose to a whole way of being in the world.

Vince nosed the skiff into the muddy bank and we clambered ashore, then struck off through the dense thickets of ground willow and alders. Back in the bush we found the decaying cabin of Solomon Prince, World War II veteran. There was animal sign everywhere—beaver, moose, eagles in the trees above the riverbank.

"Our people never tried to keep everything," Vince said of the cabin that was melting back into the underbrush, no longer needed by those who built it so long ago.

Back on the river, he took me to the spot where a proposed four-billion-dollar pipeline would cross the Stuart River. If approved, the pipeline would provide addi-

Vince Prince, who runs youth education and counselling programs at Fort St. James that reconnect young people with their traditional culture, examines hides on stretching frames. *Bill Keay/*Vancouver Sun

tional capacity for Alberta's crude oil—production from the oilsands around Fort McMurray is expected to double over the next five years—and would pass north of Prince George, south of Fort St. James to Burns Lake, south of Houston and then southwest to Kitimat for shipment by tanker to hungry international markets. A parallel pipeline going the opposite direction would pick up condensate back-hauled in tankers from Asia for shipment to Alberta. (Condensate is used to dilute heavier crude and make it easier to transport by pipe.) Although the project would create many jobs during construction, it's estimated only seventy-five people would be employed full-time after completion.

"That little island where they want to put that pipeline, that's where my oldest son shot his first moose. There's lots of moose and deer in here. There's a healthy elk population," Vince said, gesturing at the lush riverbank. "All of this will be gone, of course, cleared out to nothing, seventy-five metres on either side."

He shook his head. "My biggest concern is pollution. Salmon have always been our life. Just the thought of a pipeline cutting through here—even a small spill—that's a great risk when you have one of the world's best salmon runs here."

Vince is apparently not alone in his concern. In late August, the Carrier Sekani Tribal Council submitted to Ottawa its proposal for a First Nations review process that would parallel any federal review procedure and would invite all affected tribal groups to participate, with hearings in native Indian communities along the route. Along with hearings, the Carrier Sekani asked for a panel convened with at least two members of aboriginal background to evaluate potential impacts, costs and benefits.

In late October, the tribal coalition was in court filing a lawsuit alleging then federal Environment Minister Rona Ambrose failed to consult properly before setting up a "joint review panel" of the Canadian Environmental Assessment Agency and the National Energy Board to consider the pipeline project. They demanded that the regulatory process be halted until Ambrose consults properly, as they say she's required to do under rulings on aboriginal rights by the Supreme Court of Canada.

The start date of the proposed pipeline was postponed for several years, possibly for good, although as demand for oil grows and prices rise, all such development strategies seem likely to remain in constant play.

In an eerie replay of that first encounter between global industry in the form of the North West Company and the Carrier and Tse'Khene hunting societies, the pipeline proposal that alarms Vince appears not to be the only potential collision between past and future in New Caledonia.

Chiefs and band members of the Takla Lake First Nation, the Tsay Keh Dene and the Kwadacha First Nation gathered at Duncan Lake, about four hundred kilometres northwest of Prince George, to show concern over plans to dam the valley and use the lake as a massive tailings pond for a proposed hardrock mine. Among

Top: Vince Prince, Atsulh—"the dog that knows which way to go"—among the Carrier people of Fort St. James, demonstrates one of the drums he makes and uses to teach young people their traditional ways.
Bill Keay/Vancouver Sun

Right: Kwah's grave house is at the outlet to the Stuart River. The chief asked to be buried here so he could hear the salmon coming. Some say he shakes his rattle when the first arrive.
Bill Keay/Vancouver Sun

the two hundred who attended were kids from the Kwadacha Rediscovery Program who travelled the back roads by school bus and hiked into the site, set up camp and stayed overnight.

To Vince, who traces his genealogy back to Kwah, cultural appreciation is connected with an understanding of the natural world and its cycles. Which is why, in addition to working with troubled youth by reconnecting them with ancient traditions, he also makes drums in the traditional way—although some of the instruments give a wry nod to pop culture.

When we got back and he showed me some of the drums, I was most amused to see that among the very traditional forms was one that appeared to be illustrated with what looked like that big, slurping tongue made famous by the Rolling Stones. Well, Kwah and his people were nothing if not adaptable. So I wasn't surprised, either, when Vince showed me the mobile smokehouse he'd built. It folds up and can be trailered to sites and set up for instant demonstrations.

"I set it up at a main intersection in Prince George," he told me. "The bylaw officer came by and said: 'No open burning in Prince George.' So I said, 'there's laws against barbecues in Prince George?' He said, 'No.' I said, 'Well, it's an Indian barbecue.'"

We shared a laugh, and then he was quiet.

"I saw the first salmon fly today," he told me. "My father said after you see the first salmon fly it will be six weeks until the salmon come. I asked him, 'When shall we fish for char?' He said, 'when half of those leaves are yellow.' That's how we live."

Before we left Nu Yiz, Vince and his son Daniel, eighteen, sang me a salmon song, the rhythmic sound echoing out over the water where Kwah had tended his traps, bringing the sockeye ashore for his four wives to prepare in the smokehouse.

I asked if he'd take me over to Kwah's grave, and he generously did. The small white grave house with blue trim faces west on a small promontory just where the lake empties into the Stuart River. The grave marker is wood. It must be the third or fourth to be erected since the great chief died, Vince tells me.

It reads, in both Carrier syllabics and English, "Here lie the remains of Great Chief Kwah. Born about 1755, Died Spring of 1840. He once had in his hands the life of (future Sir) James Douglas but was great enough to refrain from taking it."

Across the water from the grave house is the low shore of the island from which he extended his salmon weir. Kwah, who was said to be a dreamer of the salmon, asked to be buried in this spot so he could hear the sockeye coming up the river and forever alert his people that the run was beginning. He was buried with his ceremonial rattle, it's said. Some claim they can hear it shaking when the first sockeye come in.

As I pondered the epitaph, the trees were alive with songbirds and a sudden wind off the lake stirred the wildflowers. Then it gusted up into the canopy of the tall alders. It set the vivid green leaves dancing and the branches rattling. Or maybe it was Kwah's rattle, letting us know that the early Stuarts were on their way to the lake.

One thing seemed certain. We are connected to our history through the determined memories and bloodlines of people such as Vince Prince. The New Caledonia that was fused from the visions and the pragmatism of Kwah and of Simon Fraser is as much a part of modern BC as are we, who inherit what they made and carry their dreams forward mingled with our own.

19

A LAND HAUNTED BY VIOLENCE

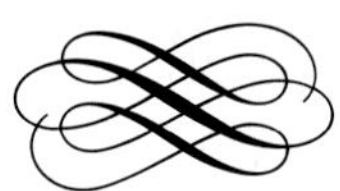

Even in bright summer sunshine, the opening in the boreal forest that's just up the Stuart River from its confluence with the Nechako is an eerie place.

A gloomy stillness hangs over it that others have commented upon, from anthropologists surveying one of the richest archeological sites in British Columbia to recreational canoeists passing by on their way down the rivers from Fort St. James to Prince George.

More than a few who planned to overnight, I'm told, have found themselves sufficiently unnerved by feelings they can't explain that they wind up hastily packing their gear and pushing off by moonlight to look for the next decent spot. Perhaps that's not so surprising.

Chinlac, for all its inherent beauty and natural advantages as both a landing site and a strategic resource centre, is still shunned more than 250 years after the massacre that made it infamous. It is too steeped in tragedy and bloodshed.

What happened there occurred so long ago, long before the kind of documentary history upon which western intellectual traditions rely, that we must piece together events from the oral histories of the Carrier nations. These histories themselves come to us across the abyss of time, bridging great ruptures in social fabric caused by epidemics that produced mortality rates so high they tore irreparable holes in a people's collective memory.

Luckily historians like Father Adrian Gabriel Morice and Lizette Hall knew

Jordie Ann Erickson, wearing traditional Carrier dress for a dance at Fort St. James, watches the sun set over Stuart Lake. *Bill Keay/*Vancouver Sun

elders of great age who themselves knew elders who knew elders with roots in that era. Thus they were able to collect accounts long ago seared into memory.

There is a tendency by some people to romanticize the period before contact between First Nations and non-native newcomers as one of blissful peace and nobility of purpose. In that idealized model, only the arrival of violent, greedy and insensitive fur traders disrupted and corrupted the social harmony and aboriginal people's engagement with the natural world. This is largely revisionist myth making.

That some fur traders could be violent and greedy is not in dispute. Some, like Alexander Mackenzie's mentor Peter Pond, were repeatedly accused of homicidal attacks upon their fellow traders, and traders were accused of murdering Inuit and Indians in what is now the Northwest Territories in order to secure trading monopolies.

The sad fact is that on a frontier beyond the reach of British law, tribes increasingly found themselves competing in a brutal new economic order and considered themselves bound by different laws than the interlopers did.

One of Simon Fraser's original crew, a Métis interpreter named Jean Baptiste Boucher, was known to the Carriers as Waccan. He served as a dreaded enforcer for the North West Company and later for the Hudson's Bay Company, imposing order with what even the company's governor, George Simpson, would come to deplore as "club law."

Violence or threats against fur traders brought swift and certain retribution and

The Stuart River is tranquil at Fort St. James where it empties from the lake on the start of its long journey to the Nechako River, then to the Fraser and finally to the sea almost 1,000 km to the south. *Glenn Baglo/ Vancouver Sun*

sometimes what amounted to a summary execution without benefit of trial.

James Douglas participated in beating to death with a hoe a man suspected in the earlier murder of two Hudson's Bay Company employees. The future governor of BC narrowly escaped a similar fate at the hands of an angry Chief Kwah, in whose lodge the victim had sought traditional sanctuary.

The First Nations who traded with the Europeans were no less capable of using violence and the threat of violence to intimidate isolated outposts. Some trading posts were attacked and burned, and entire garrisons were massacred at other forts. Violence was frequently directed at other aboriginal people to drive them from hunting grounds, monopolize trading access or avenge perceived wrongs.

In 1823, after the slaying of Joseph Bagnoit and Belone Duplantes at Fort George, Fraser's former second-in-command John Stuart wrote to James McDougall at Stuart Lake, "If no blood is shed in the Winter—I will consider the Business as well conducted—and that every one has done his Duty."

Journals kept by Alexander Mackenzie, Alexander Henry, David Thompson, Simon Fraser and Daniel Harmon, Fraser's successor in New Caledonia, recorded the outbreaks of violence with little apparent surprise. In 1813, for example, Harmon's entry for July 12 mentioned the ambush of a Tse'Khene band from Fort McLeod.

It recounted that another Tse'Khene stepped out of the woods and calmly shot dead the wife of the man who reported the incident to Harmon. Her killing was in

Bennington-born trader Daniel Williams Harmon, met Simon Fraser returning from the Pacific. Harmon's journal recounts blood feuds of the kind involved in the Chinlac massacres. *Glenbow Archives NA 3872-1*

retaliation for her husband's killing of her own executioner's cousin the previous summer. That slaying was purportedly carried out in retaliation for the even earlier drowning of her son.

This was a blood feud of the kind made famous for Americans by the Hatfields and the McCoys, or for Scots like Fraser, by the Campbells and the MacDonalds, who murdered one another in revenge killings for 450 years.

On July 20, 1813, barely a week later, Harmon recorded another incident at Fort St. James.

"Yesterday an Indian of this village killed another who was on a visit from the other end of this lake, just as he was entering his canoe to return. The former approached the latter and gave him five stabs with a lance, and ripped open his bowels in such a shocking manner that his entrails immediately fell upon the ground. He, of course, immediately expired . . .

"The people of this place are apprehensive that the relatives of the murdered will make war upon them and they will therefore set out tomorrow to go to a considerable distance down this river, where they will pass a greater part of the summer until harmony is restored between the two villages."

While all the elements of the romanticized version of precontact life were doubtless present at times, so were all the less pleasant aspects: slavery; bloody intermittent warfare over territory, resources and women; struggles between dynastic families; and eye-for-an-eye blood feuds of the kind recorded by Harmon.

One need look no further for evidence than the dramatic early history of the Carrier and Kwah's rise to political prominence. This indirectly brings us back to the eerie Chinlac site.

Around 1745, the year that Simon Fraser's ancestors rebelled against the British Crown and ten years before Kwah was born on Stuart Lake, a thriving Carrier village was located at Chinlac. It was large, rich in resources, positioned to exploit salmon runs up both the Stuart and the Nechako and probably the major population centre of what Fraser would later dub New Caledonia.

The name Chinlac, says the Yinka Dene Language Institute, is most probably derived from a contraction of the term *duchun nidulak*. This translates from the Dakelh dialect of the Carrier language as "wood floats to a terminus," which describes the way in which driftwood accumulates on sandbars thrown up in the Stuart River where it approaches the Nechako.

Linguist Bill Poser, who has long studied Carrier language and dialects, said the spelling that occurs on maps and government documents is actually incorrect.

"The proper Carrier spelling is Chunlak," he informed me, since the letter *c* never appears alone and is therefore an anglicized spelling.

"It is somewhat of a mystery how this word came to be written and pronounced with an *i* since the difference between these two vowels is one with which English speakers have no difficulty," he notes.

Archeological excavations undertaken more than fifty years ago by Charles Borden confirmed the importance of the site—however it's correctly spelled—that is now under provincial protection.

It was a rich place by the standards of its day. Once there were more than a dozen big lodges here. The depressions, filled now with a quarter of a millennium of debris, are still visible. Behind it, on the benches left over thousands of years as the post-ice-age river cut through the landscape, digs revealed more than two thousand of the storage pits used to cache food for use in the lean seasons of winter and spring.

Excavations found porcelain and glass beads, iron projectile points and awls, an iron blade, a small steel spring, miscellaneous iron fragments and even a Chinese coin from the Sung Dynasty that reigned from AD 960 to 1127, about the same times as the last Anglo-Saxon and the first Norman dynasties in Britain. The destruction of the wealthy, influential site that convention calls Chinlac was no small matter.

The story of what happened there has to be pieced together from a number of sources. Father Morice, who ministered to the Carriers of Stuart Lake for twenty years starting in 1885, knew Taya, one of Kwah's sons. In his youth Taya had lived with an earlier chief named Na'kwoel, who lived at the time of the events at Chinlac. Morice had a second and more reliable source, a woman named Samalh'ti whose mother had been married to Kwah's maternal uncle, Khadintel, the chief at Chinlac. Finally, Lizette Hall, Kwah's great-granddaughter, had the story directly from him through her father and grandfather.

A Chilcotin chief named Khalban had made it known that he intended to avenge the earlier killing of a notable person, according to the story. In 1745 he led a large war party in an attack on Chinlac village while its chief was away hunting on the Nechako with two companions.

When Khadintel returned, the scene was ghastly. A few of his people had escaped into the forest but most of the men and many women, including two of his wives, had been killed and lay in pools of blood. Those women who weren't dead had been carried off as slaves. There was worse. All the children of Chinlac had been slaughtered and mutilated, their rib cages split and their bodies hung on two long poles to mimic salmon drying in the sun.

Khadintel and his two companions gathered the dead and cremated them according to Carrier custom. Then he set about planning his revenge.

Three years later, Khadintel led a large Carrier war party he'd mustered from around Stuart Lake, Fraser Lake and Stoney Creek near present-day Vanderhoof. They proceeded to the Chilcotin settlement near present-day Anahim Lake.

This time the Chilcotin suffered the atrocity. All their children had also been butchered, split and hung like drying fish—on three long poles, one more than they had inflicted on the Carriers. In an ironic turn of fate, the Chilcotin chief, Khalban, was also away hunting and returned to find his village inhabited only by dogs.

Perhaps it's worth remembering, as we naturally recoil from the bloody and appalling image, that in the supposedly enlightened twenty-first century, supposedly advanced civilizations are still slaughtering children in the name of justice, security or retaliation for various wrongs we've suffered. Whether victims of Chechen terrorists in Russia, American air strikes in Iraq, Muslim suicide bombers in Tel Aviv, Israeli border guards in Palestine or freedom fighters in the Congo, children are still pawns in the game of adult revenge and violence.

Given the pattern, it's not surprising that the destruction of the Chilcotin did not mark the end of the bloodshed.

Kwah's father, Tsalekulhye, and two other chiefs were killed in 1780 during a raid by the Nashkhu'tins from the Blackwater River. They were convinced Tsalekulhye was responsible for witchcraft that had caused the sudden death of a prominent leader.

Two years later—while Simon Fraser suffered through the carnage and brutality of the American Revolutionary war—Kwah led his own retaliatory raid against the Nashkhu'tins, personally hacking to death and disembowelling the rival chief and his son.

War hero he might have become, but Kwah was soon on the run himself. He had killed the prominent father of a friend after the man insulted him publicly, and now he was forced to flee across the Rockies to take refuge with the Tse'Khene. He found they were under increasing pressure from the Beavers to the east, who had begun attacking them with guns obtained from the Cree.

"Parties of Beavers armed with guns would play with the fright inspired by their weapons, and, discharging them in the midst of the unsophisticated Sekanais, would kill them to the last," Morice wrote in his 1904 *History of the Northern Interior of British Columbia.*

"Thus it came to pass that no mountain fastnesses could afford them shelter or anything like real security. Moreover, as fright is contagious, the terrible deeds of the Beavers went to the ears of the far-away Carriers, who to this day have remained persuaded of their innate lust for carnage. So much so, indeed, that hardly a summer now passes without some parties of the Western Denes running home with the intelligence that bodies of Beaver Indians are lurking in the woods, evidently bent on slaughter," he wrote.

"It was but the natural result of the approach of the Canadian traders representing the North West Company," the priest wrote. "Fire arms and fire water, the one a relative blessing and the other an unmitigated curse, which are too often yoked together, were now within measurable distance of the Rocky Mountains, leaving behind them a trail of blood and indescribable debauchery."

In 1782 the Beavers, forced westward by the Cree, had attacked the Tse'Khene who had no guns, killing twenty-two. Fur-trade accounts from the same era report repeated raids and counter-raids between the Beavers, the Chipewyans and the Yellowknives into the early nineteenth century.

Slave Indians ambushed the garrison outside the palisades of Fort Nelson in 1813 and then attacked the fort, killing the North West Company trader and his family.

In 1815 the Dogribs attacked the Hareskin Indians and killed fifteen people, and then in 1823 turned to the Yellowknives, massacring 20 percent of the population and driving them into eventual extinction as a nation. Today we would call this ethnic cleansing or even genocide.

The trader and garrison at Fort St. John were ambushed and murdered in 1823. Ambushes, murders, skirmishes and full-scale raids were reported across the Yukon right into the 1840s as various bands and tribes sought to monopolize expanding trade routes or set themselves up as middlemen brokering the lucrative fur-trade transactions between less powerful groups and the Hudson's Bay Company.

For some, phantoms may still haunt the blood-soaked ground of long-abandoned Chinlac, but any ghosts there have company. The victims of violence spread all across the landscape of what became New Caledonia.

A few people were reported living at Chinlac briefly in the early nineteenth century, probably the aged descendants of the murdered families. Soon they too departed.

Today that eerie opening in the forest wall endures as one more dolorous reminder of our endless capacity for inhumanity toward one another.

Simon Fraser

20

DOWNRIVER TO DESTINY

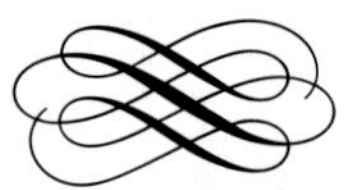

The forest that crowns steep bluffs to the south of Prince George's downtown core cast a ragged black silhouette against the dark blue of the first faint predawn blush.

I'd hauled myself out of my bed at 4 a.m., as Simon Fraser had crawled out of his on the same May morning in 1808. Not even the birds were up, and this brawny industrial city of 77,000 slumbered around me as I made my bleary way through deserted streets to the banks of the great river that now bears Fraser's name.

The river shimmered in the gloom as it must have for him on that distant Saturday morning. Luminous and alive, its current murmured behind the shadowy whisper of ancient cottonwoods, their leaves stirring in the breeze created by the billions of litres of water surging from a watershed the size of entire European countries.

For all of the scene's tranquility, there was an ineluctable menace in the river. It was in spate, as it had been for Fraser. I watched as huge boils and eddies roiled the slick surface. Uprooted trees swept into view and just as swiftly vanished. And then, to remind me that all things are relative, one small, bright green frog plopped from the bank into the water and breast-stroked calmly away downstream as though the torrent was a mere puddle.

On the dark bank I contemplated the apprehensions and questions that must have filled Fraser's mind as he went through last-minute preparations for his meticulously planned descent of the river. They were questions that would have occurred to any conscientious expedition leader, particularly one like Fraser, described by American historian H.H. Bancroft—who wasn't one of his leading fans—as "ambitious, energetic, with considerable conscience, and in the main holding to honest convictions."

Fraser must have wondered, Have I chosen the right men for the rigours of this journey? Is young John Stuart the best choice to take over if I'm lost? Do I have enough provisions? Will the people I meet be friendly or hostile? Will the canoes hold up? How many of us will return from this venture into the unknown?

On the far side of the river, counterpoint to the natural music and its invitation to think into the past, a lone truck loaded with shrink-wrapped forest products growled across Simon Fraser Bridge and laboured through its low gears, inserting some twenty-first-century punctuation into my reverie as it crawled up the hill to Highway 97 and points south.

It was a sound that I'm sure Fraser would have appreciated—he was a businessman first, with a hard head for the bottom line—although the eighteen-wheeler getting an early jump on traffic represented commerce on a scale the fur traders

Stephen Hume rose before daybreak at Prince George, BC, to visit the spot where Simon Fraser most likely launched the epic journey to the Pacific at 5 a.m. two centuries before. *Bill Keay/Vancouver Sun*

might have imagined only in a laudanum dream. And the idea of a modern paved highway running parallel to the desperate passage by water he'd be exploring in flimsy birchbark canoes likely wouldn't even enter his mind.

It occurred to me, though, since some of the back roads I'd soon be travelling on the final leg of his journey to what is now Vancouver promised to be little better than the roads in his day.

My four-year search for Simon Fraser had started in a farm field in Vermont, where his eventful life began, and had led me across a still-wild continent to this place. From here, with a thrust of his foot and the sharp dipping of paddles, he had launched his astonishing journey of exploration and a claim on immortality. His life reads like a historical epic and his account of the journey like an adventure novel. Yet I had learned, as the bicentennials of his adventures approached, that he was barely remembered even in the British Columbia he founded.

It was from near where I stood in the predawn gloom that at 5 a.m. on May 28, 1808, four canoes of the North West Company nosed into the relentless current of the muddy torrent that the Carrier people called *Lhtha-khoh* and that Sir Alexander Mackenzie had labelled *Tacoutche Tesse* on a map printed in 1801.

Once again, as has occurred so many times in following Fraser's elusive footsteps, I found myself trying to unravel a small mystery. This time it was the baffling question of his actual embarkation point. The precise spot from which the momentous journey pushed off remains unknown.

Some think it was from the mouth of the Nechako River, others from Old Fort George. But rivers wander, and judging from the old watercourses mapped in Rev. Francis Edwin Runnals's *A History of Prince George,* published in 1946, the Nechako two centuries ago entered the Fraser considerably to the west and south of where it empties today. On the other hand, the site of old Fort George has steep, undercut banks and is anything but canoe friendly.

If Runnals was right about the Nechako mouth, and Fort George Park isn't congenial, then a plausible candidate is nearby Paddle Wheel Park. Riverboats took advantage of the very low banks to discharge passengers and cargo well into the twentieth century for precisely the same reason that it makes a desirable canoe landing.

Still, no one can say for sure whether Fraser left from the Old Fort George site or from farther upstream, perhaps even from around the bend and up the Nechako where Prince George's Heritage River Trail extends from Cottonwood Island Nature Park. A strike against that site, though, is that it tends to flood at very high water. Fraser's journal did mention the river overflowing its banks in late May of 1808, but he doesn't mention flooding in the base camp.

Much history has been applied retroactively, some of it based upon erroneous assumptions. For example, historians routinely cite the founding of a trading post at Fort George by Fraser in the fall of 1807.

Packers, circa 1880, with their dog team at the Hudson's Bay Company post at South Fort George. From this point Simon Fraser launched his voyage of exploration in 1808. *Image B-00338 courtesy of Royal BC Museum, BC Archives*

Bob Campbell, curator at the Fraser–Fort George Regional Museum, said his research indicates otherwise. The first permanent fur trading fort in what is now Prince George wasn't actually established until 1820, just as Simon Fraser was retiring from the fur trade.

"He did set up an advance camp here in the fall of 1807," Campbell said, "but they pulled that camp in 1808."

Campbell pointed out that Fraser's journals and letters don't even name the departure point, and there is no reference to it in any of the trading accounts at Fort St. James prior to 1821, when a post was located up the Nechako at its confluence with the Chilako River.

"The Hudson's Bay Company moved it to Fort George in 1823," Campbell said, "then it was closed in 1824 after two HBC employees were murdered. It opened again in 1829 and operated until 1915."

His observation rang a small bell in my memory. I'd seen something similar in a report to the Hudson's Bay Company from John Stuart written at Norway House on August 18, 1824.

"Fort George temporarily established in 1807 for the conveniency of building Crafts to explore Frasers River down to the Pacific Ocean, it was afterwards in 1808 abandoned but permanently established for the purpose of trade in 1820," wrote Fraser's chief lieutenant on the expedition. It doesn't get much more specific than that.

Wherever the expedition embarked, conditions were similar then to those I encountered when I rose well before sunrise on May 28, the same day that Fraser pushed off, and I strolled the lovely Prince George riverfront.

In Fraser's day, as in mine, the river was already swollen by spring runoff, and according to the explorer's no-nonsense account of the departure was already overflowing its banks. No doubt it spilled back into what is now known as Hudson's Bay Slough, a watery intrusion into residential subdivisions that rings with the sound of redwing blackbirds and the gabble of ducks.

Today a string of lovely parks, a few old neighbourhoods still at risk of flooding at exceptionally high water, a children's playground, the district museum, a Lheidli T'enneh cemetery dating from the mid-nineteenth century—the oldest tombstone is from half a century after Fraser—and some industrial rail yards comprise the sweep of shoreline that arcs from the Nechako River to the main stem of the Fraser. Inland lie the commercial core and the central urban neighbourhoods of the bustling hub that bills itself the capital city of the northern Interior. Railways, rivers and highways all converge at Prince George, a nexus of transportation links that connect Pacific to Atlantic, industrial heartlands to resource-rich hinterlands, Alaska to California, Vancouver to Whitehorse, Prince Rupert to Chicago.

Two hundred years ago, this was just a tiny clearing in the boreal forest. There were likely a couple of rudimentary log huts—one for sleeping, one for storage—but even that's conjecture. All that is certain is that in the fall of 1807 Simon Fraser established an advanced base camp where canoes could be built and he could forward-stage supplies for his expedition down the unknown river.

Fraser, who had turned thirty-two just a week earlier, was in command of the expedition. He had been ordered two years earlier by the North West Company's officers to follow this unknown river to the sea. His mission was mercenary, not scientific, but nonetheless daring and filled with daunting risk.

Ultimately Fraser's journey would be recognized by his own peers as a feat of unsurpassed courage, diplomacy and river craft. He would travel almost two thousand kilometres to tidewater and back and pass through some of the most rugged and unforgiving terrain on the continent, sometimes under desperate conditions. He would make contact with powerful First Nations that were not always welcoming. Most telling, he would return home safely with all his men after his patience and leadership extricated them from the most threatening circumstances where lesser men might have resorted to violence.

When Hudson's Bay Company Governor George Simpson repeated the trip twenty-one years later, travelling downriver one-way in the fall when water was low, he nevertheless concluded with amazement that shooting the same rapids that Fraser's canoes took at high water would be "certain death" nine times out of ten.

In that spring of 1808, as Fraser's canoes were swept southward by "very strong current," the only other Europeans known to have ventured beyond the mouth of the river's great northern tributary, the Nechako, were on an expedition led by Mackenzie, fifteen years earlier. He had abandoned the river and struck overland, following the Blackwater River and an old grease trail to the Pacific after hearing from Indians how dangerous were the lower reaches of the river he called *Tacoutche Tesse.*

News of a successful overland trek to the mouth of the Columbia by Meriwether Lewis and William Clark in 1805–1806, however, had dashed hopes for a British commercial hegemony beyond the Rocky Mountains. The sudden prospect of American incursions into the rich pickings promised by a far western fur trade had galvanized the North West Company in Montreal. The senior partners wanted a swifter, less costly way to get furs to market from the remote interior of the continent. They also wanted to assert prior claims on the as-yet-unexploited fur resources on the western slope north of California.

And so, while David Thompson was probing the southern mountains for passes, Fraser had been dispatched to the north, first to establish a trading presence on the western slope, then to determine whether the river reported by Mackenzie was actually the upper Columbia and whether it was navigable for trade.

Fraser had crossed the mountains in late 1805 and set up trading posts at Trout Lake, later called Fort McLeod, at Nakazleh, later named Fort St. James, and at Natleh, later named Fort Fraser. But he'd been plagued by administrative and supply problems. A letter he wrote from what is now Fort Fraser dated February 1, 1807, complains about "the decay of Trout Lake" under his French-Canadian nemesis, La Malice, who had proved a challenging management problem on the initial expedition across the Rockies. And a distinct tone of exasperation tinges a further complaint about the forwarding of equipment and supplies that are "bad" and "useless," not the least of which is one pair of coat and trousers for Fraser that are "amazing large" but with "trousers so small that I cannot put them on."

Supply problems notwithstanding, Fraser was determined to complete his mission. The young trader turned explorer, recently elevated to a partnership in the fur-trade colossus, was accompanied by two carefully chosen lieutenants. Second-in-command was Stuart, a trader skilled in dealing with Indians and a master canoe-builder. Third-in-command was Jules Maurice Quesnel, fresh from two years under the tutelage of the company's leading map-maker and explorer, David Thompson.

The rest of the party consisted of two Indian guides and translators and nineteen French Canadians, only eight of whose names are mentioned in journals compiled and edited much later. W. Kaye Lamb, the historian and dominion archivist who sifted through the journals, letters and other documents, identifies them as: La Chapelle, Baptiste, D'Alaire, La Certe, Waccan—this was the nickname of the company's frontier enforcer, identified in later documents as Jean Baptiste Boucher-Gagnier, La Garde and Bourbone (perhaps a misspelling of Bourbonnais).

From a staging post briefly carved from the boreal forest, Prince George is now the busy industrial hub of British Columbia's north central Interior. *Bill Keay/*Vancouver Sun

They are part of our history now only because of the diligent work of a scholar, so it seemed fitting for me to go up the hill to the deserted campus of the University of Northern British Columbia for a last look at Prince George before setting out. A cold wind blew through the square they call the Agora, swirling around glass pyramids and balconies and buffeting the lone young woman walking down a vast, empty staircase.

At 5:39 a.m. the sun peeped above the bluffs. Suddenly the city was bathed in light. Reflected sunbeams blazed off countless windows, illuminated the huge pillars of steam above the mills from which Prince George derives its prosperity and turned the rivers into molten silver.

I gave one last thought to the tiny clearing in the boreal forest, to the four bark canoes gliding into the immense river to be carried to their destiny on an unstoppable flood and to the clerk Hugh Faries left to await their uncertain return. Then I turned south myself, heading downriver, following the paddle strokes of Simon Fraser's great adventure.

21

THUNDERING RAPIDS

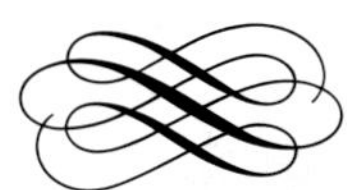

The muted thunder of the Fraser River in freshet was discernible from tremors in the ground long before the sound emerged behind the chorus of bird calls that tracked my progress through tall stands of birch, dense thickets of ground willow and tangles of wild roses that perfumed the air.

Branches of the thick underbrush still drooped, their leaves heavy with overnight condensation. Blades of grass gleamed with dewdrops. I was soon soaked and wishing I'd thought to put on my waterproof gaiters. I had put on my insect repellent, thankfully, because mosquitoes rose in fierce clouds with every step.

I was eighteen kilometres downstream from Prince George, at the dishevelled back end of Pete and Maggie Stoner's Canyon View Ranch at Red Rock. Here the fur trader's epic expedition to the sea came within a hair of disaster only a few hours into the journey.

He'd departed at 5 a.m. from his base camp near the mouth of the Nechako River, almost eight hundred kilometres north of Vancouver. The Fraser was flowing deep, smooth and wide, and swiftly enough for him to note the "very strong current," when the explorer's four canoes encountered and promptly ran the first of a series of powerful rapids.

"One of the canoes came near striking against a precipice which forms the right bank," Fraser's journals note in the laconic understatement of a veteran to whom the hazards of white water were a standard part of the job description. "A little lower down the channel it contracts to about 70 yards and passes between two

Simon Fraser came within a hair of losing a canoe in the turbulent waters of Fort George Canyon on the first day of his expedition down the Fraser River. *Image C-01310 courtesy of Royal BC Museum, BC Archives*

Fort George Canyon

rocks. After running down several considerable rapids, we put ashore at 11 a.m. to breakfast."

I wanted to look at this rapid where the river abruptly narrowed by more than three-quarters, sharply increasing the current's velocity, and that Fraser nevertheless dismissed with such nonchalance.

Fort George Canyon would be a harbinger of perils ahead that had intimidated Alexander Mackenzie into abandoning his journey down what he thought was the Columbia River fifteen years earlier. He struck out overland, reaching the Pacific by way of the Blackwater River and an ancient native Indian trade route.

Red Rock is a dispersed rural community that's little more than a name left by a now-defunct post office. From a signpost I had wound up following a gravel road westward until it petered out in front of the Stoner's rambling, age-blackened log ranch house. I found the rancher standing by a garden already exploding with the growth that comes of long hours of May sunlight in northerly latitudes. He was giving the day's instructions to his hand, Bob Lasure.

Pete Stoner, assisted by hired hand Bob Lasure, grades birch planks he mills for high-end custom flooring at his ranch near the Fort George Canyon where Simon Fraser almost lost a canoe. *Bill Keay/*Vancouver Sun

Stoner could serve as a poster boy for sustainable value-added forestry. He operates a small sawmill from which he produces specialty hardwood flooring for high-end niche markets. Lasure was getting directions on sorting and stacking beautiful white boards, freshly milled from huge birch trees Stoner selectively logs on the seventy-six-hectare property.

"If you ever want birch flooring for your house, you know who to call," Stoner grinned as Lasure tossed planks into the loft of a nearly century-old barn redolent of hay and sawdust.

"It's very high-grade tongue-and-groove with very few knots. I try and sell two to three grades above what they sell in the store. I supply cabinetmakers and homeowners putting in new flooring, and there's a steady market to the Japanese and Chinese. A lot of our customers are taking carpets out of their homes because of allergies. This clear birch is a good replacement."

Not only that, the one-time mining engineer at Stewart's Granduc Mine is keen to experiment, so he works with forest research scientists planting and harvesting new and different species on property that in Simon Fraser's day was deemed suitable only for traplines and logs.

The rancher gave me permission to cross his land to Fort George Canyon and directions about the best route—follow a skid road until it petered out, pass some trout ponds in a natural wetland, veer west and look for a trail that's hard to spot, then head for the sound of the white water reverberating from the same rock faces that nearly claimed Fraser's canoe.

Lasure shared some local knowledge to help get perspective on what I'd be looking at.

"I was talking to a very elderly lady who told me this barn was already here way back in the twenties when she was here. When you look at that river, think about what those people went through, eh? People back then crossed the river by boat and went ten miles west to the Blackwater Road and then they went north from there into town [old Fort George]."

As I went down through the groves of birch, stopping to examine rolls of the bark so prized by the canoe-builders of Simon Fraser's day, I began to feel the vibration of the river through the ground beneath my feet.

Then, on ground dappled with sunlight filtering through the branches of spruce trees that looked old enough to have been there in 1808, I popped out of the forest on a bluff above Fort George Canyon. It was just as Fraser described it, the river roaring past a sheer cliff face, then splitting into three channels around a couple of islands.

A huge rock in the narrowest channel created a foaming maelstrom, which tailed out into a series of the huge standing waves that canoeists call haystacks. The gigantic whirlpool that almost claimed Fraser's canoe still pulsed beside the precipice, although it's no longer the same menacing eddy that he encountered.

"That whirlpool, they did some blasting there," Stoner said, but he told me that it was formidable water. It had claimed the thirty-eight-metre sternwheeler *Charlotte* in 1910, and the rancher had personal experience with its threat. On September 17, 2000, he thought he heard somebody yelling. It was the lone survivor of a boat wreck in the canyon.

"A jetboat with some hunters on board tried to turn around in the narrows and they flipped her," Stoner said. "Two guys drowned. For a long time you could see the bottom [of the jetboat] going up and down in an eddy. I don't know if they ever got it out.

"Here's the strange thing, though. The two guys who drowned were wearing life jackets. They drifted down and were pulled out at Cottonwood Canyon near Quesnel. But the guy who survived, he was wearing wool and no life jacket. He got sucked down to the bottom but he kept his head and he pulled himself along the rocks and then up onto the island. I guess you could say he walked out."

From Canyon View Ranch, Stoner directed me south to Stone Creek, where Fraser's expedition is thought to have stopped for breakfast while John Stuart took a reading from the sun's lower left edge, referred to as a meridian altitude, in an attempt to establish their latitude.

Retired Kitimat mill worker Gerry Seeman was bemused to discover that Simon Fraser's expedition stopped at or near his Stone Creek RV Park and Campground north of Quesnel, BC, to take a navigational reading.
Bill Keay/Vancouver Sun

Retired engineer Nick Doe analyzed the six navigational measurements that survive in Fraser's journal—the original field notes containing greater navigational detail appear to have been lost—and adjusted them to contemporary readings in a fascinating paper in the Spring 2000 edition of *BC Historical News.*

So I used Doe's readings, my hand-held global positioning system computer and recent topographical maps to try and locate with greater precision the places mentioned in general terms in Fraser's journals, which appear to have summarized in more readable form the technical details in the original field record.

At Stone Creek, for example, Doe says that Stuart's reading of 115 9′ 45″ W actually corresponds to a contemporary map reading of 53 38.5′ N, give or take a margin of error created by the hand-me-down eighteenth-century navigational equipment available to Fraser.

My GPS unit, on the other hand, cross-references a location by triangulating from three geostationary satellites and almost instantly analyzes position to within ten metres—rather more precise than anything available in 1808, particularly when used in conjunction with a compass and a detailed topographical map.

At Stone Creek RV Park & Campground—fifteen river's-edge campsites, one guest cabin, hot showers, deck and barbecue—I found Gerry Seeman, five years retired after thirty-six years of toiling at Kitimat. He seemed unsurprised that Simon Fraser might have stopped at his establishment or nearby for a leisurely two-hour brunch almost two hundred years earlier.

Seeman is the kind of guy who glues elk antlers onto a deer skull and watches deadpan while his customers do a double-take, and the kind of guy who insists that bemused visitors in motorhomes bell their cats because the robin fledglings are just leaving the nest.

"Look," he said in excitement, first pointing to the yellow flash of a tanager in a spruce, then to the birds darting overhead. "See all the swallows. I put out boxes for them. I have six or seven nesting. They really keep the bugs down."

From the grassy opening on the riverbank, I struck off in search of the GPS reading that should indicate where Stuart took his sighting. But after struggling through tangled deadfalls and thorn bushes covering a steep 70° slope that fell directly into the river, I was convinced that wherever the landing actually occurred, it wasn't at precisely 53 38.5′ N.

There was a tiny shelf at the river's edge, barely the width of a canoe's beam. It offered protection to landward from the steep bank but had other shortcomings. First, the tiny bench beneath a thick stand of spruce wasn't easily visible from the river. Second, it was on the outer side of a sharp bend, and the current swept past at an alarming pace—not the easiest spot to land four heavily laden canoes.

When I looked downstream, however, I had a clear view of open ground, gently curving sandy beaches and a big, slow back eddy at the mouth of Stone Creek. Here paddlers could swing out of the main current and land with ease.

Seeman nodded when I asked him about it. He said, "It's an ancient Indian fishing site that's still in use."

Stone Creek curves into the Fraser River behind a sandy spit, I discovered when I went over to check it out. The back eddy would carry canoes right into flat, sheltered water where the adjacent clearing is pockmarked with fire pits left by people before and since Fraser's time who had the same idea.

The GPS reading here was well within the plus or minus 2.4-kilometre margin of error allowed by Doe's calculations. Given the difficulty of other possible landing sites inside that range, Stone Creek got my vote.

Later that day, Fraser's party sped past the mouth of the Blackwater River—Alexander Mackenzie's West Road River, the point at which he turned overland toward the Pacific in 1793—stopping briefly at two houses of a Ndazkoh (South River Carrier) chief where they courteously "left marks to let the natives know that we had passed."

By 6 p.m. Fraser was making his first camp. Putting arms in order and issuing all hands with ammunition was the first priority in unknown country, but his last journal entry for May 28, 1808, suggests that after a long, hard day of paddling, dinner was at the front of everyone's mind. "We gathered some wild onions for sauce."

With similar thoughts in mind, I pushed on for Quesnel, where Fraser camped the following night of May 29. His party had spent a harrowing day caching bales of dried salmon for his return journey, unloading canoes to run them down Cottonwood Canyon where "the river passes violently between high rocks" and enduring a night of thunder, lightning and heavy rains.

At the tourist centre, Julie Clark directed me to a public footpath leading to the confluence of the Quesnel and Fraser rivers. I strolled down through a grove of trees, each one graced by a plaque commemorating a pioneer.

Some athletic moms were briskly walking their babies, two First Nations men were listening intently to an animated narrative from a young woman and three elderly Sikhs sat in a row talking to one another. It was a calm, urban, blissfully Canadian multicultural scene that would have astounded the twenty-four explorers who camped here in 1808. In their time, on the other side of the continent, Canada was a colonial postage stamp already apprehensive about the growing tensions between Britain and the United States that would eventually lead to invasion and the War of 1812.

Before settling in for an evening of putting my notes in order and rereading Fraser's journals, I took a quick side trip to Barkerville, Richfield and Cameronton.

The gold-rush towns wouldn't be established until more than fifty years after Fraser passed the mouth of the Quesnel River, but Cameronton has a sad connection with the explorer. The explorer's fourth son, John Alexander Fraser, is buried

A white wooden headboard marks the grave of Simon Fraser's son, John, who came west with the Cariboo gold rush and is buried in a cemetery near the meticulously restored mining camp of Barkerville, BC.
Bill Keay/Vancouver Sun

in the Cameronton cemetery.

John had mortgaged the family farm he had inherited from his father at St. Andrew's West in Ontario when Simon died in 1862. He invested the funds in mining ventures in the Cariboo. They didn't pay out, his creditors foreclosed on the mortgage, he lost the family farm, a romance foundered and then—almost fifty-seven years after his father reached Quesnel—despondent and despairing, he committed suicide. One day later, one of the claims in which he was a partner struck it rich.

It was cold and there was still snow in shaded hollows when I found John's plain wooden headboard among the graves of the forgotten and misbegotten who were left behind when the gold rush ebbed away. I shrugged deeper into my jacket and listened to the wind in the treetops. The loss of the Fraser family homestead in Upper Canada that dated back to the American Revolution—and the young man's death in 1865, three years after his father's death in 1862—provided a poignant afterword to Simon's long and eventful story.

Simon Fraser

22

THE NORTH WEST COMPANY'S LAST POST

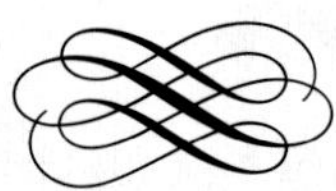

On the remote west side of the Fraser River about six hundred kilometres north of Vancouver, I turned in at the humble collection of weathered buildings that marks Alexandria Indian Reserve No. 1. To find long-abandoned Fort Alexandria, I'd crossed the river at Quesnel and turned south on the twisting West Fraser Road, watching the kilometres rattle by while suburbs gave way to acreages, then ranches, and the dense boreal forest gradually yielded to meadows of arid bunch grass.

By the time I arrived, I had left behind the trail into Deserters Creek, where Alexander Mackenzie defused a near mutiny in 1793. In my wake lay the twisting hairpin turns at Narcosli Creek, the alluvial flood plain of Diamond Island and Lt. Henry Spencer Palmer's 1863 survey trail from Bella Coola to Fort Alexandria.

The previous day, exploring around Cottonwood Canyon and Mackenzie's West Road River north of Quesnel—GPS, compass and maps notwithstanding—I had repeatedly been lost in a maze of deactivated logging roads, some of which required a little axe-work on the deadfalls. But in my trade, getting lost has its advantages.

In this case, the experience of not being where I thought I was became the richer from wildlife encounters that ranged from a nonchalant grizzly browsing on dandelion flowers to an excitable cinnamon bear with two cubs, an extraordinarily large male black bear, the grey phantom of a lynx, a herd of elk—red deer, Fraser

An abandoned log cabin at the remote Alexandria Indian Reserve on the west side of the Fraser River south of Quesnel, BC. *Bill Keay/*Vancouver Sun

Somewhere below the eerie ruins of this cabin near long-abandoned Fort Alexandria, Alexander Mackenzie turned back in 1793, then followed the Blackwater River west from Quesnel, BC to tidewater.
*Bill Keay/*Vancouver Sun

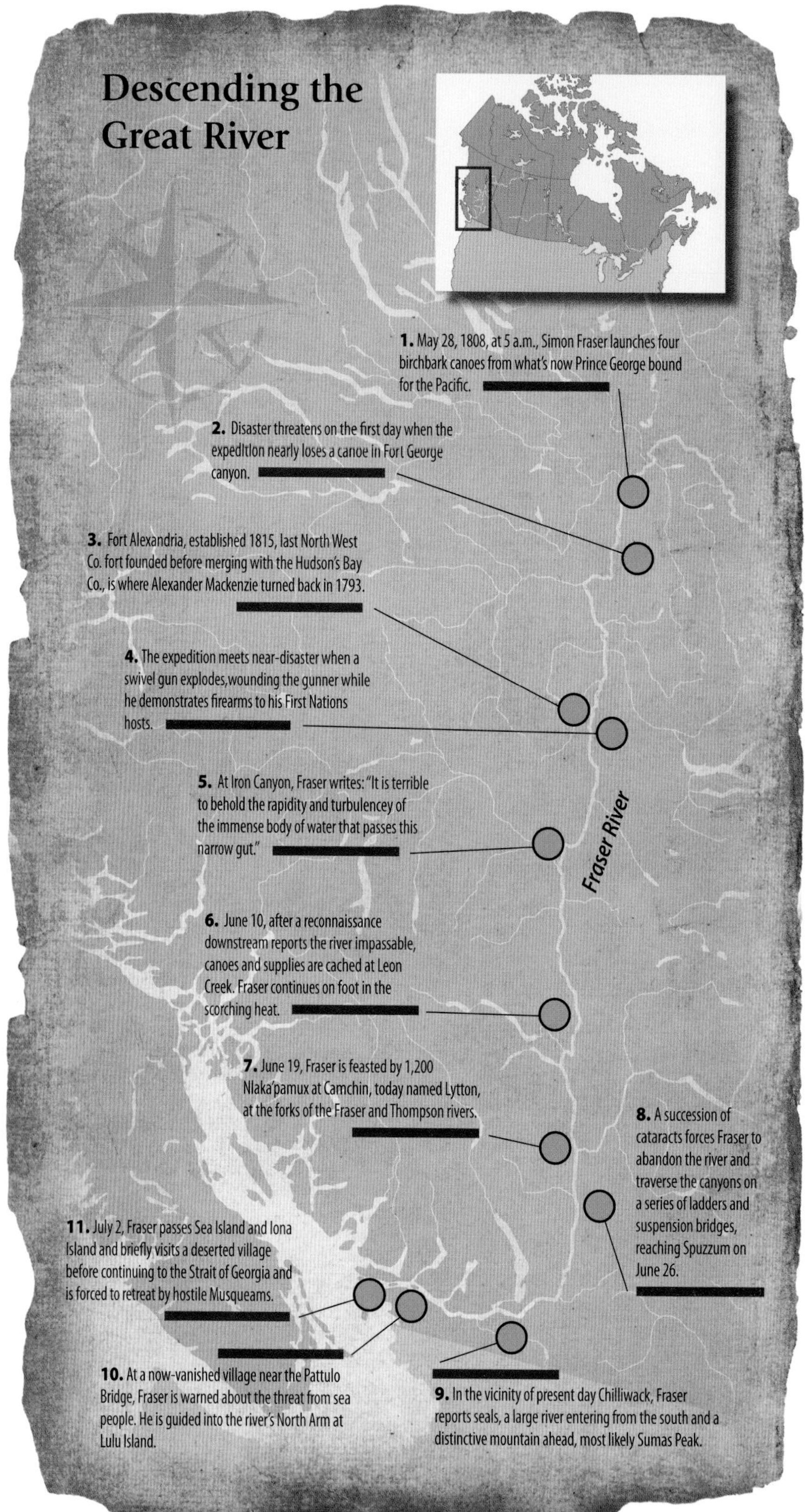
Descending the Great River
1. May 28, 1808, at 5 a.m., Simon Fraser launches four birchbark canoes from what's now Prince George bound for the Pacific.
2. Disaster threatens on the first day when the expedition nearly loses a canoe in Fort George canyon.
3. Fort Alexandria, established 1815, last North West Co. fort founded before merging with the Hudson's Bay Co., is where Alexander Mackenzie turned back in 1793.
4. The expedition meets near-disaster when a swivel gun explodes,wounding the gunner while he demonstrates firearms to his First Nations hosts.
5. At Iron Canyon, Fraser writes: "It is terrible to behold the rapidity and turbulencey of the immense body of water that passes this narrow gut."
Fraser River
6. June 10, after a reconnaissance downstream reports the river impassable, canoes and supplies are cached at Leon Creek. Fraser continues on foot in the scorching heat.
7. June 19, Fraser is feasted by 1,200 Nlaka'pamux at Camchin, today named Lytton, at the forks of the Fraser and Thompson rivers.
8. A succession of cataracts forces Fraser to abandon the river and traverse the canyons on a series of ladders and suspension bridges, reaching Spuzzum on June 26.
11. July 2, Fraser passes Sea Island and Iona Island and briefly visits a deserted village before continuing to the Strait of Georgia and is forced to retreat by hostile Musqueams.
10. At a now-vanished village near the Pattulo Bridge, Fraser is warned about the threat from sea people. He is guided into the river's North Arm at Lulu Island.
9. In the vicinity of present day Chilliwack, Fraser reports seals, a large river entering from the south and a distinctive mountain ahead, most likely Sumas Peak.

Back road travel in British Columbia brings its own perils, from washouts to deadfalls. Stephen Hume clears brush from the road with the axe he always carries. *Bill Keay/*Vancouver Sun

Simon Fraser's encounters with grizzly bears were violent and terrifying but this sleek, flower-fed specimen near Quesnel, BC, was interested only in dining on the tender blooms of dandelions. *Bill Keay/*Vancouver Sun

A herd of California bighorn sheep browses on the sparse grass of arid benches above the Fraser River near Williams Lake, BC. Simon Fraser noted their presence in his 1808 journal. *Bill Keay*/Vancouver Sun

would have called them—many mule deer, blacktail deer, marmots and a fleeting glimpse of what looked like a fisher, the large cousin of the weasel whose pelt was prized by the fur trade.

Still I wasn't sure what to expect at the site of the old fort. The last post established by Simon Fraser's North West Company before merging with the Hudson's Bay Company in 1821, Alexandria played a key role in supplying horses for the fur brigades that carried bales of goods overland to Kamloops and transportation down the more navigable Columbia River.

Fort Alexandria had a peripatetic history. Its first post was on the east side of the river. It was later moved, then moved again to the west side of the river in 1836. I wanted to visit the later site because that was the place where Fraser had landed in 1808.

In the 1830s it was the metropolis of the Interior, with a local population of 747 and a herd of two hundred horses with which it supplied the brigades. Its fields produced crops of wheat, hay and oats, and its extensive gardens produced vegetables.

At the reserve, Mary Stump kindly interrupted her preparations for a funeral to give me directions to Stella-yah, the place where Mackenzie took local advice about the impassable rapids ahead and abandoned his journey down what he thought was the Columbia River in 1793.

She was apologetic that she couldn't take time to show me down to the site herself and she'd have referred me to somebody else for guidance, she said, but the only other folks around were her niece, Tanya Sinclair, and granddaughter, Rayna Kobelt.

"It's a bad time here right now," Stump said. "We've had a death in the community. It's a young person. It's been very traumatizing for everyone."

When she pointed, I looked dubiously at a rutted track that appeared less like a road than a couple of dry ditches running side by side. It was going to take some fancy driving to avoid high-centring the foolishly sporty uptown car I was driving. Not the best vehicle for the outback, I guess, but I recalled writer Paul St. Pierre's observation that a real BC boy should be able to get just about anywhere worth getting in a standard sedan if he drives it with a little common sense.

"Drive down the rough road and cross the flats," Stump told me. "Watch out for irrigation pipe in the grass, they are watering down there. Leave your car at the graveyard. That cemetery is the old fort cemetery. There's a lot of smallpox victims buried there."

The smallpox epidemic of 1862, the year Simon Fraser died, is still a presence in many native Indian communities. It rent gaping and often irreparable holes in the social and cultural fabric, killing elders who were the custodians of oral history and traditions as well as the children who should have received them. In its own way it was a catastrophe for the oral record of similar, perhaps greater, magnitude than the destruction of libraries and manuscripts that accompanied the collapse of Rome's western empire. The BC epidemic appears worse to us because it's the closest temporally and occurred in historic times, which for a document-driven culture imbues it with a greater sense of reality.

Yet the 1862 outbreak was only the most recent of a century-long series of dreadful mortalities that afflicted First Nations' populations from the eighteenth century to the twentieth. Indeed Fraser's 1808 journal notes the presence of smallpox in one village that he was the first European to visit. These may have been among the last victims of an epidemic thought to have swept through southern Vancouver Island, the Gulf Islands and up the lower Fraser River beginning around 1800.

I thought immediately of a story I'd come across in Quesnel the day before. It gives some inkling of the magnitude of these events. Across the river from the present town is an unusual hill popularly known to some as The Sugar Loaf. Its other local name is Mt. Belgineau, after a native Indian man from the village at Quesnel described by Fraser.

Belgineau was out hunting in 1862, and on arriving at Fort Alexandria was told of a plague visiting lodges everywhere. When he got home, his village was deserted and the houses burned. All that remained of his life was ashes. Belgineau was the only known survivor. He left the area but returned in 1882 and lived alone until his death in an abandoned miner's hut at the hill. When he died in 1900, the story goes, he was thought to have died of supernatural causes, and his ghost still haunts the woods beneath the hill. There are still lingering presences at Fort Alexandria too.

"Keep going down past the cemetery and you'll cross a couple more benches," Stump told me. "When you can see our church on the other side [of the river] you'll

Rayna Kobelt sits on a rock at the Alexandria Indian Reserve overlooking flats beside the Fraser River once visited by both Alexander Mackenzie and Simon Fraser. *Bill Keay/Vancouver Sun*

be in the right place. It's one of the oldest churches in the Cariboo. We still use it sometimes."

The provincial government had promised to pave the road when it decided to close the Marguerite ferry for cost-saving reasons. The river divides the reserve, and the lack of a ferry or a good road creates a real hardship.

"If we have a sickness or an emergency we have to drive to Quesnel or Williams Lake to cross the river," Stump said, eyes flashing. "They said they would pave the road when they took away our ferry. They were supposed to finish it last year but it's still not finished. There was a washout on the other side of the river and they used our paving money to fix that."

I took my leave and made my way down the rutted track, then out into the scorching flats where I paused to examine some old log buildings. Their plank floors were falling in and the rafters were exposed. The walls were insulated with ancient Rogers Sugar boxes, yellowing newspapers and the pages of crumbling magazines, all packed behind painted canvas that substituted for drywall or panelling.

A fragment of print on the floor informed me that "many women like their homes to be of one colour tone throughout" and touted a wonderful new invention—linoleum. I doubted that the writer had this place in mind, where the flooring was two-by-twelve planking. Pencilled on a patch of cardboard in an elegant hand was a commemorative note, obviously written after the building had fallen into disuse: "Death of D.J. Partie, April 28th, 1957." Who was D.J., and who remembers now? I still don't know.

On a bench with a view over the river, I came to the cemetery. Ancient picket fences set off some grave sites, tombstones with illegible inscriptions marked others, and many were simply grassy, unmarked mounds. Here and there the raw immediacy of new graves punctuated the final resting place of people like Old Alexander, born 1878 and buried more than half a century ago.

Then, across the final vast silted flat, I came to the historic place on the river where Mackenzie turned back and the determined Fraser kept going despite warnings of the perils ahead. The landing is all that remains of Fort Alexandria today: a few bits of decaying split-rail fence, some hewn, age-blackened timbers tumbled in a grove of poplars at the back end of a clearing and a piece of rusting equipment whose purpose I couldn't discern.

Heat shimmers rippled over the hayfields, the tiny silken parachutes of seeding dandelions sailed on the breeze and sun sparkled on the wide, muddy river. I took a moment to lean on one of the fences, its decaying wood mottled with lichens, to survey the rolling benchlands that Fraser found "charming."

"This country, which is interspersed with meadows and hills, dales & high rocks, has upon the whole a romantic but pleasant appearance," says his journal entry of May 30.

Fur traders posted at Fort St. James jokingly called it "Siberia," but Fort Alexandria was, according to historian Margaret Ormsby, "the paradise of New Caledonia. The post was situated in lightly wooded, rolling country where there was shooting and fishing and where good crops of grain and vegetables could be grown if the frosts did not come too early."

Somewhere near here Fraser stopped to cache dried fish, took some fresh fish from a native Indian cache, left payment and took note that he was indeed in different country now, for his journal says that he "observed some vestiges of horses at this place."

Exact locations remain almost impossible to determine. The site to which Stump had directed me certainly looked welcoming. Fort Alexandria itself was not established until 1821, thirteen years after Fraser passed. It would later become the flashpoint in a grisly exchange of hostilities between Carrier and Chilcotin peoples, but in 1808 the region seemed relatively tranquil.

On the west side of the river a bit farther south, Fraser wrote, the expedition "landed at a large house. Our Indians then called out to the strangers on the opposite shore, informing them that we were white people going to the sea."

Fort Alexandria, the last trading post established by the North West Company before its 1821 merger with the Hudson's Bay Company was located near this gentle stretch of river above Williams Lake, BC. *Bill Keay*/Vancouver Sun

An ancient fragment of split-rail fence is likely all that remains of one incarnation of Fort Alexandria, once the staging point for pack trains carrying furs to the Columbia River via the Okanagan Valley. *Bill Keay*/Vancouver Sun

On this stretch of river Fraser observed horsemen for the first time on his journey when couriers galloped ahead to inform the next village that strangers were coming by water. I bid farewell to the sleepers in the vanished fort's graveyard, gave a thought to D.J., half a century dead now, left Mary Stump to her community's mourning and pushed south for Soda Creek.

On Monday, May 30, 1808, after what appears to have been a relatively uneventful day on a swiftly flowing but not overly rough section of river, Fraser recounts his first encounter with people he called "the Atnah nation." Readers who trivialize the native Indians' insistence that they comprise nations and deserve consideration as such should take note: that's how they were defined two centuries ago.

Fraser's Atnah were almost certainly the Secwepemc, once commonly referred to by non-natives as Shuswap. He was passing through the western tongue of broad tribal territories that extended from just north of Soda Creek to Pavilion, just north of Lillooet, and eastward beyond Revelstoke to the Rockies.

This western wedge of territory, which extended across the Fraser, was important because it gave the Secwepemc access to fishing sites where they could harvest salmon, although they relied to a much greater extent than other peoples on hunting big game.

Somewhere between Tingley Creek and Beaverdam Creek—W. Kaye Lamb thinks in the vicinity of Macalister, since the journal says the next day's run to Soda Creek was about nineteen kilometres—Fraser landed to parley with people who began arriving on horseback.

"They seemed peaceably inclined, and appeared happy to see us, and observed that having heard by their neighbours that white people were to visit their country this season, they had remained near the route on purpose to receive us," Fraser's journal says.

Despite the language barrier—communications had to be passed through two different interpreters—it proved a fortuitous meeting, although it was almost ruined when the fur traders' exhibition of firearms went awry. The traders' small brass swivel gun, old and obviously suffering metal fatigue, blew up when a demonstration shot was fired, wounding Gagnier, the party's gunner.

Fraser tried to look on the bright side. It was fortunate that the cannon, being "cracked in many places of old," failed in the way it did, he noted, with only a moderate charge, because "was it to break amongst a large band of Indians the consequences might be fatal.

"This accident alarmed the Indians, but having convinced them that the injury was of no great consequence, they were reconciled," Fraser reported. This was a good thing, because the Secwepemc had vital intelligence for him on two counts.

First they warned the explorer that "the river below was but a succession of falls and cascades, which we should find impossible to pass, not only thro the badness of the channel, but also thro the badness of the surrounding country, which was rugged and mountainous. Their opinion, therefore, was that we should discontinue our voyage and remain with them."

Fraser told them that he was determined to continue. He then got the second bit of crucial intelligence: "They, then, informed us that at the next camp, the Great Chief of the Atnaugh had a slave who had been to the sea."

On May 31, accompanied by an interpreter, Fraser set out at 5:30 a.m. for Xats'ull, the Great Chief's camp near Soda Creek. After a late lunch of apples and cheese beside the roaring river, with swallows darting and the blue shadows beginning to lengthen as the sun slid toward the Coast Range, so did I.

23

EVERY MOMENT AT THE BRINK OF ETERNITY

A faint pungent scent—maybe wood smoke, maybe sweetgrass—drifted up through the dense thickets crowding the narrow, dusty track that led me down to Xats'ull where the Fraser River boils into a tight gorge.

The local Indian band at Soda Creek—the prosaic English name for the place derives from the white rime of alkali that dries on the rocks—runs a heritage and cultural camp here. Tourists have been known to follow the tantalizing aroma of traditional pit-baked salmon down to the site. There are authentic pit houses, drying racks for salmon and a nomadic people's simple and efficient summer shelters made from wooden frames and evergreen boughs. Observers from the time of Simon Fraser called these structures "shades."

A row of tipis graces the meadow too. The people here were known to ride their horses beyond the Rocky Mountains to hunt bison, a fact that impressed Fraser in 1808, but manager Rhonda Shackelly confessed the tipis were imported from Alberta, a necessary concession to the expectations of German visitors.

Shackelly, who lived fifteen years in Merritt before getting her degree from Simon Fraser University and coming home to run the heritage site, has had more interesting problems than finding ways to market Xats'ull heritage to European culture campers. There's also the occasional squatter to evict.

"There was a bear living in the pit house last winter," she laughed. "We had to kick him out."

Above: At Xats'ull Heritage Village near Soda Creek, BC, manager Rhonda Shackelly stands by what Simon Fraser called a "shade," the traditional Secwepemc summer shelter. Tipis in the background are imported for foreign tourists. *Bill Keay/*Vancouver Sun

Right: Secwepemc chiefs at Soda Creek provided Simon Fraser with invaluable assistance. This view shows where a rawhide suspension bridge once crossed the river; some say the bridge was burned to prevent travel during a smallpox epidemic. *Bill Keay/*Vancouver Sun

Xats'ull is no Disneyfied concoction, though. It's the real deal. For millennia, people have camped on dry benches just like this one above Soda Creek canyon, 580 kilometres north of Vancouver.

"There were once a thousand to fifteen hundred people living here at Soda Creek, so many they used to have a bridge across the Fraser made of rawhide. Now there are only a few hundred," Shackelly said. "They got the smallpox and they all died."

Xats'ull had been a fishing site since time immemorial for several reasons. Migrating salmon concentrate in the huge eddies and can be caught with dip nets. And the furnace winds of the cordilleran rain shadow are ideal for drying fish.

On this day elder Minnie Phillips was only talking about fishing, however, or more properly about not fishing, while she gave her four-year-old grandson Kenneth Phillips a lesson in how to scrape a deerskin for tanning. She was lamenting the fact that so often the peoples who inhabit the upper sections of the Fraser seem to come last in line for allocations of the food resource that has sustained their families since time out of mind.

Legally and constitutionally—but in actuality only theoretically—First Nations have a right to harvest traditional resources for food and ceremonial purposes. That right is trumped only by conservation needs.

But salmon runs that were once numberless now dwindle in the face of climate change, pollution, habitat loss and overharvesting. At the same time, a noisy clamour intensifies from commercial and recreational interests that need bigger shares of a smaller pie in order to remain economically viable. This is paralleled by the growing risk that politically influenced management decisions will create a culture that encourages miscalculations regarding stock abundance, run timing and the minimum escapement necessary for the survival of small populations co-migrating with healthy ones.

In reality people like Minnie Phillips on the upper river often find their fishing opportunities restricted for conservation reasons long after commercial, recreational and First Nations interests downstream have exercised their opportunities to intercept the salmon either at sea or in the estuary.

"They weren't allowing us to catch anything but spring salmon," the soft-spoken elder complained. "You'd catch twenty fish and throw them back just to catch one salmon you could keep, because if they caught you fishing other salmon, they'd take away your net and take your car too."

While she grumbled about the ironies of greed and mismanagement on the other side of the mountains that prevented her from fishing where her ancestors had fished, I observed that she didn't once miss a stroke in cleaning her deerskin.

Preparing hides is an old and much-admired skill. Even Fraser, who after a life on the fur-trade frontier had an educated eye for good buckskin, commented on the quality of Secwepemc craftsmanship when he first encountered it in 1808.

"They had bows and arrows both extremely well made, which they laid down on coming to us," he wrote. "Most of their bows were of Juniper or Box wood and Ceader and covered with the skin of rattlesnake, which they say are numerous in this quarter, and their arrows are pointed with stone of flint kind but dark, and their clothing consisted of dressed leather, leggings and shoes with robes of the Chivirease [buckskin], Carribo [caribou], Biche [doeskin] and Beaver skins most of which were dressed in the hair."

While Kristen Sellars pulled the hide taut, Phillips swept her scraper in methodical arcs, taking the hair off the hide in slow, steady strips. Kenneth seemed bemused.

"For the kids," his uncle, Ike Phillips, told me, "the only fun part of this is stretching the skin. When I was a kid, I used to do this but, really, the only fun is stretching."

In the background the silt-laden river boomed and rumbled through the canyon. It was high water, the highest in many years, yet barely submerged rocks still scarred the surface with arrowheads of glistening white froth. Immense eddies formed and whirled away, sucking and hissing along the vertical rock faces.

At the quickest glance it was instantly evident why Fraser decided to pause in his journey, reconnoitre the rapids, gather local information about what lay ahead and try to find and talk with the slave he was told had been to the sea.

It was at Xats'ull that Fraser met with "the Great Chief of the Atnaugh," who welcomed him, spoke on behalf of the strangers to his followers and produced a man who had seen the sea.

More important for Fraser, said Shackelly, "he didn't want to risk the river from here, and so one of the Soda Creek chiefs took him from here all the way down to Lillooet."

Fraser never names this powerful chief, who so graciously offered both to guide the party and to serve as an ambassador, smoothing their way with the next nations they would meet. Some argue that it's evidence of the fur trader's ethnocentric arrogance and bigotry, even racism.

Yet, after living with his journals for years I'm not certain this criticism isn't merely expedient. It enables someone with an agenda to justify today's revisionist point of view by retroactively applying judgments to people whose prejudices were shaped in the eighteenth century.

Time and again Fraser and his men met with First Nations strangers, ate with them, negotiated with them, presented them with gifts, deferred to their superior knowledge in many areas, spoke of them respectfully—if roughly, on occasion—and even with admiration. Certainly they seemed fully aware of their own dependence upon First Nations, and firearms notwithstanding, their ultimate vulnerability.

Struggling with unknown languages, trying to express in his own alphabet unfamiliar sounds for which he had no orthography, trying to communicate through one and sometimes two interpreters without breaching protocols or giving offence, yet driven forward by the mission itself, seldom staying in any camp for more than a day, perhaps it's not surprising that Fraser's account often lacks names. Indeed he often doesn't name his own men.

At Soda Creek the explorer refers only to The Chief, although Fraser clearly holds him in some esteem for his integrity, courage and kindness—"all the Indians in this place were very civil to us," the journal says.

But research by James Teit, an educated British adventurer—who went to live among the Thompson Indians, took a native Indian woman as his wife and became an informant for the great anthropologist Franz Boas of the American Museum of Natural History—lifts the veil of anonymity for a man who, as much as Fraser, deserves credit for the expedition's success.

In an account of the Secwepemc published in 1908, Teit recounts an interview with Setse'l, who was then a very old man. He had been born at a place named Peq on Riske Creek but was living at Alkali Lake when interviewed, his village being one of those obliterated in a series of smallpox epidemics.

"He was a small boy when Simon Fraser's party came down Fraser River with canoes," Teit reported.

"Xlo'sem, the Soda Creek chief, accompanied the party as guide and interpreted for them. Kolpapatci'nexen was at that time chief of the Canoe Creek band and Haxkw'est was a noted war chief and wealthy man. He had three wives and was tall and wore only a breech-clout, excepting in winter time.

"Some of the Soda Creek Indians were the only Shuswap who had seen white men prior to Fraser's party," Teit recounted. "Fraser gave presents of tobacco, beads and knives to almost all the Indians he met. The tobacco was black twist and much stronger than the native tobacco and many men who smoked it became sick."

The feeling may have been mutual, for Fraser mentions, in a rather masterful understatement, that Xlo'sem provided them with food—dried salmon and roots—but "the last though considered as excellent by the natives, we could not very well relish."

After frequent inquiries, Xlo'sem was persuaded to bring forward the slave who had been to the sea and had knowledge of the country that lay ahead. Fraser laid out a pair of oilcloths and asked for a sketch of what lay between him and the Pacific. Although the map was skimpy and required input from one of the chief's elderly relatives, the information was daunting.

"In his sketch, we could plainly see a confirmation of the badness of the navigation and thereby the necessity of leaving our canoes and as much of our baggage as we could spare, in order to prosecute our journey by land," Fraser wrote. In the meantime, however, he intended to run the river for as long as possible.

On May 31, having left four bales of their precious dried salmon in the custody of Xlo'sem's brother, the expedition once again embarked, this time with the Secwepemc chief as guide. They were whisked along by the strong current "through many bad places" until—with the wind "blowing a hurricane from the south" and faced with a very long and dangerous-looking rapid where the river passes to the west of what is now Williams Lake—Fraser camped.

"I inquired of the Chief, if the Indians were in the habit of running down this rapid: he said no; he conceived that the whirlpools would swallow up or overpower any canoes."

The next morning Fraser, John Stuart and six voyageurs went to scout the rapid. It was intimidating. I found it equally scary when I got a look at it myself. It hasn't changed much in the nearly two hundred years since Fraser described its steep canyon walls contracting to a gorge about fifty metres wide.

"The immense body of water passing through this narrow space in a turbulent manner, forming numerous gulphs and cascades, and making a tremendous noise, had an awful and forbidding appearance," Fraser wrote. But since the surrounding terrain made carrying the canoes impossible, he decided to run the more than three kilometres of white water.

He put his best five men in a canoe from which most of the supplies had been removed and they put on a demonstration of canoeing skill that's still exhilarating to read, even today in a world of extreme sports.

The canoe was caught in a whirlpool, the paddlers powerless to escape, "every moment at the brink of eternity," then it was spat out, "flying from one danger to the next." Despite heroic efforts, more whirlpools finally forced it against a rock projecting from the canyon wall. The men and their commander concurred wordlessly, the Secwepemc had been right and "of course to continue on the water would be certain destruction."

But the crew still had to be rescued. Fraser had the remaining crew plunge their daggers into the bank to prevent themselves sliding into the maelstrom below. They cut steps into the canyon sides, got a line down to the vital canoe and half hauled, half lifted it up the cliff.

"Our lives hung as it were upon a thread," he wrote, "for failure of the line or a false step of one of the men would have hurled the whole of us into eternity."

A lesser leader might have taken the Secwepemc advice at this point, abandoned the canoes and travelled by horseback to the east where they were told they would find a great river and smooth water all the way to the sea.

Stuart obviously tucked away this intelligence. He later returned and charted a trail that eventually did permit the North West Company and later the Hudson's Bay Company to transport furs from the north by pack train from the Fraser to Kamloops, the Okanagan and a navigable canoe route to the Columbia River and the sea.

"But going to the sea by an indirect way was not the object of the undertaking," Fraser wrote. "I therefore would not deviate and continued our route."

It was now June 2, and the river was cresting. It rose almost three metres overnight and any lingering thoughts about risking the rapids must have evaporated. Fraser obtained four horses from the Secwepemc and began a long and painful portage. One of the horses lost its footing, however, and fell down the cliff. Stuart's small writing desk was smashed and medicines and papers lost into the river. The next day, once again faced with either running canoes down a violent rapid or abandoning them, cargo was unloaded for carrying by land and the canoes shot the white water crewed by five men each.

"The struggle which the men on this trial experienced between the whirlpools and rocks almost exhausted their strength; the canoes were in perpetual danger of sinking or being broken to pieces. It was a desperate undertaking," Fraser wrote.

The trail proved as dangerous as the river. The exhausted men with their thirty-kilogram packs clambered along the edge of a precipice among loose stones and gravel that continually gave way beneath their feet. One got himself stuck in a position where he could go neither forward nor backward nor remove his pack. Leadership meant leading; Fraser himself went to help.

"Seeing the poor fellow in this predicament, I crawled to his assistance; but not without great risk, and saved him, however his load dropped off his back over the precipice and into the river."

By the time they'd reached their next camp, their moccasins were in tatters, they were all plagued with severe blisters and "very sore with much walking."

There was a ray of light in the gloom, however. A few more days of rough country, Fraser was told, would lead him into a country of plenty where the people were hospitable. Furthermore, "they informed us that white people had lately passed down the large river to the left." This most likely referred to David Thompson's expedition through the Rockies to the upper Columbia the previous year.

Fraser was determined to complete his mission by whatever means available. In the same spirit I decided that following his route meant it was time for me to venture onto the wild river itself and under similar conditions to those he faced.

A redwing blackbird lands on bulrushes in a wetland near Williams Lake River, which Simon Fraser passed heading south on May 31, 1808. There was once an extensive settlement at the river mouth. *Bill Keay*/Vancouver Sun

Simon Fraser

24

A NARROW ESCAPE FROM PERDITION

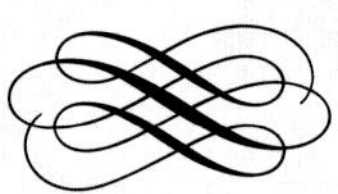

An eddy rolling off the walls of Iron Canyon punched the jetboat sideways, and the rigid eight-metre hull flexed. My head snapped and my teeth rattled in the force of the whiplash. As the boat corkscrewed, I felt an intense desire to cinch even tighter the straps on my life jacket. The feeling was momentary. I didn't dare let go of the grab-hold to which I was clinging like someone in the front seat of the Big Dipper Roller Coaster.

Simon Fraser had passed this unrelenting place in a birchbark canoe almost two hundred years ago on his journey to the Pacific Ocean. It was just as formidable for my trek—even using the latest and most sophisticated of twenty-first-century technology.

A wall of muddy brown water foamed past the tilting rail, then vanished again—sucked down into a whirlpool the size of a small suburban bungalow—as the boat gave another sickening lurch in the opposite direction. This was a boat that at a touch of the throttle generates as much power as seven four-cylinder cars like the old Dodge sedan that zips me around comfortably at freeway speed.

Doug Green gunned his boat's two engines. The surge from their 650 horses was discernible even with the force of the river. He hauled on the controls. The acceleration from the boat's powerful jets combined with the centrifugal force of the whirlpool to flick the vessel out of the vortex and into the next huge eddy.

But not before a slick patch of what looked like calm water suddenly erupted,

Stephen Hume (left) and wilderness guide Doug Green prepare to enter the dangerous Iron Canyon where Simon Fraser commented upon "whirlpools and eddies that surpass any thing of the kind that I ever saw before." *Bill Keay*/Vancouver Sun

Doug Green's jetboat needed all 650 horsepower to escape this sucking whirlpool in Iron Canyon between Riske Creek and the Chilcotin River. *Bill Keay*/Vancouver Sun

boiling up from below. Steep waves jackhammered the bottom—almost three centimetres of solid metal—causing the boat to buck and lurch alarmingly, first to one side, then the other.

"It's like wrestling an anaconda," Green yelled over the din of the engines. "It just keeps twisting away from me. This is total chaos. Anything can happen in here."

We were in Iron Canyon, a thirty-metre-wide notch in the bedrock between Riske Creek and the Chilcotin River where the entire Fraser River spurts around a dogleg. Water piles up against sheer cliffs even as it changes direction, creating undertows and cross-currents that wash across the main flow at right angles. Beneath it all, the river roars along in volumes and velocities that must measure in the tens of millions of litres per second.

"It is terrible to behold the rapidity and turbulence of the immense body of water that passes in this narrow gut," Fraser noted in astonishment in his journal when he surveyed the rapid in 1808. "No less do the numerous Gulphs and whirlpools it forms constantly striking from one rock to another. The rocks are amazing high and craggy, particularly on the right side, and the water in a manner seems to have forced a passage under them and flows out here and there in numerous whirlpools and eddies that surpass any thing of the kind that I ever saw before."

Small wonder that Fraser—after his men had dragged their canoes and cargo over a gruelling portage rather than risk running the river—broached a carefully hoarded keg of "shrub," a concoction of lemon juice, sugar and rum. He ordered a dram for all hands.

Using the boat's global positioning system, we'd already clocked our downstream drift on one of the Fraser's calmer stretches above Iron Rapids at close to twenty kilometres per hour. In the deep, constricted canyon the flow was even faster.

As it had during Fraser's journey, the river had come up close to a metre overnight. Its already complicated hydraulics were constantly changing, Green said, making it almost impossible to predict what the current would do.

"Those great big whirlpools open up, and you just get going around and one opens up going the other way. You have to be ready for anything. I'm comfortable with it. You learn to become calm and focussed, so you can see your way through the chaos as it unfolds, eh?"

I admired his Zen-like approach. It reminded me of Fraser's description of the philosophical calm with which his men faced the terrifying challenge of another rapid near French Bar Canyon that left no alternative but the route by water.

"Skimming along like lightning, the crews cool and determined, followed each other in awful silence. And when we arrived at the end we stood gazing on our narrow escape from perdition," Fraser wrote. After taking a few deep breaths, they went on to where their Secwepemc advance party was camped.

"Here we were happy to find our old friends, the Chief and the Interpreter, who immediately joined our party." There's a clear sense of relief in Fraser's entry.

I'd explained to Green before chartering his boat that I wanted to experience the river in its raw power as Simon Fraser's party had experienced it. He'd taken me at my word, showing me the formidable stretch of water between Williams Lake River and French Bar Creek, just west of Clinton.

"The water must have been about like this when Fraser's canoes went through," Green had said as we ran down some lesser rapids toward Iron Canyon. "Man, oh man, it's hard to imagine. This is a real handful, even for this boat. That's big water in there. No fooling around, boy."

Green should know. He and his partner Charlene Lupien operate Cariboo Chilcotin Jetboat Adventures. They have been running charters and tours, mostly in the summer months after the runoff has subsided and the river is much gentler, for almost ten years. "We've had twelve mountain bikes back here." Green nodded toward his boat's stern. "I've had a ninety-three-year-old woman and I've had a three-year-old, so I've had the full range."

At high water these passages are not for the faint of heart, he acknowledged, even with twin engines generating 650 horsepower. But the trip put Fraser's descent of the river by canoe into a context that I couldn't have imagined simply by reading his journals, however vivid the accounts. It wasn't all frightening white water and terrifying canyons, either for me or for Fraser's expedition. As we idled along in the calm stretches that the old log books describe as "good going," Green helped me try to identify places Fraser mentioned.

"This would be where he crossed the river," he said in the vicinity of Chimney Creek. "He talks about a house and there are the remnants of a house here. You can see a gravesite and even vestiges of the trail they cut in the bank [for a portage]. California bighorn sheep can be seen here—this is one of the few places you see them because it's their northernmost range."

Fraser noted finding the horn of a "Sasyan or Rocky Mountain ram" with which he was familiar from his experiences with Tse'Khene hunters. And later we did see the rare sheep, some silhouetted on an escarpment, another small herd browsing on bunch grass on the steep banks close to the water's edge.

His campsite above Riske Creek was easy to spot. It is now Toosey Indian Reserve No. 3, and Green is from Toosey.

"I'd imagine the village site would be here," he said. "There are lots of flat spots, there's good hunting, there's good sturgeon fishing right there"—pointing to a back eddy—"there's a couple of ways in; there's quiet water and a good beach. Lots of kikwillie holes [remains of old pit houses] up there. Yeah, this is the place."

But it turned out there were other signals of human habitation.

"Look for giant rye grass," Lupien said. "That's not native to this area. It was traded in from the Okanagan. The people would seed their village sites with it

Tiny in the desert landscape of British Columbia's Interior, Charlene Lupien looks over the turbulent Fraser River downstream from Riske Creek. *Bill Keay/*Vancouver Sun

Giant rye grass, here examined by wilderness guide Charlene Lupien at a site near the Chilcotin River, was imported for weaving mats. It is an indicator of First Nations encampments. *Bill Keay/* Vancouver Sun

and then use it to weave mats and linings for their pit houses. So you can spot the village sites by looking for the giant rye. Then you'll find kikwillies. Look for big bush sage—you use that to cleanse your house. Wormwood sage, that's a natural mosquito repellent, common yarrow too."

As we drifted, ran rapids and drifted again, Green pointed out the other signs of changing demography. Where possible we paused to examine ancient petroglyphs carved into riverside boulders; stone ovens likely built by the Secwepemc who occupied this territory before smallpox depopulated many villages and the Chilcotin expanded eastward; portage cuts left by Fraser himself; the tiny sod-roofed cabins left by prospectors in the 1858 gold rush; a building with one stone wall and a tiny stone spillway for a spring that's since gone dry—as many have since the advent of irrigation on the benches—most likely left by Chinese prospectors.

"It's a strange feeling seeing these things," Green mused. "Everybody's life is meaningful. Somebody spent some of his life here, built these things and now there is nothing left but these little ruins, and they are disappearing too."

Just as Fraser had sent scouting parties ahead to assess the risks before putting his men to the dangers of running a rapid, I'd mounted my own reconnaissance before making my rendezvous with Green, a Chilcotin who now lives near Riske Creek.

I'd begun by hiking to the mouth of Williams Lake River, now part of a regional park, where the riverbed cuts through a series of glacial lake bottoms. I was

Stephen Hume hikes the Williams Lake River to its confluence with the Fraser where the expedition to the Pacific made a brief stop. *Bill Keay/*Vancouver Sun

fascinated by the sedimentary record in the steep banks, which revealed the water levels of eleven thousand years, sixteen thousand years and twenty thousand years ago.

Mostly I wanted a look at the long-abandoned village site at Ckemtsitsen, the creek mouth where Fraser would have stopped in 1808 on his journey down the big river that the Secwepemc call *Setekwe.*

The creek widened into a lagoon protected by a long sandy spit while the river beyond was broad and placid, except for a riffle along the west side where the Fraser swept past a ledge of striking red and black rock.

This was a major village site before smallpox reduced the Tlexelc, as the Williams Lake Indian band calls itself, Chief Willie Alphonse told me. Numbers had dwindled from thirty-five hundred to five hundred, and in the twenty years after the gold rush in 1858, the surviving members found themselves with no land—it had all been taken by white settlers. The present reserve was obtained only after the band wrote to Queen Victoria expressing the injustice. Five local ranches were finally bought on their behalf.

Fraser's accounts of his meetings with the Secwepemc offer lessons for today, Alphonse said.

"That's a good demonstration of how the different bands recognized the boundaries of the different nations. The Carriers passed Simon Fraser on to us and we passed him on to the Lillooets," he said.

"You know, Simon Fraser always camped at village sites because he was smart. It was for protection. If you just camped anywhere, you'd be considered to be trespassing and maybe an enemy. You might get yourself killed. But if you camped with people, you were a guest and you were under the chief's protection and you got fed."

At the creek mouth, not far from the depressions where abandoned pit houses eventually collapsed, I got a reminder that there are tribes older than any of ours. Ravens began to gather overhead, scores of them. Wheeling and soaring in an immense circle, they swooshed down, one by one, touched briefly on the edge of a high bluff, then took off again. On the other side of the river, hundreds more perched in the trees at the edge of the bank, cronking and croaking in that distinctive raven language. In the trees where I stood watching this mysterious ceremony, a large flock of crows—normally sworn enemies of the raven clan—sat muttering and mumbling in numbers that bowed the branches.

What it meant I don't know, and I haven't found any references in the scientific literature that can help me understand. The ravens vanished as suddenly as they had gathered, abruptly peeling off and flying away to all points of the compass. Later I thought of something Green said while we stood on a sandbar beside the river.

"When you are in the bush a lot by yourself, you realize that everything—the

Doctoral candidate Erin O'Brien checks the feathers of a male mountain bluebird chick as part of a research project in the arid country southwest of Williams Lake, BC, near Dog Creek.
Bill Keay/Vancouver Sun

An ancient, water-worn petroglyph near Iron Canyon, a signal of the supernatural world carved into a boulder at the river's edge, is gradually being erased by the abrasive, silt-laden current of the Fraser River.
Bill Keay/Vancouver Sun

sky, the clouds, the rivers, the animals—they are all telling you things, but sometimes, coming from our modern world, it's hard to comprehend what they mean," he said.

Soon the mystery of the ravens and their ritual was behind me as I travelled hundreds of kilometres on remote back roads on both sides of the Fraser. On a series of cruel switchbacks rising to the Gang Ranch, I met Doug Clawson of Seattle, riding his bicycle solo across the outback to Bella Coola. And on the other side, somewhere between Dog Creek and Alkali Lake, I met Erin O'Brien, a doctoral candidate in biology from the University of Northern BC. She was doing the lonely, gentle work of counting bluebird chicks, banding them and returning them to their nests.

I crossed the river again heading south for Farwell Canyon, where I hoped to look at pictographs and compare them with those stunning images I'd seen on Stuart Lake far to the north. The road was closed, and I was forced to turn back.

That disappointment waned, however, when I learned that my river guide had some unusual pictographs to show me that he'd recently discovered right on the Fraser River. Green found them by accident when he was out hunting the previous winter. "I was following cougar tracks. I saw a kill down on the ice—this was all covered with a glaze of ice—and I slipped and fell. I went down about 150 feet," he said, wincing at the memory.

Luckily he was able to break his fall by jamming his rifle sideways so that the stock and barrel caught on some trees, but he still wound up on the frozen river. When he looked up, there were the pictographs, hidden from casual view. It was as though he'd been led there.

From the river I made out what looked like five human figures painted inside a bowl that had been hollowed out of the rock by a boulder rolling around in some past age when the river level was higher. In the middle was a white figure. It appeared to be holding hands with red figures on either side.

Dream images? Perhaps a depiction of some supernatural being, like the transformer who created the distinctions between animals and humans? Or was it a depiction of a transformative event so unusual that it entered the realm of myth—the first encounter with white-skinned people?

Green shrugged. "Maybe that goes right back to Simon Fraser. There are things that go back a long time before him. I've heard a story out west about how they hunted woolly mammoths, how they would shoot the arrows straight up in the air and the arrows would come down on the mammoth's head, where there's a soft spot."

I finally bid farewell to this remote and relatively untouched and unvisited stretch of the river to turn south again. I followed winding roads cut from hardpan clay through the same terrain that plagued Fraser with "a violent pain in my groins which prevents me from being able to walk any distance." His men were wearing out a pair of moccasins a day, and their feet were "full of thorns."

Still Fraser pressed the expedition forward past Dog Creek, Churn Creek, Canoe Creek, China Gulch, Grinder Creek, Lone Cabin Creek, Deadman Creek, French Bar and Big Bar, while the warnings from his Secwepemc guides of what lay ahead became ever grimmer.

By June 9, the journal entry shows an uncharacteristic sense of pessimism. The rapids, Fraser says, are now the worst yet and seem to have no end.

"I scarcely ever saw any thing so dreary and seldom so dangerous in any country; and at present while I am writing this, whatever way I turn, mountains upon mountains, whose summits are covered with eternal snows, close the gloomy scene."

Finally at Leon Creek, listening to the advice of Xlo'sem, the chief from Xats'ull at Soda Creek, Fraser decided to continue by land. A scaffold covered with branches was erected to store the canoes and protect them from the scorching sun. Food and unnecessary supplies were cached. In the middle of the night a second, secret cache was made of items deemed absolutely necessary to survive a return journey. Then they set off for the country of the St'at'imc who live at Lillooet.

I tuned in the forecast on my weather radio. The forecast was for rain. I considered how quickly a sprinkle would turn the clay to slippery gumbo, thought about the narrow switchbacks and hairpins I had to negotiate and made a decision similar to Fraser's. On the theory that a bit of backtracking was better than having to get my car pulled out of a creek, I abandoned camp and high-tailed it for Lillooet.

Simon Fraser

25

INTO THE SUNBURNT CORDILLERA

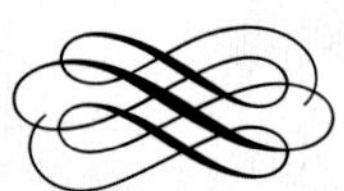

The wind announced itself about 3 a.m., shaking me awake with a hail of needles and twigs that exploded against the sides of my tent as if sent as a reminder to expect the unexpected.

Fraser's journal noted the propensity of the canyon through which he was passing to spawn powerful winds—"blowing a hurricane from the south," says one entry—and my weather radio had been forecasting a low pressure front moving inland from the coast.

In fact the arid winds that consistently sweep through the sunburnt cordillera are one of the reasons that so many First Nations had extensive fishing camps along the river. Families travelled hundreds of kilometres because the combination of heat, low humidity and diminishing fat content in sockeye salmon as they swim upstream creates ideal conditions for drying salmon in preparation for the lean winter months. People had already begun to gather at their fishing sites when Fraser's expedition passed by on its journey to the Pacific Ocean in the late spring of 1808.

The evening had been dead calm and a bit sultry when I pitched my tent across the Fraser River and a bit upstream from Lillooet about 320 kilometres north of Vancouver. Not far from my campsite, people still gather to dip net and wind-dry sockeye on wooden racks much as they did in Fraser's day.

Fraser's party was feasted here on fish, roots and berries. I dined alone on

A combination of heat, canyon winds and just the right fat content in salmon migrating through the arid rain shadow cast by British Columbia's Coast Range create ideal conditions for much prized wind-dried sockeye, dried on racks like these near Lillooet. *Glenn Baglo/*Vancouver Sun

Fishing with a dip net as his ancestors did in Simon Fraser's time two centuries earlier, Nolan Alec lands another salmon at the Bridge River rapids near Lillooet, BC. *Glenn Baglo/* Vancouver Sun

military field rations left over from an earlier trip into the bush on patrol with the Pacific Rangers militia unit—scalloped potatoes and apple sauce in foil pouches heated by adding water to a catalyst. I reviewed my notes, tapping the interactive screen of my hand-held computer, a device that would have been mind-boggling to the man I was writing about. I'd become obsessive about my own notes since reading in Fraser's journal about how John Stuart lost his irreplaceable notebook in 1806 when one of his men accidentally flipped it into the Parsnip River.

Stephen Hume pitched his tent beside the river near Lillooet where Simon Fraser spent the night and, to his surprise, found a wireless hot spot that let him e-mail home. *Bill Keay/*Vancouver Sun

Somewhere near this same spot, the explorer made his own journal entry with a quill pen and India ink that he'd have mixed himself by adding water to powder shaved from a solid block of pigment. The wooden pencil with graphite "lead" and the straight pen using a steel nib had just been invented, but they wouldn't come into widespread use for years. It seems unlikely that the high technology of 1800 had made its way to a fur-trade frontier where most men still hunted with bow and flint-tipped arrow.

The entry for June 15, 1808, suggests Fraser was assailed by a deepening sense of isolation and menace. The terrain had defeated his plans to paddle down the river. He'd been lucky in encountering friends among the Secwepemc, but a few days earlier he'd described the snow-covered mountains through which he was forced to travel on foot as "the most savage that can be imagined." And his first encounter with the St'at'imc or Lillooet Indians had been tense.

The meeting had been peaceful enough. Fraser wrote that the St'at'imc—he used the Secwepemc name, Askettih—"looked manly and had really the appearance of warriors," and he'd personally shaken hands with 137 men. Still he was aware of hostility between the two tribes. The St'at'imc observed pointedly that they'd been attacked by a Secwepemc war party the year before. Some even suggested that Fraser and his men were really enemies in disguise. It took some statesmanlike diplomacy by their guide from Soda Creek to calm things down.

The flare-up left Fraser nervous. He made camp and mounted a military-style watch from a defensive position on the opposite side of the river from the village. Protected by nine-metre-high palisades, it lay across from present-day Lillooet.

"Here we are, in a strange Country, surrounded with dangers and difficulties, among numberless tribes of savages who never saw the face of a white man. Our situation is critical and highly unpleasant; however we shall endeavour to make the best of it; what cannot be cured must be endured," he wrote.

Fraser may have felt that he was now well and truly off the map of European knowledge. I discovered, on the other hand, that I'd pitched my tent in a wireless hot spot. My hand-held computer automatically logged itself onto an open network, with the swollen Fraser thundering along a few strides away as it had two hundred years ago. With the little iPAQ's backlit screen and light from a tiny LED lantern that runs off a rechargeable AA battery, I was able to pick up my email from home and the office, send a few messages of my own and upload a slew of notes via web mail to the safety of my desktop on the other side of the mountains. Fireless cooking and wireless communications—if things have changed this much in a couple of centuries, I wondered, what will the world be like in 2208?

Some things are eternal, for example, the weather. By 5 a.m. steady lashings of rain spattered across the tent fly. The wind gusted strongly enough to pull pegs from the loose, sandy soil and soon began lifting the tent. Then the fly tore loose and began flapping like a loose spinnaker sail. I decided to break camp, collapsed the tent, rolled a large river boulder onto it while I extracted the poles and then jammed the whole soggy bundle into a stuff bag.

It wasn't the most elegant departure, but then Fraser's party wasn't burdened with high-tech conveniences. His men slept in the open and got wet, crawled under their canoes or threw together a quick lean-to, and simply walked away the next morning. I could drive into town, get myself coffee and a croissant and sit in my rented car at Lillooet's Hanging Tree Park, taking a leisurely breakfast while the rain squalls marched down the canyon and across the flooding delta of the Seton River.

A day earlier I'd been sitting on a deadfall at Leon Creek where Fraser stowed his canoes and all but the most essential gear. He had surveyed the next rapids and concluded they were so violent "it was impossible for canoes even to approach with safety." Leon Creek gave me a moment of blissful tranquility, even though the mosquitoes were fierce. The temperature had topped out at 37 degrees Celsius. Even the parched landscape seemed breathless. Sitting in the deep shade from a

A cool strip of green in the dry landscape, Leon Creek tumbles toward the wild Fraser River. Simon Fraser cached canoes near here in 1808 and continued on foot. *Bill Keay/Vancouver Sun*

grove of old-growth fir that must have stood when Fraser passed, cooled by mist from the tumbling stream, I found a moment of respite in which to imagine what the explorers must have felt as they contemplated what lay behind and what might lie ahead.

For me, the seventy kilometres of rough forestry road between Leon Creek and Lillooet meant an hour's drive at most, even with steep, hair-raising switchbacks on loose gravel and sheer drops into the canyon below. For Fraser, it meant four days of hungry, thirsty bushwhacking burdened by forty-kilogram packs. His men's moccasin-clad feet were continually bruised and cut by sharp stones on a trail that took them almost a kilometre high on the shoulder of the Camelsfoot Range.

At one point the men's thirst reduced Fraser to digging out a seep, the journal says. He let the hole fill with "a substance something like Borax, which had a saline or sulphurous taste" and they drank "this nauseous liquid."

High on this same mountainside, Fraser had made first contact with the St'at'imc people he called Askittihs or Askettihs. Silent as phantoms, they materialized out of nothing.

"All at once, and when we least expected a surprise, seven Askittihs presented themselves before us with their bows and arrows in readiness for attack; they conceived us to be enemies, but upon coming nearer they discovered from our appearance and demeanour their mistake, laid by their weapons, joined us and we shook hands."

Fraser's guide and interpreter from Soda Creek had gone ahead, so he and the St'at'imc warriors were unable to understand each other, but they stayed together. Once they caught up with the Secwepemc chief and the purpose of the expedition was explained, the warriors left, promising to return with provisions for the hungry visitors.

"Soon after our new friends accompanied by our old chief, who had gone ahead to the lodges of these people, joined us, and brought different kinds of Roots, wild onions formed into syrope [syrup], excellent dried salmon, and some berries," Fraser writes.

But there was more to satisfy Fraser than the generous hospitality. "These Indians say the sea is about ten nights from their village," says his journal. "One of the old men, a very talkative fellow, and we understand a great warrior, had been at the sea; saw great canoes and white men. He observed that the chiefs of the white men were well dressed and very proud, for, continued he, getting up and clapping his hands upon his hips, then strutting about with an air of consequence, 'This is the way they go.'"

Significant sections of the old trail by which Fraser was led from Leon Creek to Lillooet are intact and can still be hiked. (To find it, cross the Bridge River north of Lillooet and then take the West Pavilion Road.) According to the Lillooet Naturalist Society, hikers intending to cover the whole trail should expect some rough going, take plenty of water and allow for about half a day's travel for the round trip, with a little extra time to eat lunch and savour some of the spectacular views of the river and its canyons.

The trail is ancient, possibly one of the oldest human-made transportation features in British Columbia. At Keatley Creek, for example, about midway between Leon Creek and Lillooet, Simon Fraser University archeologist Brian Hayden spent a decade excavating one village. It extended more than a kilometre along the Fraser River and featured some of the largest pit house depressions found in western Canada.

People inhabited the complex in three phases reaching back seven thousand years. Its pit houses had been occupied for four thousand years before the Shang dynasty arose in China, which should give pause to those who assume our history began with the gold rush, or even with Fraser's founding of New Caledonia. Yet after six thousand years of occupation, residents abruptly abandoned the Keatley Creek site about eleven hundred years ago—one more mystery to unravel.

Approaching what is now Lillooet, Fraser's party camped at Bridge River, a stunningly beautiful place where people still gather at the rapids each summer to dip net salmon and hang them on the racks, where the rich, red flesh of wind-dried sockeye makes a vivid splash of colour on the drab desert browns. The next morning Fraser probably crossed on the ingenious St'at'imc suspension bridge that was still there when two American miners tore it down, put up their own bridge and began charging their fellow prospectors a twenty-five-cent toll in 1858. From Bridge River, Fraser continued to the forks of the Seton River and observed "the metropolis of the Askettih Nation," a well-fortified site on the east side of the river just across from Lillooet's present townsite.

The St'at'imc helpfully mapped the next section of the river for him. It was difficult and dangerous, they said, and they depicted another large river to the east running parallel to the Fraser River. This can only have been the Columbia, and their knowledge of it serves to indicate how widely the Indians—that later settlers considered "primitive"—travelled and traded. Although Fraser was the first European to arrive at Lillooet, for example, European trade goods had preceded him. He saw a new copper tea kettle and a large gun that he guessed was of Russian make.

At Lillooet, Fraser bartered a file and a kettle for thirty dried salmon and a canoe. The next day he obtained a second canoe for medicines he provided to a sick man. The canoes must have seemed a godsend. The heaviest packs could travel by water while the rest of the party continued, still on foot but now travelling light.

An ancient stone oven collapses back into the parched sagebrush desert near the Churn Creek Protected Area about 120 km north of Lillooet, BC. *Bill Keay/*Vancouver Sun

Fraser's Secwepemc guides handed Fraser off to the St'at'imc chief, then slipped away home. The new guide agreed to lead the expedition to the next nation, whom Fraser called the Hacamaugh; they were called the Thompson Indians in anthropological literature. They call themselves the Nlaka'pamux.

Once again I turned to Nick Doe's translation of John Stuart's meridian observation into contemporary navigational values. Then I used my hand-held GPS to find the spot where it was taken. Fraser, the device confirmed, was in the vicinity of Texas Creek and travelling on the west bank of the river. Texas Creek and its spectacular canyon held special interest for me. Daniel Boersma, a prospector at Lillooet, told me about a strange feature he'd found there while looking for jade boulders and provided directions.

"I was following a trail along an old bench on the north side of the creek," he said. "I found a large kikwillie [pit house] hole, and while I was looking at it, I saw something unusual in the bush. Just above the river, I found a large stone fire circle.

"It's very, very old but it's not Indian, it looks European. I think it's too big for something left by miners [in 1858]. It's a size more appropriate to a brigade-sized group of twenty men or so [Fraser's party numbered twenty-four or more]. And here's the interesting thing, one of the stones has been pushed out of place by a tree that grew under it. From the size of that tree, it's probably 150 to 200 years old."

Unfortunately the dirty weather became a deluge, the creeks boiled and the muddy roads became too slippery for my rental car to risk. I had to leave the search for the fire circle for another day. Boersma's tale reminded me that plenty of mysteries surround Fraser's exploits, however, and some of them created conundrums even for the explorer. What was the "sword of tremendous size made of sheet iron," for example, that he said was carried by one of the people he met near Texas Creek?

Another first encounter occurred on June 16 as the two canoes proceeded downriver while Fraser and the rest of his party followed on land. A party of Nlaka'pamux horsemen rode up, and with them were two riders from another tribe. Fraser called them Suihonie, and they were probably Shoshone, whose home territory was in Idaho, Montana, Wyoming and Utah. A Shoshone woman, Sacajawea, had been the guide and interpreter for the Lewis and Clark expedition to the mouth of the Columbia in 1805.

"All were exceedingly well dressed in leather, and were on horseback," Fraser wrote. "They have a great quantity of shells and blue beads, and we saw a broken silver broach such as the Sauteus [a tribe from east of the Rockies] wear, among them. They were kind to us, and assisted us at the carrying place with their horses."

His description makes poignant reading, considering that in 1862 an American militia in Utah would massacre the western Shoshone.

"The chief invited us to his quarters; his son, by his orders, served us upon a handsome mat, and regaled us with salmon and roots. Our men had some also, and they procured, besides, several Dogs which is always a favourite dish with the Canadian voyageurs," Fraser wrote of the Nlaka'pamux.

Not far from the site of the dog feast, I encountered Lloyd Stock, who lives on the banks of the Fraser close to where Stuart recorded his meridian observation. Stock took me out into his backyard, but not just to admire his prolific tomato plants. He pointed to geological evidence of an immense landslide that had crossed the Fraser at Texas Creek about eleven hundred years ago, in all likelihood damming the river—an impoundment, in scholarly language—and preventing the salmon from getting farther up stream. Famine would certainly have followed. Written there in the earth itself, Stock said, was a likely answer to the mystery of that abandoned village at Keatley Creek.

But like the explorer, I was impatient to get moving, so I said goodbye to Stock, his wife Gladys and her wonderful garden and pushed on past the Stein River to where Fraser arrived at a village of about four hundred people.

"Some of them appear very old; they live among mountains, and enjoy pure air, seem cleanly inclined, and make use of wholesome food," Fraser wrote. "We had every reason to be thankful for our reception at this place; the Indians shewed us every possible attention and supplied our wants as much as they could. We had salmon, berries, oil and roots in abundance, and our men had six dogs. Our tent was pitched near the camp and we enjoyed peace and security during our stay."

The expedition had now reached present-day Lytton or Camchin, as the Nlaka'pamux call the confluence of the Fraser River and its largest tributary, the Thompson. Fraser named the river for his friend and colleague David Thompson, who was exploring its headwaters far to the east.

Yet if Fraser felt he could relax a bit with his new Nlaka'pamux friends on his journey to the sea, ahead lay the most difficult stretch of all—Hell's Gate and the Black Canyon.

Simon Fraser

26

THE GATES OF HELL

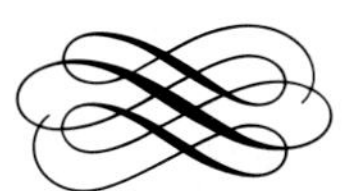

At the place the Sto:lo call Th'exelis, the sun beat down like a copper hammer and thermal shimmers rebounded from naked rock in a blast so fierce it seemed to congeal the dry air. Beneath the ledge on which I stood, the mighty Fraser River churned by, its milky green whirlpools peeling off the turbulent edge of an eddy and then expanding as they pinwheeled away on the tireless current. A bit farther downstream they'd be consumed by the devouring grandmother of all whirlpools—Hemq'elq to the Sto:lo—a guardian at the gates, set there to menace any coastal raiders foolhardy enough to assume the river meant easy passage for their great seagoing war canoes.

Despite the heat the water was icy, having melted from snow fields and glaciers on a quarter of a million square kilometres of mountains. Even the breeze from its chill passage offered no relief in the summer furnace that the canyon becomes above Yale, about 175 kilometres upriver from Vancouver.

Place names like Th'exelis and Hemq'elq, I:yem and Aseláw, Lhilheltalets and Sxwóxwiymelh don't appear on conventional maps of British Columbia. Colonizers throughout time have exerted their symbolic sovereignty over newly annexed territory by replacing the names of the old order with the names of the new, in our unimaginative case mostly the names of explorers, settlers, soldiers and politicians. Yet the old names endure in the mental landscape of the native peoples who were absorbed into a new and inescapable reality, and increasingly they are reborn on the maps prepared for treaty-making that can shape a new future capable of fully

As the river thundered through canyons like Hell's Gate that were truly impassable by water, Fraser said it was a place where no human being should venture. *Rick Blacklaws*

acknowledging the rich and often repressed past from which it springs.

I'd asked at the Sto:lo tribal administration for directions to this dramatic spot because Simon Fraser was brought here in 1808. He was shown the same landmark and had stood, I had little doubt, just about where I placed my feet. And in more human terms, he likely seized the same opportunity that I did, staining his fingers with the juice of the fat, blue-black Saskatoon berries that grow in profusion along the river. All the accounts, both native Indian and his own, remark that the berries were ripe and rich when he passed through the country.

Fraser's expedition to the Pacific had spent the previous eight days struggling down more than a hundred tortuous kilometres of near-continuous rapids to get here. These hardy men had been ejected into white water when their canoes were upended or smashed to splinters on the rocks. Miraculously nobody had drowned, but Fraser's tough voyageurs had become so reluctant to use the few dugout canoes they could buy or borrow from the native Indians that Fraser himself had embarked in the bow paddler's key position to lead them down some dangerous rapids.

Eventually he had abandoned the water, leading his men as they clambered along the slippery bluffs above. They watched as packs, a valuable kettle and stones displaced by their scrambling feet bounced and bounded into the abyss. Frequently

In the sheer Fraser Canyon, the explorer's journal compared ingenious native suspension bridges and lashed scaffolding to a sailing ship's rigging. *John Innes, "Simon Fraser in the Fraser Canyon on His Journey to the Sea," A.D. 1808 [1925], Simon Fraser University Collection, commissioned by Native Sons of British Columbia*

they traversed apparently impossible cliff faces, led over a spindly latticework—it resembled the shrouds of a sailing ship, he wrote—of native Indian ladders and suspension bridges. Made with poles lashed together, they dangled above the torrent from ropes woven out of rawhide and vegetable fibre. Sometimes the passage was so precarious that Fraser permitted the nervous men to part with their precious guns, passing their only means of defence hand-to-hand to Nlaka'pamux guides as they edged forward, their arms spread for balance and their faces pressed against the cliff walls.

"A safe and convenient passage to the Natives," Fraser observed wryly, "but we, who had not the advantages of their experience, were often in imminent danger."

Despite these trials, Fraser nevertheless maintained an alert curiosity about everything he saw, filling his journals with observations about the people he met—"very civil"—and their customs, from burial practices to public ceremonies. Just upstream from where I stood, he described "tombs of a curious construction . . . superior to any thing of the kind I ever saw among the savages. They are about fifteen feet long and of the form of a chest of drawers. Upon the boards and posts are carved beasts and birds, in a curious but rude manner, yet pretty well proportioned."

A little farther on, having crossed a suspension bridge at Siwash Creek, Fraser first encountered Sto:lo people—he called them the Ackinroe nation—"where we were received with as much kindness as if we had been their lost relations. Neat mats were spread for our reception, and plenty of Salmon served in wooden dishes was placed before us.

"They have rugs made from the wool of Aspai, or wild goat, and from Dog's hair, which are equally as good as those found in Canada. We observed that the dogs were lately shorn," he wrote.

He noted their ornamentation, "shells of different kinds, shell beads, brass made into pipes hanging from the neck or across the shoulders, bracelets of large brass wire," their weaving patterns, "stripes of different colours crossing at right angles resembling at a distance a Highland plaid," the construction of their fishing nets, the shape of their hats, "which are made of wattap [the spruce root cord used to make bark canoes] had broad rims and diminish gradually to the top" and methods for making canoes, "hollowed with fire and then polished."

Near what is now Yale, he saw "an excellent house 46 feet by 23 feet and constructed like American frame houses . . . On the opposite side of the river there is a considerable village with houses similar to the one upon this side."

It was here, "a little distance above the village where the rapids terminate, the natives informed us, that white people like us came there from below; they shewed us indented marks which the white people made upon the rocks, but which, by the bye, seemed to us to be natural marks."

Albert "Sonny" McHalsie agreed to guide me to the place. His great-great-great-

Near Yale, BC, Stephen Hume examines the ruin of a stone fortification used by the Sto:lo to defend important fishing sites in the Fraser Canyon from coastal raiders. *Bill Keay/*Vancouver Sun

grandfather, Sexyel, a famous hunter of grizzly bears, had been there when Fraser was feasted near Siwash Creek, and his grave is at the since-abandoned village site at Aseláw.

A few hours earlier, McHalsie—Naxaxalhts'i in his own language, a *sí:yá:m* (influential leader) in his own culture, but Sonny to just about everyone—had been working in the cool glow of the computer screen in his Sto:lo Research and Resource Management Centre office at Chilliwack.

Now, in the unrelenting glare of the sun, he kneeled beside the smooth saddle of rock that is one of the important places in Sto:lo cosmology. He pointed to the most obvious of what I later counted as twenty-five marks on the stone's surface.

"Th'exelis means 'gritting his teeth,'" McHalsie explained. He slipped into the saddle and sat facing the river. His blunt fingertips traced the gouges in the stone, some deep polished grooves, some barely discernible, thin as knife cuts.

"X:áls sat here," he said. "Every time he used his power, he marked the rock where he gripped it. He was gritting his teeth from the effort. That's from his right hand, that's from his left. He threw a thunderbolt from here. You can see where it struck over there."

I looked along his pointing arm. It directed my eye to a jagged streak of quartz in the distant rock. These marks, he said, were left to forever remind the Sto:lo of what he did. X:áls, McHalsie explained, is a being from the beginning of time, from

On June 28, 1808, Sto:lo guides brought Simon Fraser to Th'exelis—"gritting his teeth"—near Yale, BC. Elder Sonny McHalsie points to the spot where the the transformer X:áls left marks in the stone during a supernatural battle. *Bill Keay/*Vancouver Sun

the age known as *sx?xwijoh* (when the world was mixed up), when animals spoke like humans and people could change their shape. So X:áls travelled the world setting things right, giving things the shapes they have today, putting all in its proper place, transforming the deserving for good or ill.

He changed a good and generous man named Xepáy into the cedar tree so that he might continue giving to the people for eternity. Another he transformed into the sturgeon so that the people might have food in the winter months when few salmon enter the rivers.

Some he punished, turning them to stone: the three wise *sí:yá:ms* to whom X:áls taught writing but who kept this knowledge to themselves; a woman who had food and wouldn't share with the hungry; a powerful Indian doctor—on the Great Plains he'd be called a medicine man, and an anthropologist might say shaman—who used his powers to benefit himself instead of his people. Farther upstream the Nlaka'pamux called the transformer Kex.xoiem. He took the form of Coyote, travelling up the canyons with his assistants and fulfilling the same mythic function, giving good people their places on the land and changing bad people into rocks to remind those left behind of the consequences.

So the "white people" that the Sto:lo told Fraser had travelled upstream and marked the rock were not other European explorers from the coast, but the supernatural transformers who in the ancient past had changed their world into its present form.

For McHalsie narratives like these are framed within a universe of references and allusions, both conscious and unconscious, spoken and unspoken, of which only fragments are accessible to an audience like me, not being steeped from birth in the cosmologies from which they emerge. As I listened to his evocative descriptions, I was acutely aware that at best I'd be able to offer readers only a pale reflection.

Nevertheless, Fraser came to this spot late on the afternoon of June 28, 1808, for reasons that were rooted directly in that world view. After journeying downstream from Camchin, now Lytton, his party had reached Spuzzum by land the previous day. They'd stopped at a camp of about sixty people and spent the night after being "hospitably entertained" with roasted and boiled salmon, green and dried berries, oil and onions.

Spuzzum, Fraser observed, was a territorial boundary between the Nlaka'pamux and the Sto:lo. Just as the Secwepemc had handed him off to the St'at'imc, who had handed him off to the Nlaka'pamux, now he was being handed off to the Sto:lo. All had stories of pale-complexioned, blue-eyed supernatural beings who had travelled up the canyon wielding their powers, never to be seen again.

Word of Fraser's journey downriver had preceded him at every stop, as it had since he left Soda Creek. Now, just as native Indian prophets had foretold, a white-skinned transformer had returned. As X:áls had done in the mixed-up time, this one was once again travelling down the river for mysterious reasons, accompanied by helpers who carried sticks capable of hurling thunderbolts.

As I listened to McHalsie, the horn of a diesel locomotive sounded, a thin wail on the far side of the river. Brown boxcars and flatbeds laden with colour-coded shipping containers flicked past in apparent silence, the train's brassy signal mostly subsumed into the roar of white water foaming down chutes around a glistening black outcrop.

We call the outcrop Lady Franklin Rock, named in honour of a brief visit in 1861 by the widow of Sir John Franklin, who disappeared in 1847 while exploring the Arctic. To Fraser, trying to decipher its story through at least four languages, it was Bad Rock. To the Sto:lo, McHalsie told me, it is Xéylxelamós, all that remains of that strong but self-serving Indian doctor whom X:áls had changed to stone in a fierce battle involving supernatural powers.

"He had a third eye," McHalsie said of the stone sorcerer, whose attributes included the power to summon underwater monsters. "On the back side of that rock is his third eye. We're not allowed to look at it." Then he pointed abruptly to the large eddy below the rock. "There's an underwater black bear that lives there. That's his home, in that little bay."

Up the hill and behind us, traffic whizzed by on Highway 97, one world passing through another, oblivious. Here and there pickup trucks were parked in highway pullouts, intermittent evidence of Sto:lo families making early preparations at ancient fishing sites where they have harvested the summer and fall runs since there have been salmon in the river.

As Fraser had been two hundred years earlier, the train and the traffic were a momentary intrusion, visitors passing through the looking glass at one of those strange interfaces where different worlds appear as transparent palimpsests, the ghostly images of one reality superimposed as imprints upon the other. If the train was a messenger from the present world of science, industry and commerce, a direct descendant from the eighteenth-century enlightenment for which Fraser himself served as an envoy in 1808, it was passing through a far more ancient world of myth and prophecy, miraculous transformations and inexplicable supernatural forces.

It is likely that Fraser—although his journal suggests he was aware of their presence—could no more comprehend the complexity and depth of the spiritual worlds inhabited by the Secwepemc, St'at'imc, Nlaka'pamux and Sto:lo, to whom he suddenly appeared, than they could comprehend his own.

"I don't think Simon Fraser had the ghost of an idea as to how he was perceived by the nations through which he passed," said Andrea Laforet, the director of ethnology at the Canadian Museum of Civilization and co-author of *Spuzzum: Fraser Canyon Histories, 1808–1939,* a study of Fraser Canyon oral histories published in 1998.

"There were no other people like him there. There were no other people of that cultural origin for local people to make comparisons. Nor were their actions entirely explicable to the Nlaka'pamux," she said over an air-conditioned lunch in Ottawa.

"Nor did they understand, entirely, what they encountered. He would not have dreamed that once he passed through he'd be recast as Coyote and other supernatural beings." One aged informant, reaching for a metaphor that was comprehensible in contemporary terms, even cast Fraser as an analog of Jesus Christ, one more example of alien worlds seeping into one another.

In fact Fraser's behaviour of skilfully attempting to wheedle, barter, buy and in some cases extort the help he needed to complete his mission, Laforet said, helped reinforce the cultural metaphors by which the Nlaka'pamux attempted to comprehend who he was.

"Fraser's party tried to take some canoes. Well, Coyote was a trickster and quite capable of doing shady things. It was a fixed enough impression that it made it into the oral tradition and persisted over five or six generations," she said.

In another story, recorded by University of Victoria historian Wendy Wickwire in a remarkable paper published more than a decade ago in the *Canadian Historical Review,* Fraser startled some girls bathing at the river's edge. While they stared at him, naked and dumbfounded, he "sized them all up." Coyote, too, was known to have an eye for women, often when they were other men's wives.

Wickwire examined Fraser's journals and compared them for points of congruence with accounts of his first contact with the Nlaka'pamux, both in the stories collected by nineteenth-century ethnologist James Teit and in oral histories she acquired from contemporary elders Annie York and Louis Phillips, both of who have since died.

Among the descriptions of Fraser's arrival collected by Teit was one by Semalitsa, a woman from Stein River, whose grandmother was present as a young girl.

"She saw two canoes with red flags hoisted, come downstream. She ran and told her mother and the people gathered to see the strange sight. Seeing so many people gathered, the canoes put ashore and several men came ashore. Each canoe carried a number of men [perhaps six or seven in each], and many of them wore strange dresses, and everything about them was strange. Some of the men looked like Indians, and others looked like what we call white men. Among them was a Shuswap chief who acted as interpreter. Our people were not afraid of the strang-

The growing turbulence of the river forced frequent portages of increasing difficulty and began to frustrate Simon Fraser as he approached the dry mountains around Lillooet, BC. *Bill Keay/Vancouver Sun*

ers, nor were they hostile to them. The strangers produced a large pipe, and had a ceremonial smoke with some of our men. After distributing a few presents, they boarded their canoes and went on to Lytton."

Word had also reached Lytton before Fraser arrived. He was met by twelve hundred people, sitting quietly in rows. They had come from far and wide to witness the visit of a supernatural figure appearing in human form. They came on foot and on horseback from up the Botanie Valley, from Spence's Bridge, from Fountain Valley, from the Stein Valley and Siska Creek, from Nikaia and Pooeyelth creeks.

"The principal chief invited us over the river," Fraser wrote on June 19. "We crossed and He received us at the water side, where, assisted by several others, he took me by the arms and conducted me up the hill to the camp where his people

This elaborately adorned chief's grave photographed near Lytton, BC, in 1860 is similar to those noted by Simon Fraser in his journal half a century earlier. *Frederick Dally, Glenbow Archives NA-674-16*

were sitting in rows . . . I had to shake hands with all of them."

"Then the Great Chief made a long harangue, in course of which he pointed to the sun, to the four quarters of the world and then to us, and then he introduced his father, who was old and blind, and was carried by another man, who also made a harangue of some length. The old [blind] man was placed near us, and with some emotion, often stretched out both his hands in order to feel ours."

The chief who made the great oration was Tcexe'x, and he had run the fifteen kilometres from Botanie Valley. When he was pointing at the sun and then at Fraser, he was telling his people that this was the "son of Sun." He later guided the expedition through the difficult terrain to Sto:lo territory, prompting Fraser to comment, "The chief of the Camshins is the greatest chief we have seen; he behaved towards us uncommonly well. I made him a present of a large silver broach which he immediately fixed on his head, and he was exceedingly well pleased with our attention."

The journal corroborates the Nlaka'pamux oral histories. A woman named Waxtko, a relative of Tcexe'x, told Teit almost a century later, "This chief so pleased Sun, that he gave him a present of a large silver broach, or some other similar ornament, which he had on his person. On several occasions Tcexe'x used this attached to his hair in front, or on the front of his head. When I was a girl, I saw it worn by his sons . . . it was probably buried with the third brother who had it, as it disappeared about the time of his death."

Wickwire's paper quotes Annie York, who says that the old Lytton chief CexpentlEm, another orator—his equally great descendant David Spintlum, who was born in 1812 and died in 1887, ended the bloodshed when miners and native Indians fought for control of the Fraser Canyon fifty years later—also told his followers that Fraser was "sent by Sun."

In this oral tradition, York reported that "Fraser's captain"—that must have been either John Stuart or Jules Quesnel—warned people not to touch them or they would catch a lethal disease. She said that CexpentlEm reiterated that the party was not to be harmed. Did Fraser's lieutenant offer such a warning? Or was this a conflation with a later memory from 1864 of William Brewster, a road foreman who made a similar threat about sending smallpox among the Chilcotin and pulled the trigger on a bloody uprising?

Oral histories are not precise in the way the mainstream documentary record purports to be—although it is also rife with conflations, misinterpretations and outright error. Often oral history is rendered as metaphor or parable, and those telling it must cast the story within the framework of their own understanding.

Wickwire, for example, compared two accounts of one of the close calls that afflicted the expedition in the worst sections of the canyon. For Fraser the voyage had deteriorated beyond Lytton into an almost continuous series of impassable rapids. In the vicinity of what's been called Jackass Mountain since a pack animal

A jagged rim of wind- and water-eroded hoodoos looms above the Fraser River south of Williams Lake, BC. Simon Fraser's journal comments on the "grotesque banks or pinnacles." *Bill Keay/*Vancouver Sun

fell to its death there during the gold rush, the voyageurs were still game to try and run the white water. They undertook this foolhardy project while Fraser and Stuart were in their tents writing up their logs about the amazing events of the previous few days.

In the first cascade they attempted, one of the canoes swamped and capsized. The crew made it ashore save for one paddler named D'Allaire who became entangled with the thwarts, finally extricated himself, and with no alternative, rode astride the upturned canoe as it was swept down the boiling chutes.

An anxious Fraser, after finding D'Allaire making his way wearily back to camp, quoted the paddler's own words: "In the second or third cascade (for I cannot remember which) the canoe from a great height plunged into the deep eddy at the foot, and striking with violence against the bottom, splitted in two. Here I lost my recollection, which however, I soon recovered and was surprised to find myself on a smooth easy current with only one half of the canoe in my arms. In this condition I continued through several cascades, until the stream fortunately conducted me into an eddy at the foot of a high and steep rock."

D'Allaire lost his grip, but at that moment a large wave deposited him on the shore. After surveying the rapid, Fraser expressed astonishment at his survival. The Nlaka'pamux telling of the event, as collected by Teit, differs considerably.

"In the middle of the river, a short distance below Lytton, the Moon, who was steersman of the canoe, disappeared with it under the water. The others came out of the water and sat down on a rock close to the river. Then Skwia'xEnEmux [arrow-armed person] fired many lightning arrows, and nmu'ipEm [diver] dived many times into the river. The Sun sat still and smoked; while Coyote, Kokwe'la, and Morning-Star danced. Coyote said, 'Moon will never come up again with the canoe;' but Sun said, 'Yes, in the evening he will appear.' Just after sunset, Moon appeared holding the canoe, and came ashore. All of them embarked, and going down the river, were never seen again."

The Nlaka'apamux may have seen events involving Fraser as evidence of supernatural fore-knowledge and power, but for the explorer things seemed to be going from bad to worse.

"I have been for a long period among the Rocky Mountains," Fraser wrote on June 26 as he proceeded downriver following the near-drowning, "but I have never seen anything equal to this country, for I cannot find words to describe our situation at times. We had to pass where no human being should venture."

Having passed safely through the canyons with the help of his Nlaka'pamux and Sto:lo guides, Fraser reached Lhilheltalets, an island just above Hope, where he stayed two hours for a feast of salmon, oil, roots and fresh raspberries before pushing on. At the next village, somewhere in the vicinity of Chilliwack, he saw the first real evidence that he might be closing on his goal. The country was opening out, the land was flattening and "the river is more than two miles broad and is interspersed with islands."

More important, as Fraser and his weary men prepared to settle in for the night—after being fed sturgeon by their hosts, whose politeness seemed so extreme that he jotted his worries about their sincerity—he saw European trade goods from the sea, "a large copper kettle shaped like a jar, and a large English hatchet stamped Sargaret with the figure of a crown."

His quest for the Pacific was now within days of its objective. The greatest threat to his success lay not behind him in the boiling canyons of the great river, however, but ahead in the gentler landscape of its vast and fertile flood plain.

Simon Fraser

27

"AS THE FIRE CONSUMES THE DRY GRASS OF THE FIELD"

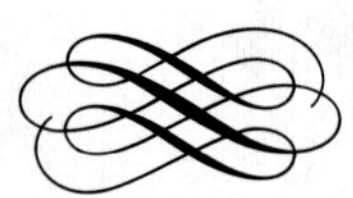

The shallow depressions left by long vanished pit houses were lined up in a neat row along the banks of the Fraser River. Nine were visible. Another twenty-seven lay hidden in the scant underbrush. Thirty-six in all, they'd probably been home to about two hundred people.

Sunlight filtered in through a rustling canopy of leaves, and the Fraser slid silently by its polished gravel banks, a river of sparkling green light just beyond a whispering screen of willow and spindly alder reaching for the sun. But no birds sang in the shadows, and there was an strange, cool stillness to the place.

Simon Fraser likely didn't even notice the slight opening in the trees when his brigade passed, finally out of the mountains and riding the booming freshet late on the afternoon of June 29, 1808. That's because there was nobody there. Sxwóx-wiymelh, on what is now the Chawathil Indian Reserve, about ten kilometres west of Hope on Highway 7, had been abandoned for more than twenty-five years by the time Fraser passed in his canoes bound for the sea.

The turf-clad log roofs had already collapsed into the subterranean dwellings, burying the woven mats, the decorated cedar baskets and carved wooden utensils, the colourful dog-hair blankets and the earth floors packed so smooth they seemed like a synthetic material. Season after season, as the rotting wood slumped, the depressions had filled with leaf drift and storm debris. All that remained after a couple of centuries was a hint of their presence so faint that I'd never have noticed

Sto:lo elder Sonny McHalsie takes a reflective moment at Sxwóxwiymelh, a village near Hope, BC, obliterated by smallpox during an epidemic about twenty-five years before Simon Fraser passed on June 29,1808.
*Bill Keay/*Vancouver Sun

them if Sto:lo historian and cultural advisor Sonny McHalsie hadn't guided me.

Those shallow depressions were more than archeological curiosities; they were mass graves, enduring evidence of a culture-shattering event that had traumatized entire societies for many generations. Translated from Halkomelem into English, Sxwóxwiymelh, the name of the abandoned village, means something like "a lot of people died all at once."

According to Sto:lo elder Susan Peters, McHalsie said, people at Sxwóxwiymelh had died at the rate of twenty-five to thirty victims a day. Those still alive placed the bodies in their pit houses, then burned them and collapsed the roofs to cover corpses that were piling up too fast to be disposed of according to traditional burial rites. Any survivors fled. What killed them so suddenly and in such numbers may have been a hemorrhagic form of smallpox, a pestilence that moved swiftly and with horrific effects that were almost always lethal.

Accounts reported by a Roman Catholic missionary in 1847, cited by Elizabeth Fenn in her book *Pox Americana: The Great Smallpox Epidemic of 1775–82*, give an inkling of the cataclysm. Jesuit Gregory Mengarini said, Fenn wrote, that he was told of a plague about seventy years earlier by Flathead informants who had been neighbours of the Kootenays in what is now northern Idaho and Montana. He was told the victims developed either red pustules, after which they died a few days later, or black pustules, from which death was almost immediate for nearly 100 percent of those infected.

The latter symptom, Fenn suggests, sounds like a hemorrhagic form of smallpox in which those infected bleed out through the eyes, nose and other orifices as the virus attacks internal mucous membranes. Those afflicted thus succumb more quickly and in much greater numbers than those suffering the more usual symptoms. The mortality rate tops 97 percent.

In another account cited by Fenn, Asa Bowen Smith wrote in 1840 that very old members of the Nez Perce, neighbours of the Okanagans in Washington state, told him of a plague in their childhood that had killed almost everyone. The disease, Smith concluded, was "the most virulent form of smallpox."

These accounts are important because they help map a route for the disease across the Rocky Mountains, westward along the Snake River and then into the Columbia River system, where the Lewis and Clark expedition of 1805 reported survivors with the characteristic scarring of smallpox.

It was a small leap from the Columbia by swift seagoing canoe to the densely populated Fraser Valley, and by horse to the southern Interior of BC—where Simon Fraser reported Shoshones from the Great Plains were present in a Secwepemc camp during his journey down the river. Whichever variant of smallpox swept across the Northwest Coast at the time that Sxwóxwiymelh was depopulated—perhaps both types, perhaps even accompanied by some other opportunistic communicable disease—it visited an almost unimaginable cataclysm upon the wealthy, complex and highly organized societies of what is now BC.

It may also have changed the course of history on the eastern side of the Rocky Mountains. In the spring of 1780 a flood of independent traders—some doing business with integrity and respect for aboriginal trappers, others predatory and irresponsible, some coercive and violent—had begun to enter the Great Plains around what is now Southern Manitoba and North Dakota. The worst shot each other, debauched native women, cheated clients and traded for prime furs with bad liquor laced with everything from hot pepper to gunpowder.

The fur trade was in "a forlorn state," wrote Alexander Mackenzie, at that time employed in the counting house of a small trading company in Montreal. When one trader tried to shut up a noisy, importuning drunk by spiking a drink with what proved a lethal dose of the opiate laudanum, violence erupted. A trader and several voyageurs were killed in the fray. Then Indians overran two trading forts on the Assiniboine River, and several Europeans and many Indians who had come there to trade were killed in the fighting. Traders abandoned their trade goods and the previous season's furs, took to their canoes and fled as fast as they could.

The British government would send no help. It was occupied with a ferocious civil war in the American colonies, and anyway, it looked with disapproval upon any interference with aboriginal nations. The Royal Proclamation of 1763 specified that such nations "should not be molested or disturbed."

Just as resistance to these independent traders was coalescing among the Cree, Sioux and Assiniboines, the most powerful tribes on the northern plains, smallpox changed everything.

In 1798, about the time of Simon Fraser's ascendancy in the North West Company's Athabasca District, Mackenzie wrote, "Nothing but the greatest calamity that could have befallen the natives, saved the traders from destruction: this was the smallpox, which spread its destructive and desolating power, as the fire consumes the dry grass of the field.

"The fatal infection spread around with a baleful rapidity which no flight could escape and with a fatal effect that nothing could resist. It destroyed with its pestilential breath whole families and tribes; and the horrid scene presented to those who had the melancholy and afflicting opportunity of beholding it, a combination of the dead and the dying. . . .

"To aggravate the picture, if aggravation were possible, may be added, the putrid carcasses which the wolves, with a furious voracity, dragged forth from the huts, or which were mangled within them by the dogs, whose hunger was satisfied with the disfigured remains of their masters. Nor was it uncommon for the father of a family, who the infection had not reached, to call them around him, to represent the cruel sufferings and horrid fate of their relations, from the influence of some evil spirit who was preparing to extirpate their race; and to incite them to baffle death, with all its horrors, by their own poinards.

"At the same time, if their hearts failed them in this necessary act, he was himself ready to perform the deed of mercy with his own hand, as the last act of affection . . . ."

The pestilence depopulated vast swathes of the western landscape, leaving the demoralized tatters of once-great tribes to negotiate future treaties. This created a still-prevailing misconception among those who came later to claim their land that it had always been unoccupied and under-used by its aboriginal inhabitants.

Some aboriginal cultures never recovered from the spiritual and psychological blow of the smallpox epidemic. Others endured almost two centuries before their populations rebounded into the mainstream. Yet many Canadians, ignorant of their own history, would increasingly describe the federal duties to compensate First Nations for their annexed land as "handouts."

When Fraser and his canoes swept down the river past the ghostly, unseen presence of Sxwówiymelh, he was the harbinger of a great demographic change. As the first visitor from the first European settlements west of the Rockies, he was a forerunner of the settler cultures that would come to occupy the depopulated landscapes of a biological catastrophe. The reverberations from those events continue to echo in the twenty-first century.

On July 1, 1808, the day before he reached the Pacific, Simon Fraser visited a powerful chief's house with carved posts like this one, depicting Chief Capilano. Harlan I. Smith photographed it with Charlie, Capilano III, at Musqueam Village in 1898. *American Museum of Natural History, New York: 411717*

Robert Boyd, a Portland-based anthropologist, more than twenty years ago began studying the epidemiology of introduced diseases and their impact upon what's popularly known as the Pacific Northwest. He pieced together oral traditions, historic accounts, archeological evidence and statistical analysis. What emerged was a truly frightening picture of the catastrophic effects of smallpox upon a West Coast population with no natural antibodies or immunities. In doctoral research that he refined into his book *The Coming of the Spirit of Pestilence: Introduced Infectious Diseases and Population Decline among Northwest Coast Indians, 1774–1874,* Boyd estimates—conservatively, he acknowledges—that an epidemic that entered what is now BC in 1784 had a mortality rate of at least 30 percent.

The Sto:lo people themselves in *You Are Asked To Witness: The Sto:lo in Canada's Pacific Coast History,* edited by University of Saskatchewan historian Keith Thor Carlson, who also serves as historian to the Sto:lo, estimate that two-thirds of the population perished within weeks of contracting the disease.

We can place that demographic event in a contemporary perspective. Imagine returning to Greater Vancouver from a summer vacation to find 1.5 million of your neighbours dead, many of their houses razed, those still standing full of corpses, the streets littered with bodies decomposing where they fell and the stunned, grieving survivors starving in the ruins because the entire infrastructure for food procurement was in a shambles.

Many of us are moved by the iconic image of an abandoned Chinese baby crying in the ruins during the Japanese occupation of Nanking just before World War II. Among the Sto:lo there is a similar image, although rather than a physical representation it is one flashed into the collective memory of what was and in part remains an oral culture.

You Are Asked To Witness recounts the story told by Peter Pierre, an elder from Katzie who was born in 1861. His story was collected by the great New Zealand-born ethnologist Diamond Jenness, who later served as chief anthropologist at the National Museum of Canada. Pierre told of his great-grandfather whose wife had recently given birth to twins. Custom required the parents of twins and their babies be sequestered away from the community for several months, and he had taken his family up into the mountains.

When he returned to the village, which was located where Pitt Lake empties into the Pitt River, "all his kinsmen and relatives lay dead in their homes; only in one house did there survive a baby boy, who was vainly sucking at his dead mother's breast. They rescued the child, burned all the houses together with the corpses that lay inside and built a new home for themselves several miles away. If you dig today on the site of any of the old villages you will uncover countless bones, the remains of Indians who perished during this epidemic of smallpox."

Valerie Patenaude, the archeologist who is curator at the Maple Ridge Museum, found just such physical evidence when she did rescue excavations at a Pitt River site near the Fraser that was threatened by highway expansion.

"It was a huge site, well over a kilometre long," she told me. "There were two occupation periods. The first was from 4,800 to 2,400 years ago. Then it was reoccupied from about 1,500 to 250 years ago. Then it was abandoned quite abruptly."

Patenaude's excavations found all kinds of artifacts that weren't supposed to be there, for example, a form of women's lip ornament called a labret that was normally not found at grave sites because it was passed from generation to generation, mother to daughter to granddaughter.

"But at the Pitt River site we found hundreds of labrets, all charred and blackened with fire. It was probably a smallpox epidemic. Yet neither the Katzie nor the Coquitlams claimed descent from those people. It's a strong possibility that site was used by people from South Vancouver Island who just never came back after the catastrophe."

And 150 kilometres to the southwest at Port Angeles in Washington state, the excavation of a Clallam village site uncovered during a construction project yielded similar evidence. Archeologists found burned house planks, abandoned tools, graves with multiple interments, unusual rituals and "children, dozens of them 12 years old or younger," reported Lynda Mapes for the *Seattle Times* in 2005. Radiocarbon samples from the site dated some of the burials to the period between 1780 and 1800.

If the Sto:lo assessment of mortality is correct, the disaster that befell the people of the Northwest Coast from 1782 to 1784 was of greater magnitude—considered as a percentage of population—than that visited upon civilians by the worst horrors of World War II, including the atomic bombs dropped on Hiroshima and Nagasaki. The atomic bombs killed 40 percent and about 25 percent of those cities' populations respectively. Smallpox on the West Coast appears to have killed a far greater percentage of the population in a few weeks.

The horror of the experience certainly entered the collective consciousness of the grieving survivors. It did so with such power and pervasiveness that the stories later collected by ethnologists are frightening even today. Geographer Cole Harris, writing in the journal *Ethnohistory* in 1994 in a paper entitled "Voices of Disaster: Smallpox around the Strait of Georgia in 1782," quotes another Sto:lo elder. Jimmy Peters said that when he was a child shortly after World War I, he was forbidden to play near sites such as Sxwóxwiymelh because he might dream about the victims and what happened to them. If he experienced those dreams, he might soon afterward die suddenly like them.

The survivors sought to frame their understanding of what had happened in the metaphors and imagery of their own cosmology and oral literature, not by using the clinical explanations that descend from western European science and scholarship.

Harris cited an 1899 paper in the *American Antiquarian* by Ellen Webber of Vancouver, who wrote that some years earlier a Kwantlen had told her that the disease came from a supernatural creature whose breath caused sores to break out on the skin of anyone whom it touched. "They burned with heat and they died to feed this monster."

Harris also cited a story recounted by Vancouver anthropologist Charles Hill-Tout, who interviewed a Squamish elder named Mulks in 1896 who told of "a dreadful skin disease loathsome to look upon" that afflicted people who had been forced by hunger to eat salmon covered with sores.

"Men, women and children sickened, took the disease and died in agony by hundreds, so that when spring arrived and fresh food was procurable there was scarcely a person left of all their numbers to get it," Mulks told Hill-Tout. "Camp after camp, village after village was left desolate."

Another account Harris mentioned, from Salt Spring Island, said the pestilence was thought to have come on a contaminated wind from the south and that the clean north wind wasn't strong enough to block it away. The wind blew all winter "until most of the tribe were dead and there were too few left to bury their bodies."

In 1792 Capt. George Vancouver, charting the coastline from Cape Flattery along the Strait of Juan de Fuca, around Puget Sound and up the coast to English Bay and beyond, reported the physical evidence of Mulks's account. He observed a whole series of villages in which the buildings were in decay, weeds overgrew the footpaths and everywhere there was evidence of a sudden death that had overwhelmed the inhabitants' ability to cope.

Some of them, like the "extensive" deserted village he found at the north end of the Strait of Georgia, had buildings and defensive fortifications "so skilfully contrived, and so firmly and well executed" that the naval commander found it difficult to attribute their construction to "untutored tribes" until the abandoned weapons, implements and clothing of the vanished inhabitants convinced him otherwise.

I turned to Edmond S. Meany's entertainingly annotated 1907 excerpt from the original journals, *Vancouver's Discovery of Puget Sound,* for the explorer's observations regarding the apparent depopulation of the Georgia Basin.

"In our different excursions," Vancouver wrote, "particularly those in the neighborhood of port Discovery, the scull, limbs, ribs, and backbones or some other vestiges of the human body, were found in many places promiscuously scattered about the beach in great numbers.

"Similar relics were also frequently met with during our survey in the boats; and I was informed by the officers, that in their several perambulations, the like appearances had presented themselves so repeatedly, and in such abundance, as to produce an idea that the environs of port Discovery were a general cemetery for the whole of the surrounding country."

Vancouver found evidence of traditional ceremonial burials—some in canoes, some in baskets—and was at pains to prevent any "indignities" by his crew toward the human remains. But he also noted the signs of mass cremations, one in which the skulls and bones of twenty individuals were counted, hasty burials in which bodies had been tumbled into holes and only lightly covered with earth, and most distressing, many bodies obviously left to decay where they fell.

Whether these mortalities were the result of an epidemic or by recent warfare, Vancouver said he couldn't venture, but he was a shrewd observer and took note that whatever had happened, it hadn't been in the ancient past. Although the deserted villages were rank with weeds, shrubs hadn't yet grown to any size, indicating that the events occurred "not many years since."

Clearly Vancouver suspected smallpox was more likely than war. "This deplorable disease is not only common, but it is greatly to be apprehended and is very fatal amongst them, as its indelible marks were seen on many; and several had lost the sight of one eye, which was remarked generally to be the left, owing most likely to the virulent effects of this baneful disorder."

Ethnologists, anthropologists and native Indians themselves have long been aware that a smallpox epidemic either preceded or occurred at about the same time as first contact with European explorers and traders. Now scholarship has begun to confirm the catastrophic magnitude of the event recorded in oral traditions.

The Chinook, the Snohomish, the Clallam, the Nitinat and the Dididaht, the Straits Salish in the Gulf Islands, the Cowichans, the Lummi, the Tsawwassens, the Semiahoo and all the Sto:lo tribes of the lower Fraser rapidly fell victim to the smallpox catastrophe of 1782.

When Simon Fraser passed through the canyon into Sto:lo territory wearing the reputation of a returning supernatural transformer, the awe and dread with which he was greeted by local peoples is understandable. If Boyd's analysis is right, Fraser may have arrived in the immediate aftermath of a second wave of smallpox (he'd noted the disease was present in a camp he visited in the Interior) that had pulsed through the region from 1800 to 1805.

The arrival of the fur trade from New Caledonia represented change, but Fraser was entering a landscape that had already been transformed and thrown into utter disarray by what can only be described as a demographic collapse. According to a telling quote by Karl W. Butzer that appears in the Harris paper, it had led to widespread settlement discontinuity.

"To grasp the implications of such discontinuity, one must imagine what almost total depopulation would mean in Italy or Spain . . ." Butzer wrote in 1992.

Power balances that had endured for centuries must have been overturned, some once-great nations had been obliterated, others had expanded into power vacuums left by the departed, the social order had been altered, great gaps had been rent in the traditions, histories and genealogies of an oral culture and survivors jockeyed for access to resources.

People may also have shared feelings of despair, despondency, numbed emotions and personal guilt for not having died with the rest—"my senses have been charred" wrote soldier poet Wilfrid Owen in the carnage of World War I—the same feelings that modern psychology now describes as survivor's guilt.

When Fraser entered Sto:lo territory in 1808, his canoes sweeping past the ruins of Sxwóxwiymelh without even noticing, he wasn't just passing into exotic new terrain, he was also encountering a grieving survivor culture and everything that it entailed.

British Columbia was built not just upon the enterprise and ingenuity of the newcomers like Fraser who came to develop an empty, unused wilderness and wound up dominating the cultural landscape we share today. It was also built on the bones of its previous inhabitants, their wealth and resources annexed by the ignorant and the uncaring, wrested from the massively diminished, despondent and psychologically traumatized survivors of a shattered world.

28

AT LAST, THE SEA

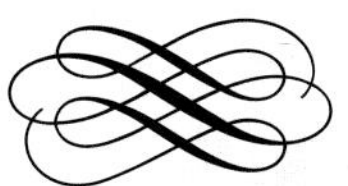

The sea was a crescent of pearl. It flooded across shining mudflats, picked up the delicate filigree of weed left by the tide's earlier retreat and carried it once again toward a ragged foreshore of salt marshes, sloughs and brackish side channels.

Water seeped into my shoes as I paused at the shoreline, ignoring the massive transformations caused by industrial dredges, urban development, sewer outfalls and agricultural drainage. I concentrated instead on what remained of the view that greeted Simon Fraser at the river's mouth almost two hundred years earlier. Except for the vast panorama of sea, sky, islands and mountains, almost everything was transformed.

My search for Simon Fraser had begun almost four years earlier with another sliver of light, one defining a dark horizon on the far side of the continent. It had led me, like the young explorer, up immense rivers and down pounding rapids, past brooding eighteenth-century battlements and into aboriginal encampments so ancient even their descendants have forgotten who lived there. I had passed through the gloom of subarctic forests and the desert hiss of wind-burnished sagebrush, and through winter blizzards, spring freshets, summer storms and the crisp, vivid palette of fall.

For every day I'd spent in the bush, I'd spent another immersed in old journals and the still air of archives where the only life seemed to be the golden dust motes dancing in sunbeams. I had travelled more than twenty thousand kilometres by air,

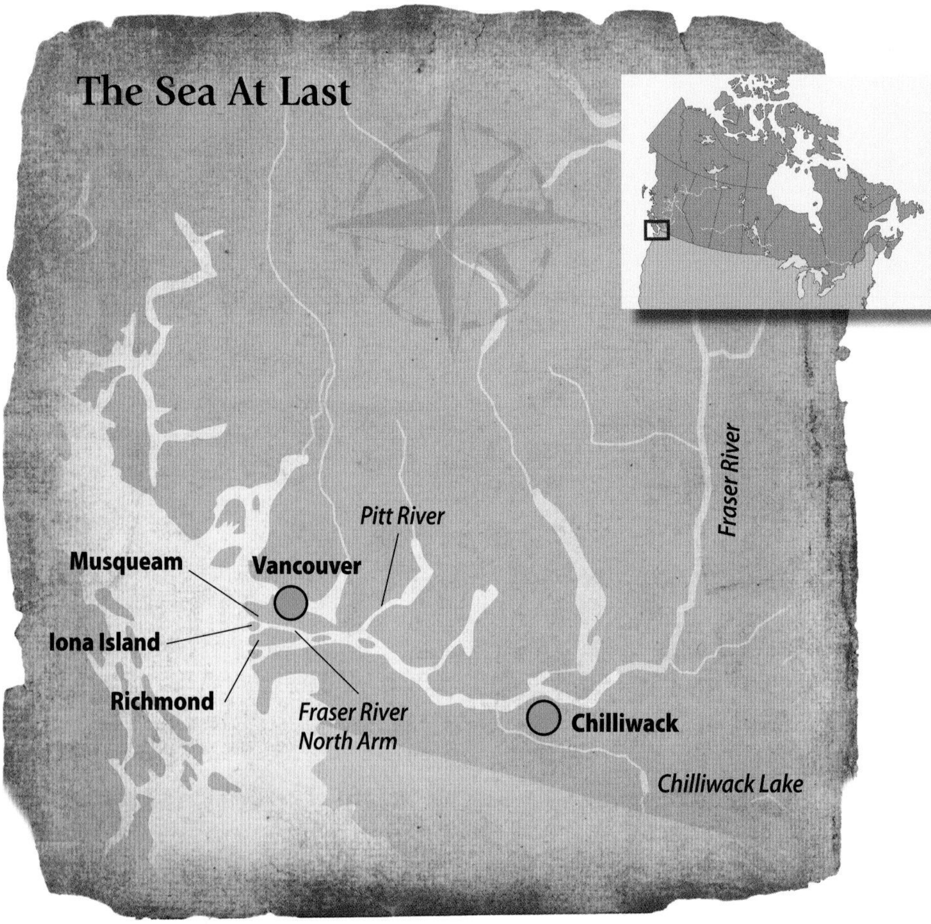

The Sea At Last

Fraser River
Pitt River
Musqueam
Vancouver
Iona Island
Richmond
Fraser River North Arm
Chilliwack
Chilliwack Lake

Two centuries after Simon Fraser ventured down the river that bears his name, Stephen Hume stood on a small gravel spit on Iona Island. Somewhere near here, the explorer first saw the Pacific Ocean. *Bill Keay/* Vancouver Sun

river and road, on foot, in four-by-fours, in jetboats and by canoe in a trek equal to nearly half the distance around the equator.

My journey had begun at sunrise in the same place and on the same day that Fraser was born in 1776. Now it was ending in the glow of a sun descending toward the edge of the Pacific Ocean. I'd begun in a farm field; I was ending in the pulsing heart of one of Canada's three great urban areas. I'd made my way to the same place where his quest had ended. I arrived on the same day of the same month after studying Fraser's reports of tides and distances travelled to work out my best guess as to the time of day he'd actually sighted the sea.

Behind me was the Musqueam Indian Reserve. In 1808 the village had several rows of cedar plank houses separated by footpaths. It extended about five hundred metres along the shore of a small tidal lake, and Fraser described it as a fort. Today the lake is long gone, filled in by progress. Much of the creek that drained into the Fraser River has disappeared into ditches and culverts. Residential houses are tucked in behind the busy clubhouse and pro shop that serve a minigolf and driving range. The streets and crescents are indistinguishable from any other Canadian residential subdivision.

To my right there's a lovely, lonely expanse of seagrass and driftwood. Once another village stood there—Mahli or Ma-li or Mâ'lê, depending upon era and orthography—in a long single row of houses facing the North Arm of the Fraser. Beyond it, along the shoreline of Point Grey, archeologists unearthed evidence of perhaps a dozen more village sites inhabited before Europeans arrived. Scattered across the river's lower estuary are the relics of perhaps a hundred such villages, camps and extended-family sites. Exactly who occupied these sites and when

Where the Fraser River approaches the Pacific, Stephen Hume explores the "greasy grass" where threatening Musqueam warriors ended the explorer's plans of continuing to the open ocean. *Bill Keay/Vancouver Sun*

during the West Coast's ten thousand years of sometimes turbulent human history is often a matter of conjecture, despite the work of archeologists, anthropologists, linguists and ethnohistorians.

Just upstream from where I stood, Fraser had paddled his commandeered canoe almost a kilometre up winding Musqueam Creek, only to find the village deserted but for a few old men and women. Raiders from the sea were menacing the river, and the villagers had apparently taken to the woods at the sight of strangers. I knew that the village was located where it was for just such tactical defensive reasons. Sto:lo tribes made a practice of locating villages in sloughs and side channels where they were out of sight of raiders; inhabitants had retreat routes and they could be better defended in a fight.

At Musqueam the shallow, winding creek was accessible to a big canoe only on a high tide. So once the Canadian Hydrographic Service had told me the time of high tide for the same date 200 years ago, I could estimate what time of day he'd gone up the creek.

High tide on July 2, 1808, occurred at 2:12 p.m. I knew from his journal that he'd spent an hour looking about the village, and I knew that the tide was falling

At the mouth of Musqueam Creek in Vancouver, BC, Simon Fraser had an ominous encounter with fierce warriors; their descendants Brett Sparrow and Taylor Guerin play beside the river. *Bill Keay/*Vancouver Sun

because it left his canoe high and dry. He was forced to drag it "some distance" back to the river before his brigade could paddle it again. So he'd glimpsed the sea about 2 p.m. and travelled farther downstream for a more complete view, probably approximately 3:30 p.m.

On my way to the water's edge, I'd stopped to look at the creek. Even today it's just a trickle at low tide, a narrow ditch between grassy banks that submerge only at high water.

There I chatted briefly with Graham Allen Guerin, whose ancestors were here when Fraser arrived. His father, former Chief Delbert Guerin, just turned seventy, had left his name on a famous court case that held the federal government accountable for failing to protect the best interests of the Musqueam band and establishing its constitutional obligation to do so for all bands in Canada henceforth. Graham (named for the lawyer who fought the case) was taking a break from netting spring salmon—"I got twenty of them yesterday, about twenty-five pounds average, nice big fish"—to take the kids, Taylor Guerin and Brett Sparrow, both twelve, for a promised round of minigolf. There's a prospect that would have astonished Simon Fraser.

As I approached the sea, spongy ground underfoot oozed water, and the marsh grass and sedges rustled and rippled. The sea breeze over what remains of the old marsh left frost-coloured cat's paws on the waving field of green.

Barely 10 percent of the biologically rich wetlands that surrounded Fraser and sustained scores of villages as the explorer made his way to the river's mouth have survived the subsequent dykes, dredging, runways, storm drains, bridge footings, log booms, farm drainage, pilings and rip-rap, wash from tugboats and pleasure craft, three sewage treatment plants that discharge more than a billion litres of wastewater a day, residential subdivisions, strip malls and the whole vast metropolis that now sprawls across the flood plain and up the mountainsides. On the North Arm almost 2,800 hectares of the original 2,900 hectares of wetland have vanished, says a 1996 habitat study by the federal government. Attempts to rehabilitate these biologically important sedge marshes had achieved a less-than-stellar result, restoring only 3.4 hectares.

Most of the villages didn't survive either. Smallpox ravaged them in the late eighteenth century, then again in the early 1800s, again in the 1830s and once more in 1862. When Sto:lo populations had declined from as many as sixty thousand people or more to as few as twelve hundred, they were finally displaced and dispossessed in the great immigrant land grabs, reserve reductions, cutoffs and transfers that frequently cleared indigenous occupants off the most valuable farmland.

Some things haven't changed. Sunrise and sunset, the rhythmic rise and fall of the tides, the changeable marine weather, the annual spring freshet and the subsequent return of the salmon and migratory bird flocks are all the same. The great plume of silt that's visible from space continues to spill across the Strait of Georgia all the way to the Gulf Islands, a lens of fresh water riding over the cold oceanic currents from the open Pacific. And even today Fraser would recognize the view from the estuary to the western horizon—except at night when the electric lights come on.

I stood mulling the changes that have taken place over the ten generations that separate us from the explorer. It was a Canada Day holiday. When the fur trader reached this spot in 1808, Canada as we know it wouldn't come into existence for another fifty-nine years.

Here and there birdwatchers scanned the intertidal zone and its teeming shorebirds. They peered intently through binoculars, telescopes and massive camera lenses. Joggers in flimsy synthetic quick-dries, young moms pushing baby strollers, teenagers sharing earbuds and holding hands, couples walking the family dog and kids on mountain bikes all enjoyed a tranquil Saturday afternoon outing at what is now Iona Beach Regional Park.

For Fraser, reaching the Pacific had proved anything but tranquil. At the moment of his expedition's success its very survival was in question. As he scrambled back into his canoe and pushed off into deep water, the riverbank was suddenly lined with fierce Musqueam warriors who had emerged from the forest wearing armour, wielding war clubs and "howling like wolves." Canoes bristling with spears, archers notching their bows with arrows, paddlers banging the gunwales with the short, sharp-pointed war paddles that the warriors stabbed at the faces of their foes, were closing rapidly from upriver. One had come so close alongside that Fraser's voyageurs fended it off with the long muzzles of their flintlock muskets until the belligerents gave up and paddled to the Musqueam village.

Although a concentrated volley from his guns would have blown the threatening canoe to splinters and massacred much of its crew, to Fraser's credit he fired no shots in anger but instead calmly, if speedily, withdrew up the river. He hoped to refresh provisions and return the next day to reconnoitre farther, maybe even travel on to what he called "the main ocean."

"The tide was now in our favor [it had turned at 6:50 p.m.], the evening was fine and we continued our course with great speed until 11, when we encamped within six miles of the Chief's village [where he had obtained the canoe]," he wrote. "The men being extremely tired, went to rest; but they were not long in bed before the tide rushed upon the beds and roused them up."

Some suggest that Fraser had misinterpreted welcoming ceremonies for hostility or had unwittingly breached the protocols required of visiting strangers in a time when slave raiders could arrive unexpectedly at any moment. Former Musqueam chief Delbert Guerin once told me, however, that his grandparents had told him that the natives' intent was certainly to drive Fraser away. Whatever the cause, it must have been enormously frustrating for Fraser to have his moment of triumph evaporate in a miasma of fear and menace. The next day he complained of his "great disappointment." Yet it speaks to his cool head and leadership skills that his men did not panic in the face of imminent disaster. A successful retreat without losses, any military officer will tell you, is far more difficult to achieve than a successful attack.

I thought about that as I looked west and northwest into the vista that had greeted Fraser. First I'd walked down the north bank of the North Arm, parking near Musqueam Creek and squelching through the "greasy grass" of the estuary while tugboats churned against the current, working to position log booms in the channel.

Somewhere nearby, Fraser's canoe had come abreast of what he called the "second village" beyond Musqueam—probably the abandoned site at Mahli—and he'd seen the bluffs of Point Grey and the Strait of Georgia. Or as long-time North Arm fisherman Terry Slack suggests, maybe these assumptions are wrong. Maybe he'd turned into a major channel, since filled, which once separated the west end of Iona Island and the islet from which a man-made jetty now juts far into the strait.

Alan Morley, a former *Vancouver Sun* writer who published a history of Vancouver in 1961, was even more skeptical. "Despite enthusiastic modern Vancouver pageantry, Simon Fraser never saw the Strait of Georgia, he never rounded Point Grey and he never paddled across English Bay to land on Kitsilano Beach among the plaudits of friendly Indians," Morley wrote. "He did see and land on the southern slope of South Vancouver or Marpole somewhere along the riverbank."

Fraser, on the other hand, claims unequivocally in his journal that he saw the sea.

Slack had thumped his hand—fingers blunt and calloused from half a century of net-minding and mending—on old maps to show me where the channel ran and to point out, just where it opened to the sea, another long-abandoned Musqueam village.

"See the bulrushes in that indentation over there," Slack had said, pointing to a section of riverbank where the Iona sewage treatment plant now stands. "That's where the channel was. It became a slough later. I used to go in there as a kid. Now it's all filled in."

Nothing whets a reporter's appetite like the prospect of an unsolved mystery. I crossed the river, threaded my way through the maze of roads around the airport and went down to the jetty to examine the view from the edge of the mudflat where the old channel appeared to have opened.

Fraser, too, had looked from the low vantage point of his canoe to the west, where clouds from the open Pacific tumbled over the spine of Vancouver Island. As they had on that afternoon, snow fields gleamed on the Comox glacier and Mt. Arrowsmith. To the north the stark, snow-clad massifs marched away behind West Vancouver and the Sunshine Coast. Curving to the south lay a jumbled arc of dark green Gulf Islands that today bear Spanish names: Gabriola, Valdes, Galiano and Saturna.

But why does Fraser's journal say the Strait of Georgia runs from southwest to northeast when it so obviously runs from southeast to northwest? Was this a copying error? One more mystery for some historian to solve, I thought.

As I looked, I savoured the mingled scents of wet earth, salt air, the brackish smell of sedge marsh and the sharp iodine tang of seaweed. All those odours the explorer would have known when he looked into the Strait of Georgia with the flooded lowlands of the great Fraser River estuary stretched out behind him.

The acrid whiff of ground level ozone from the immense, throbbing conurbation behind me, the explorer would not have known. Nor the almost subliminal rumble of traffic over the bridges into Richmond, a city with a population today that is more than double that of all Upper Canada in 1808, its subdivisions snug behind the dykes where Fraser saw only sodden marshes and low-lying vegetation.

It's difficult to imagine now, but so much of the river's delta was subject to flooding on a combination of high tides and summer freshet that Capt. George Vancouver had sailed the whole shoreline from Point Roberts to Point Grey in 1792 without spotting any of the river's great channels. The Spanish who preceded him in 1791 had missed it, too, although they knew from its muddy plume there was a major river somewhere nearby. There's a theory that Jose Maria Narvaez walked from Boundary Bay to the river during his explorations, but as historic maps expert Derek Hayes points out in his *Historical Atlas of Vancouver,* there's no discovered documentary record, and Narvaez's own map presents no evidence he did.

So as far as the historical record is concerned, credit for being the first non-natives to actually lay eyes on the lower river where it meets the sea at what is now Vancouver must thus remain with Fraser and his brigade. Exactly where he saw the Pacific, as Slack points out, can only be a surmise.

Fraser described both the historic event and the stunning vista in perfunctory terms.

"At last we came in sight of a gulph or bay of sea; this the Indians call Pas-hil-roe. It runs in a S.W. & N.E. direction. In this bay are several high and rocky Islands whose summits are covered with snow. On the right shore we noticed a village called by the Natives Misquiame; we directed our course toward it," he wrote.

In fairness, the scenery wasn't high on Fraser's agenda at the moment he jotted his entry. He'd reached the Pacific all right, but the river he'd been exploring wasn't the Columbia. Furthermore, it didn't offer a navigable—and thus less costly—route for the shipment by water of furs and trade goods to and from New Caledonia, thirty-six days of arduous travel to the north.

"If I had been convinced of this fact where I left my canoes [at Leon Creek], I would certainly have returned from thence," he wrote.

More important, I suspect, his practical commander's mind had already engaged the more pressing tactical problem of how to extricate himself from the confrontation with the Musqueam that threatened his survival.

Fraser had begun his final progress to the sea on Thursday, June 30, breaking camp at a Sto:lo village somewhere downstream from present-day Hope. Determining exactly where he made his stops on the river is difficult and perhaps even impossible, given the vagueness of his account and the enormous social disruptions caused by a series of virulent smallpox epidemics. They resulted in sequential depopulations and movements of people. Villages later documented may have been deserted in Fraser's day, places he recorded may have subsequently been

Simon Fraser commented on the unpleasant odour at one Sto:lo village near Hope, BC. Perhaps, as this Musqueam family is doing, strong-smelling oolichans were being processed. Swilth, near Jones Creek which he passed, was a large processing complex. *Image C-09289 courtesy of Royal BC Museum, BC Archives*

abandoned and then reoccupied by newcomers, and the political and economic influence of tribes certainly waxed and waned and their affiliations changed.

Judge F.W. Howay, who in 1914 co-authored with provincial archivist E.O.S. Scholefield the first major history of British Columbia, placed his first stop in the Lower Mainland near present-day Ruby Creek. Nic Doe, writing in the *BC Historical News* in 2000, makes a well-argued case—based on his analysis of John Stuart's solar observation—for the present-day Ohamil Indian Reserve.

Either way, the expedition was delayed there in its departure because Fraser's guides had returned to their upriver village and he had to negotiate the use of canoes. He got underway about 11 a.m. and just before noon, his journal says, he landed at a village of four hundred people.

"Here we saw a man from the sea, which they said was so near that we should see it tomorrow. The Indians at this place seem dirty and have an unpleasant smell," he wrote, "they were surprised at seeing men different from Indians and extremely disagreeable to us through their curiosity and attention." Why the unusual note about the odour? Were these people engaged in some kind of specialized food processing—extracting oolichan oil or sockeye oil? There was a huge processing site for oolichan at a village called Swilth, located in a side channel at the mouth of Jones Creek below Hope.

Since his guides from the morning had returned upriver, he spent several hours dickering for canoes so he could continue downstream. By 2 p.m. he had them and ran about fourteen kilometres with a strong current to "where the river expands into a lake." Here Fraser got the first visible evidence that he was close to the ocean—at a spot where a large river flowed in from the south and there was a distinctive round mountain. He saw seals.

Most likely this was shallow Sumas Lake, long since drained for agricultural use. But in Fraser's time it covered about fourteen thousand hectares just south of Chilliwack and flooded to eighteen thousand hectares during the spring freshet. There was a major outlet to the Fraser where the Sumas and Chilliwack rivers, now channelled by the Vedder Canal, joined at the foot of Sumas Mountain. Sumas Lake was valuable as a source of sturgeon, and some villages were built on stilts.

Having continued paddling until sunset—hungry, tired and with their provisions exhausted—the expedition camped on the north bank in a stand of immense cedars. Fraser remarked on the size of the trees, "five fathoms in circumference" [about nine metres]. He also complained for the first time about dense clouds of mosquitoes, so the bugs must have made it an unpleasant night.

29

RETURN OF THE GIANT

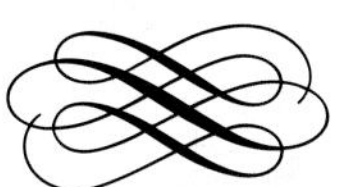

On the morning of July 1 at 8 a.m., the explorers were once again handed off by their guides to the next village, a community of about two hundred. Fraser took note that its cedar plank houses were contained in one immense structure whose front was greater in length than a present football field. At first, Fraser wrote, he was struck by the fair complexions of the villagers until he realized that they were using white paint to alter their features. Or perhaps it was dust from the processing of dog hair blankets, since clay was a component in the weaving process. The name of a village site at Seabird Island, for example, means "lumpy clay."

"They evinced no kind of surprise or curiosity at seeing us," Fraser observed, "nor were they afraid of our arms, so that they must have been in the habit of seeing white people." Trading vessels had certainly been off the coast in previous years, but it seems less likely they were in proximity to the Fraser River or ventured much into the Strait of Georgia in sufficient numbers for local people to become accustomed to their presence.

Hands were shaken all round, and presents were exchanged. Fraser received what he called a "coat of mail," presumably of thick tanned leather used for protection against arrows but that he prized for making moccasins. His Nlaka'pamux guide and interpreter, identified only as Little Fellow, received prized white shells.

"I gave the Chief in return a calico gown, for which he was thankful and proud," Fraser wrote.

Simon Fraser marvelled at the sturdy plank construction and the large carved houseposts in Sto:lo dwellings similar to this example of a Musqueam residence. *Image AA-00234 courtesy of Royal BC Museum, BC Archives*

The visitors, non-native and native alike, were then invited to dine with the chief and served fish, berries and dried oysters in large troughs while a dance was performed.

"In this room the posts or pillars are nearly three feet in diameter at the base, and diminish gradually to the top. In one of these posts is an oval opening answering the purpose of a door, thro' which to crawl in and out. Above, on the outside, are carved a human figure large as life, and there are other figures in imitation of beasts and birds," he marvelled.

The feast, the presents, the dance ceremony, the size of the big house and its decorations, and the ornate entry through a house post all indicate that the chief must have been powerful and wealthy, although he's never named. Who the chief was and the location remain an intriguing puzzle for history buffs, because it was here, at what's been dubbed "the mystery village," that Fraser's later troubles with the Musqueam likely began.

A Sto:lo Coast Salish Historical Atlas places the village at Matsqui, based on some oral traditions and what Sto:lo know of paddling times and distances below Yale, according to editor Keith Thor Carlson, whose editorial advisors include archeologist Dave Schaepe and Sto:lo elder Albert "Sonny" McHalsie.

Nic Doe's paper in *BC Historical News* argues that Matsqui must be excluded because it lies too far outside the range of Stuart's meridian altitude observation that placed him at 49° 10.9′ N, plus or minus 2.4 kilometres to allow for the imprecision of his eighteenth-century instruments. Doe lists a dozen possibilities but argues that the most likely is a long-abandoned village site at what was formerly Port Hammond. It now lies under the Interfor cedar mill in what is now Maple Ridge.

Barbara Rogers, who has been researching the minutiae of Simon Fraser for nearly twenty years and wrote the article on Fraser for *The Greater Vancouver Book,* also leans to the Port Hammond site. Denys Nelson, who published a history of Fort Langley in 1927, thought it was at Coquitlam River. Others argue for sites near Pitt River or Barnston Island. Still others say we'll likely never get beyond best guesswork.

"To say whether a particular population occupied a particular site at a particular time—I don't think it's possible to retrieve that information," said Valerie Patenaude, curator of the Maple Ridge Museum and an archeologist who excavated a major site on the Pitt River in the 1990s. It extended more than a kilometre and yielded more than fifty thousand artifacts and was abruptly abandoned more than two hundred years ago—archeological evidence of mass cremations suggests a catastrophic epidemic, probably smallpox—yet neither the adjacent Katzie nor Coquitlam peoples claimed descent from whoever lived there, she told me.

"It's a strong possibility that the site was used by people from south Vancouver Island who just never came back after the catastrophe," Patenaude said. "I would say it's impossible to precisely locate the actual place [of the chief's mystery village where Fraser took the canoe]. That's because of the enormous disruptions to the demography."

Perhaps Fraser's expedition itself, making first European contact with previously isolated populations, was one of the unwitting agents of such change.

In his book *The Coming of the Spirit of Pestilence, Introduced Infectious Diseases and Population Decline among Northwest Coast Indians, 1774–1874,* Robert Boyd includes a story collected from Joe Splockton at Tsawwassen half a century ago that may link Fraser's journey and his perception as a supernatural being to later events. It tells of two Tsawwassen men who journeyed far up the Fraser River where they met a giant named Stalacom, clearly an analog for the Halkomelem word *stl'áleqem* that refers to a being with supernatural powers.

The giant rode back down the river in their canoe, but when people became frightened and shot at him, he fled back up the river and was never seen again—but after he was gone, everywhere he had passed, all the people died.

Fraser found himself stranded in the mystery village, wherever it was. He was unable to procure canoes "for any consideration," he wrote, until the chief agreed to loan his big canoe the next day and to accompany them on their journey downriver to the sea. But on the morning of July 2, he found the chief had changed his mind about lending his big canoe, which must have been a large vessel to accommodate twenty-four voyageurs and assorted guides and companions. Desperate, Fraser took matters into his own hands—literally.

"I applied to the Chief in consequence of his promise of yesterday for his canoe, but he paid no attention to my request. I, therefore, took the canoe and had it carried to the water side. The Chief got it carried back. We again laid hold of it. He still resisted, and made us understand that he was the greatest of his nation and equal in power to the sun. However as we could not go without we persisted and at last gained our point. The chief and several of the tribe accompanied us."

Who was this powerful chief? According to journalist and historian Bruce Alistair McKelvie, born in 1889 and at one time editor of the *Victoria Daily Colonist,* his name was Whattlekainum, although it is variously spelled Whottlekaimun, Whotleakenum, Whittlakainum and Whittlekainum in other accounts.

McKelvie, writing in *Fort Langley, Outpost of Empire,* quotes an informant identified as "old Staquisit" who was present for the events of July 2, 1808. Denys Nelson wrote that his information came from "Staquoisit, a Kiwantlen friend of Jason Allard." Allard's father, Ovid Allard, was born in 1817 and died at the old fort in 1874.

A Kwantlen chief named Whotleakenum was mentioned in the early journals from Fort Langley as having met James McMillan's survey party for the fort in 1824. He was described then as "a good Natured old man," so it seems plausible that he was chief in 1808, just sixteen years earlier.

A young visitor to the riverside market at New Westminster, BC, scrutinizes the bust of Simon Fraser that keeps watch over now-bustling commerce on his "River of Disappointment."
Mark Van Manen/Vancouver Sun

An entry in George Barnston's journal from Fort Langley for August 28, 1827, says Whittlakainum was at his residence on the Quoitle River. Where was that? In an earlier entry for July 24, 1827, Barnston wrote, "We were opposite the Quoitle or Pitt's River about 5 p.m."

On July 2, about 11 a.m., accompanied by the chief who may have been Whittlekainum, Fraser arrived at another village. Both McKelvie and Nelson identify this village as Kikait, a summer fishing site for the Kwantlen who inhabited Skaiametl, a village near Sapperton Landing in New Westminster. Nelson, quotes "Gabriel," presumably Chief Alfred Gabriel who was born at Fort Langley in 1893, or perhaps his father, as saying his grandfather was present when Fraser visited Kikait in 1808.

Kikait, spelled Qiqá:yt in the Sto:lo atlas, was on the Surrey side near the Patullo Bridge, although once again there are conflicting accounts as to precise location. One says the village was where saloonkeeper Ebenezer Brown built a hotel at the foot of Old Yale Road in 1861; another says it was at a site later occupied by the Liverpool Cannery, which Dianne Newell, writing in *Tangled Webs of History: Indians and the Law in Canada's Pacific Coast Fisheries,* locates directly across the river from Sapperton.

At Kikait, Fraser was warned not to go any farther downstream.

"The Indians advised us not to advance any further, as the natives of the coast or Islanders were at war with them, being very malicious, and will destroy us," he wrote. But he was not going to be deterred so close to his destination. He prepared to embark again, only to be physically prevented from leaving.

"Islanders" probably referred to the warlike Cowichans who were powerful enough to hold village sites in the delta—one of them south of Lulu Island—and often raided up the river. It's not clear whether the perceived threat from "natives of the coast" meant the Musqueam, who lived at the river mouth, or to the people the Sto:lo referred to as coastal raiders. War parties from the Haida, Tsimshian and Kwakwaka'wakw frequently ventured up the river in search of slaves and booty, much like the Vikings of European history.

Fraser pushed on regardless, using the big canoe he'd "borrowed" after some insistence, although the chief declined. The fur trader's loyal Nlaka'pamux interpreter, Little Fellow, also demurred, "saying that he was also afraid of the people at the sea."

The explorer picked up one local guide from a following canoe, who steered him into the North Arm and later up the winding, shallow creek to the Musqueam village. Was he leading Fraser away from the fierce Cowichans or into an intended ambush? We'll never know, although the journal says that "convinced of his unfriendly disposition, we turned him out and made him and the others, who were closing in upon us, understand, that if they did not keep their distance we would fire upon them."

The size of the chief's canoe proved a blessing because it was apparently too large for the smaller canoes to approach and capsize it, which would likely have occurred if Fraser and his party had been using several smaller vessels.

In the end he saw the ocean for perhaps ninety minutes, then was forced to retreat back up the river, never to return to the West Coast. Fraser had to retrace his difficult passage and get word of his disappointing discovery back to the North West Company headquarters in Montreal, almost five thousand kilometres to the east. My own journey was ending at the sea's edge in a new city that looks to Asia for its economic future.

Up in the Fraser Canyon, I'd learned how the auburn-haired, blue-eyed, pale-skinned traveller had been mistaken by native peoples for the return of a transformer, one of the supernatural beings from the beginning of time who changed the world and its contents into the one they knew.

Looking around at the modified landscape, the glittering towers, the freeway bridges, the tank farms, the log booms strung like a bizarre necklace of raw wood along the riverbanks, the gambling casino, the container yards, the vinyl, brick and stucco subdivisions where cedar longhouses once stood, I realized that the prophets of the Secwepemc and the Nlaka'pamux had been right—the coming of Simon

Simon Fraser is an icon of exploration gracing a stained glass window at Canadian Memorial Church, 16th and Burrard, in Vancouver, BC. It appears to acknowledge the assistance of First Nations, as Fraser himself did. *Glenn Baglo/*Vancouver Sun

Fraser was indeed the coming of a transformer.

"It's a bittersweet thing for me," my Chilcotin guide Doug Green on the upper Fraser had said, musing on the formidable skills and tenacity of Fraser's expedition in shooting wild rapids that were a challenge for his jetboat. "I have to admire those men but, of course, their arrival marked the beginning of the end for us and everything we knew."

And so it was, although—as with everything in the complex tapestries that human lives weave for both good and ill—endings and beginnings are always tangled up with one another. Some things that ended deserved to end, including slavery, the institutionalized abduction and traffic in women and murderous eye-for-an-eye blood feuds that went on for generations. Some things that began, no one would forfeit for a golden age that never was. Today we boast of hospitals and health care, public education and great universities, democratic institutions that uphold human rights and a civil society that now strives, however imperfectly, to right the injustices of the past.

Whatever Fraser was in the world of the imagination, in the physical world of thundering white water, towering mountains, brutal winters and burning sun, starvation and thirst, he proved a remarkable force of courage, leadership, initiative and dedication.

He had just led his expedition eight hundred kilometres over terrain that would challenge the abilities of the best-trained military special forces unit today. For most of us his accomplishments would simply be impossible. He completed his mission from present-day Prince George to present-day Vancouver and back in seventy-one days. He talked his men out of a near-disastrous mutiny when things appeared most bleak, brought every man for whom he was responsible home safely, negotiated the support of powerful Indian nations, and despite circumstances fraught with threats of violence, killed not one enemy.

His story is also indubitably a poignant milestone in a narrative of transformation and transition. The permanent network of forts that Fraser established west of the Rocky Mountains forever altered the economy and thus the lives of the nations he had visited. The trade routes he explored down the river that bears his name launched the permanent state of commercial enterprise that would shape British Columbia. They became the transportation and staging infrastructure that made the gold rush of 1858 possible, and from that infusion of sudden wealth came a new settler society.

Eventually the fur trade that had eclipsed the hunting and gathering economies it encountered was itself surpassed in importance by the mining, fishing and forestry industries. These in turn were surpassed by the information age and the knowledge-based industries upon which it relies. Today the Lower Mainland is home to almost a dozen universities, colleges and technical schools. One of the

A bald eagle soars above the pristine Stuart River south of Fort St. James. Rumbles of possible pipeline development trouble First Nations in the area. *Bill Keay/*Vancouver Sun

universities bears Fraser's name, although his astounding exploits remain little known or understood by most British Columbians.

Like the giant Stalacom in the Tsawwassen story, as much as he was a harbinger of all that's good about the present, Simon Fraser was also a transformer, the herald for a future that would descend like a whirlwind to disrupt, destroy and dispossess the nations that once greeted him with such awe and trepidation.

30

JOURNEY'S END

The Rivière aux Raisins was a lazy brown curl through a screen of scrubby trees just bursting into vivid green leaf. A light rain drizzled out of the overcast to dimple its muddy surface. Behind it sodden farm fields rose to the hedgerows of Ontario's Eastern Townships.

I leaned on the time-worn stone wall surrounding the old burial ground at the crossroads in St. Andrew's West and looked at the replica of the first Roman Catholic Church, a tiny six-by-seven-metre structure of hand-hewn logs erected by Loyalists fleeing the American Revolutionary War in 1784.

The original was long gone, replaced in 1801 by a stone church that served as a hospital during the War of 1812. It had been built with contributions solicited from the fur traders of the North West Company and bore a startling architectural resemblance to one of the company's fur warehouses. Simon Fraser—he was later married in that church on June 7, 1820—was one of the contributors. Although it still stands, it too was replaced in the march of progress, this time by the neo-Gothic structure begun in 1858 and completed in 1864, whose imposing spire rose into the grey sky behind me. Fraser, having ended his earthly journey on August 12, 1862, was dispatched from here upon his last expedition into eternity.

I'd come to this tranquil and historic crossroads a few kilometers inland from the mighty St. Lawrence River because this was where Simon Fraser's story ended, more than five thousand kilometres from the great deeds of his youth on the far side of the Rocky Mountains, long after they'd largely been forgotten by all but a few old men and women.

Once this was a stagecoach stop on the main road between Kingston and Montreal; today it is just another sleepy footnote in the sweep of history. Across the small, neatly trimmed cemetery, tombstones tilted this way and that on the uneven ground. They marked the graves of people born before the United States invented itself in the chaos and catastrophe of its first civil war.

The burial ground is today being restored thanks in part to the efforts of Maureen McAlear, whose farm along the same river frontage shared by Fraser has been in her family for two hundred years. Funds for the restoration were raised by the Cornwall Township Historical Society, grants from the Ontario government, the Hudson's Bay Company History Foundation and Simon Fraser University.

I let myself in and walked among the sixty tombstones; their shapes made a timeline of society's changing tastes in grave markers. I thought of Fraser's own careful observations of tombs and what they told him about the nations through which he passed in 1808 on his way to the Pacific. There was an ornate red granite pillar that represented the high Victoriana of the late nineteenth century. It marked the grave of John Sandfield Macdonald—tavern keeper at this crossroads, at whose

The plain granite tombstone above the grave Simon Fraser shares with his wife, Catherine Macdonell, wasn't erected until fifty-nine years after he was buried at historic St. Andrew's Church in St. Andrew's West, near Cornwall, Ontario. *Rachelle Labreque/*Vancouver Sun

inn Fraser doubtless took a dram now and then—former premier of the Province of Canada and first premier of Ontario, buried in 1872. Moving backward in time, there was Nancy Munro, born in 1766, died in 1809. Other markers were more austere but no less striking, comprised of weather-stained obelisks, stone cairns, Celtic crosses that signalled Scottish origins and rows of the plain rectangular markers that were indistinguishable from those I'd seen marking the graves of British and American soldiers killed in the Revolutionary War.

The little log church had been erected the same year that Fraser's mother fled the new American republic for Canada to escape the persecutions of Loyalists after the revolution—today we might call it the political equivalent of ethnic cleansing—and the big stone church had gone up two years before he died on August 18, 1862.

Yet after his death at the age of eighty-six, it was almost another lifetime before the Hudson's Bay Company would put up a monument to mark the humble common grave Fraser shares with his wife, Catherine Macdonell, who died one day later and was interred beside him.

Today the polished granite block—installed in 1921, the hundredth anniversary of the merger that absorbed Fraser's North West Company—leans slightly on a weather-worn concrete footing. The terse memorial notes that: "While in the employ of the North West Company he conducted important exploration and pioneer work principally in the area now known as British Columbia which he helped to secure for the British."

As I bent to trace the chiselled words with my fingertips, I thought how the dry prose was as distant from the dramatic reality of that summer in 1808 as I was from the untamed Fraser River.

His voyage of discovery had ended in disappointment at the edge of the Pacific when he confirmed that the river he was exploring was neither the Columbia nor the navigable waterway the North West Company sought to link New Caledonia to transoceanic trade routes. But if his exploration was finished, the expedition had yet to survive growing hostility among the tribes of the Fraser River and return more than eight hundred kilometres through the dangerous canyons and up the thundering rapids.

The hostility of the Musqueams at the mouth of the river may have been triggered by Fraser's abrupt and unannounced appearance at a time of tension and fear caused by raiding parties from the sea. Or it may, as some Musqueams maintain, have resulted because word had preceded him about a serious breach of protocol in which he forced a powerful chief to surrender a canoe, causing him to lose face before his followers.

Whatever the cause was, Fraser and his men were forced to flee through growing darkness, finally camping in exhaustion shortly before midnight, only to then be flooded from their beds by the rising tide a few hours later.

A torrent of silver at the close of day, the Fraser River twists its way into the rugged desert mountains near Lillooet, BC. *Bill Keay/*Vancouver Sun

On July 3, returning to the village where he'd been forced by desperation to seize the canoe, he'd found his friendly Indian guide from upriver had been taken prisoner as soon as the expedition was out of sight.

"He informed us that the Indians after our departure had fixed upon our destruction," Fraser wrote. "He himself was pillaged, his hands and feet tied, and they were about to knock him on the head when the Chief of the Ackinroe appeared, released him and secured his escape to this place, where he was now detained as a slave."

This "unpleasant recital" and growing evidence of "insolence and ill nature" convinced Fraser to shelve any plans to return to the sea for more exploration. He decided to get his increasingly frightened men out of danger as swiftly as possible. The extent of their fright is evident from the behaviour of one, whom Fraser identifies only as G.B., as they prepared to embark again.

"The fellow being afraid had fled into the woods and placed himself behind a range of tombs, where he remained during the greatest part of the time we tarried on shore and it was with difficulty we prevailed upon him to embark," says Fraser's journal entry for July 3.

It was not a moment too soon. As Fraser's crew struggled upstream against a strong current, they saw that the insulted chief and a flotilla of canoes, "well-manned and armed," was paralleling their course, "singing with unwelcome gestures all the while." When they began to close in with the apparent intention of capsizing the canoe, Fraser startled them into withdrawal with "threats and vehemence of speech and gestures."

His men observed that one of those menacing them wore a large belt suspended from his neck garnished with locks of human hair. The implications can't have been lost on people whose own parents and grandparents had endured the scalpings and ambushes of both the French and Indian Wars and the American Revolutionary War.

Now his main objective was to get back to friendly territory, and his men didn't need much incentive to forego the comforts of camp and keep on paddling.

"The night was dark and the current strong; we pressed on," he wrote, but the immediacy of the threat did not diminish a sense that the company's great venture had proved a failure.

"Here I must again acknowledge my great disappointment in not seeing the main ocean, having gone so near it as to be almost within view," he wrote.

"For we wished very much to settle the situation by an observation for the longitude. The latitude is 49 degrees nearly, while that of the entrance of the Columbia is 46 degrees, 20 minutes. This River, therefore, is not the Columbia. If I had been convinced of this fact where I left my canoes, I would certainly have returned from thence."

The next morning Fraser put in at another village where he saw canoes scattered along the beach. He thought he might obtain some, and surrendered to the pursuing chief the one that he had forcibly "borrowed" two days earlier. While he, John Stuart and Jules Quesnel were being entertained by the local chief, however, his men interrupted. They went outside to find the whole village assembled around their baggage, armed to the teeth and showing hostile intentions.

"It was then, that our situation might really be considered as critical. Placed upon a small sandy Island, few in number, without canoes, without provisions, and surrounded by upwards of 700 barbarians," he wrote. "However, our resolution did not forsake us.

"We now applied for canoes in every direction, but could not procure any either for love or money, so that we had to regret the inadvertency committed on our arrival by parting with the one we had before.

"There being no alternative we had again recourse to the chief, notwithstanding our experience of his illiberality. He asked his price—I consented—he augmented his demand—I again yielded—he still continued to increase his imposition. Feeling highly provoked at the impertinence of his conduct, I exclaimed violently. He then ordered the canoe to be brought."

It leaked, but it was a canoe. When Fraser and his men sought to leave, however, the villagers began to seize their equipment and baggage, and he ordered his party into a "posture of defence," most likely deployed to deliver a musket volley. Once embarked, having had only a few hours sleep in the previous two days, they paddled again until late into the night, making camp on a small island they could easily defend. As the men slept, Fraser and Stuart alternated on sentry duty.

The next day, as they continued upriver, the growing threat became sufficiently intense that Fraser had his men fire musket shots across the bows of the canoes harassing them, at which point their pursuers withdrew.

On July 6, when the party arrived at another village, some inhabitants launched canoes while others lined the shore "and all were advancing upon us." While pushing them off with their musket muzzles, Fraser's own canoe was shoved into the current, carried back down a rapid and beached at the foot of a steep bank. Stuart went ashore to establish a defensive formation and the show of force succeeded. Once again, the would-be assailants withdrew upriver.

But now the young expedition commander faced the greatest challenge of all. His team—exhausted, hungry and afraid of their pursuers—was falling apart. When he asked the men ashore to get back in the canoe, several refused the order. They said they were going to cross the mountains on foot to the friendly villages around present-day Lytton.

Fraser went ashore to talk them out of a decision he considered desperate and foolhardy. They told him their plan was fixed and that "they saw no other way by which they might [save] themselves from immediate destruction, for continuing by water, said they, surrounded by hostile nations, who watched every opportunity to attack and torment them, created in their minds a state of suspicion, which was worse than death."

Joined by Stuart and Quesnel, Fraser remonstrated, threatened and cajoled. Finally, after much debate, he persuaded his men to swear an oath that the crew would never separate during the voyage or forsake a crewmate in distress.

"By this time it was near sun set. We, however, decamped full of spirits, singing and making a great noise. The Indians, who were waiting ahead, observing us so cheerful, felt disheartened, kept their distance, and some of them thought proper to paddle downstream," he wrote.

As they progressed upriver, they noticed an increasing propensity for pilferage when they stopped at villages. A kettle, Fraser's own tobacco pipe and small items from their baggage began to disappear. Then they encountered two friendly Hacamaugh chiefs on the river. They were so surprised and pleased that they loaned Fraser's party their two canoes and set off on foot to alert those upstream.

Once again handing off their guns and equipment, they were guided past the seething waters of Hell's Gate and the Black Canyon on a latticework of spindly ladders, suspension bridges and swaying scaffolds. They reached the forks of the

Thompson River on July 14 to find new people in the village they didn't recognize but who were called Swhanemugh.

The inhabitants appeared to be afflicted with some unidentified disease. Furthermore, Fraser observed, there was famine in the camp and some had been reduced to killing and eating their horses, possibly because instead of dispersing to their hunting territories, all twelve hundred people had been waiting for him to return.

When parents brought three or four emaciated children for help—Fraser indicated the symptoms were from some serious disorder, not hunger—he made a tincture of laudanum, a popular opiate of the day, dipped his finger in it and stroked it on their foreheads. Soon he'd had to do the same for four score. The party left immediately afterward and pushed upstream, passing through the rapids and over the portages that had wrecked their canoes and blistered their feet on the way down, with the same consequences.

At Leon Creek, they found their canoes and the cached provisions and equipment intact.

"For this good fortune we felt grateful to the Indians who continually attended to their security during our absence," Fraser wrote.

On July 27, he once again found a cache of provisions intact, and after distributing supplies to his men, gave the rest to the Atnah man who had been guarding it on their behalf.

"He immediately divided the same among his friends who were greatly in want," Fraser noted. "Having been in a state of starvation for some time previous to our arrival, they deserve much credit for having abstained from the cache."

The next day the expedition passed out of the worst part of the canyons with clear paddling for the rest of the journey. About to depart from Atnah country, Fraser presented the chief who had been of such great assistance with a gun, ammunition and other necessaries while to his brother he presented a dagger.

With the worst of the journey behind him, Fraser turned his observations to the landscape, fish traps and technology, and the presence of a white sea shell that he said seemed to be the principal medium of exchange. "This is to them what money is to us."

On August 6, after a return journey one day shorter than the voyage downstream, his canoes beached at Fort George. There he found the junior clerk, Hugh Faries, and two men keeping the watch for their return.

For Fraser the travelling was not done. By September 21, he was in Fort Chipewyan for the annual rendezvous at which trade outfits were distributed to the various posts around the Athabasca district. Daniel Williams Harmon, the new clerk who had been born not far from Fraser's birthplace, noted in his journal for that day:

"People from almost every corner of this extensive Department have been flocking in—one of whom is a Mr. Simon Fraser from New Caledonia (on the West side of the Rocky Mountain) who accompanied by Messrs. John Stuart and J.M. Quesnel and a Dozen of the Canadians as well as two of the Natives, is just returned from a voyage to the Pacific Ocean," Harmon wrote, aware that he was in the presence of history being made. "He says they met with some ill treatment from the Indians who live along the Sea-coast, but were hospitably received by all those they saw further up the Country."

Just before Christmas, Harmon reports Fraser passing through Dunvegan on his way back to winter quarters and on May 16, 1809, his journal mentions him again, this time with four canoes bound for Rainy Lake, presumably to report on his mission at Fort William.

After founding New Caledonia, Fraser spent some years in the Mackenzie district to the north of Fort Chipewyan, then became embroiled in the increasingly violent struggle between the North West Company and the Hudson's Bay Company for control of the fur frontier. In 1815 Miles Macdonell, governor of Lord Selkirk's new Red River Colony, sought to restrict access to the pemmican supplies upon which remote trading posts depended. He was "arrested" by the North West

A sign identifies the muddy Fraser River as it gathers momentum near Soda Creek, BC. Simon Fraser would have appreciated a similar landmark – he thought he was on the Columbia. *Bill Keay/*Vancouver Sun

Company, and Fraser was one of the officers who transported him to Fort William, at present-day Thunder Bay.

Two years later, after the new Red River governor, Robert Semple, and nineteen men were slain in what became known as the Seven Oaks Massacre, Fraser was one of the North West Company officers arrested and charged with treason and conspiracy. He was acquitted in 1818 and no evidence was introduced that showed he had anything to do with the events.

Fraser retired from the fur trade after the trial, however, and settled on his farm at St. Andrew's West, just outside Cornwall, Ontario. On June 7, 1820, he married Catherine Macdonell, the well-connected daughter of a local military man.

During the rebellion of 1837–38, loyal as his father had been, he served as a captain in the local militia and suffered a serious injury during a night march that would plague him until his death twenty-four years later.

His long and eventful life had spanned the reshaping of the continent, from his birth on May 20, 1776, to his death as the political events leading to Confederation gathered momentum. His work for the North West Company in establishing the fur trade west of the Rockies had helped secure what is now British Columbia for Canada.

In a way Fraser and his fur-trade companions—Little Fellow, James McDougall, David Thompson, The Chief and his brother, John Stuart, Jean Baptiste Boucher, Jules Quesnel, Kwah and the voyageurs both named and unnamed—were among the real Fathers of Confederation.

And while there's room for endless debate about which Europeans founded what would become Canada's westernmost province, only one man left his name on the river that would eventually be recognized as the "Soul of British Columbia"—Simon Fraser.

READER'S GUIDE TO ABORIGINAL PEOPLES ENCOUNTERED BY SIMON FRASER

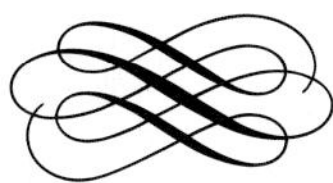

The human occupation of the territory we call British Columbia extends back more than 11,000 years, perhaps much longer. And so, long before the arrival of the first Europeans, the cultural landscape of what's now Canada had taken shape and was waiting to greet Champlain and Cook, Vancouver and Quadra, Mackenzie and Fraser. The broad shape of that pre-contact ethnolinguistic map survives today, though sometimes masked beneath the overlays of the dominant settler culture that imposed itself upon the existing template.

At Fort St. James, thoroughly modern dancer Shelby Erickson rests behind a pair of the ancient dugout canoes carved from cottonwood trees that were favoured by her Carrier ancestors on river highways of the Nechako Plateau. *Bill Keay/*Vancouver Sun

IROQUOIS

Among the first aboriginal peoples in Canada to come into contact with Europeans, the Iroquois were soon drawn into struggles for supremacy between the Dutch, French and English settler societies and often sought to draw these powers into their own conflicts. The Huron, allies of the French, for example, were destroyed by the Iroquois, allies of the British, in the war to control North America, which both exploited and was exploited by aboriginal societies.

The Iroquois were displaced from traditional lands in the United States, particularly in the Mohawk Valley of upstate New York after they allied themselves with the British during the American Revolution. The Indians that Simon Fraser's father commanded at the Battle of Bennington included Iroquois.

The politically sophisticated Iroquois practised agriculture, growing corn, beans, squash and ceremonial tobacco in addition to their hunting and gathering. They lived in fortified villages of bark-covered longhouses that were occupied by family groups. Society was organized into clans, and descent was matrilineal.

In Fraser's time the Iroquois were located to the south and east of Lake Ontario and the St. Lawrence River. They are perhaps best known for the Five Nations Confederacy under which the Seneca, Cayuga, Oneida, Mohawk and Tuscarora formed a federation that was governed by a council of fifty chiefs.

Some Iroquois came west with the fur trade, and their descendants still live in Alberta and British Columbia.

OJIBWA

This cultural grouping of peoples, who also call themselves the Anishinabe, originated around the north shore of the upper Great Lakes, initially concentrated around the fish resources at Sault Ste. Marie. They expanded their territory rapidly in historic times, invading Iroquois lands in southern Ontario, pushing the Dakota westward out of what's now Wisconsin and Minnesota, occupying the western end of the Ottawa Valley, Lake Nipissing, the shores of Lake Huron, Manitoulin Island and moving northward into the Canadian Shield.

Ojibwa society consisted of larger hunting bands, headed informally by chiefs who derived their authority from their demonstrated success as hunters, warriors or shamans. These bands dispersed into small units based on families during the fall and winter but regathered in late spring and early summer. Some early accounts report up to 2,000 meeting at Sault Ste. Marie, for example.

Ojibwa hunting prowess was widely recognized, but they also relied on fish, made maple sugar, harvested wild rice and gathered and preserved wild berries. They were masters of construction of the birchbark canoe, which was ideally adapted to their terrain and practices. They lived in wigwams constructed of bark sheets laid over a frame of saplings.

CREE

The name "Cree" is an anglicized contraction of the French term Kristinaux, which underwent numerous variations as it was mangled in the mouths of fur traders. Alexander Mackenzie calls them the Knisteneaux. Originally located on the shores of James Bay, where they were first mentioned by a French missionary in 1640, the Cree obtained firearms earlier than many of their neighbours and expanded their territory aggressively in the post-contact period.

"As for the Knisteneaux, there is no question of their having been and continuing to be, invaders of this country from the eastward. Formerly they struck terror into all the other tribes they met," writes Mackenzie.

Eventually they occupied much of the territory from Labrador to the Rockies north and west of the Great Lakes, the largest geographic area covered by a single aboriginal nation. As the Cree adapted to local conditions, their language evolved into numerous dialects by which sub-categories were identified: Naskapi and Montagnais in Labrador and eastern Quebec; Attikamek in the St. Maurice River region of Quebec; East Cree in Quebec east of James Bay; Moose Cree south of James Bay; Swampy Cree west of Hudson Bay; Woods Cree across the forests of Manitoba and Saskatchewan; Plains Cree across the grasslands of the central prairies.

The Cree were primarily hunters who lived in small social groups organized on the basis of families, which came together to form small hunting bands. These small bands themselves owed allegiance to larger regional bands scattered across the vast territory they occupied. Because they spoke variants of the same language across most of the interior fur trade route, they proved indispensable allies of the trader and provided guides, hunters, interpreters and wives—and occasionally armed protection.

CHIPEWYAN

Across the sub-Arctic fringe of the boreal forest ranged speakers of the Athapaskan language group. The most numerous and widely dispersed of these were the Chipewyans.

The Chipewyans inhabited the transition zone where forest gives way to tundra but frequently ventured into the barrens. There they hunted large herds of caribou as they migrated from calving grounds on the tundra to winter pasture in the forest and then back in the spring and fall. In winter they hunted moose and had developed methods and technologies for fishing beneath the ice in frozen lakes. They were hardy and highly adapted to a harsh climate where winter was long and temperatures could plunge to far below zero for months at a time.

They were accomplished winter travellers, using snowshoes and dog teams to hunt big game. These were the people upon whom Samuel Hearne relied for his long trek to the mouth of the Coppermine River. The basic unit of social organization was the small, highly mobile hunting band built around the nuclear family of a man, one or more wives, children and surviving elderly parents.

Chipewyan people were less affected by the fur trade than other aboriginal nations because the populations of the most prized fur-bearing animals were not so dense in their harsh climatic zone. They did expand their territory southward into the forested areas, however, in response to trading opportunities. In Simon Fraser's time, Chipewyan peoples had pushed into northeastern Alberta around Lake Athabasca and present-day Fort Smith in the NWT and would have been frequent visitors to Fort Chipewyan, his main base of operations.

BEAVER

These Athapaskan speakers occupied most of the Peace River region extending from Lake Athabasca to the Rocky Mountains. Mackenzie says they had once lived farther to the east, but had been forced westward when the Cree obtained guns while they still had only stone weapons. A peace made between the two tribes gave the river its name.

In the late eighteenth century, just as Fraser was arriving in the Athabasca district as a junior clerk, Mackenzie reported that there was still great hostility between the Cree and the Beaver, who had obtained guns themselves in 1782 and were far more warlike than their Chipewyan cousins.

Anthropologist Robin Ridington describes Beaver social organization, based on the family hunting band, as being "like a series of partially overlapping circles within an area bounded by geography, common history, language and culture."

The Beaver were primarily buffalo hunters who used some of the methods and technologies—driving herds into a pound where they could be enclosed and slaughtered, for example—that were common among Plains Indian cultures farther to the south. Moose, elk, deer and smaller game were all hunted as well.

In one marked way the Beaver differed from the Cree and the Chipewyans: "the abhorrence they profess of any carnal communication between their women and the white people." Another interesting difference was noted by the explorer. "There are many old men among them." This suggests a higher survival rate than among those people inhabiting the harsher climatic zones to the north.

TSE'KHENE

This culture, sometimes called the Sekani, was the first group from the far side of the mountains that Simon Fraser encountered. These are probably the "Big Men" mentioned in his journals from the McLeod Lake area in 1806. They are members of the Athapaskan language group.

Tse-Khene territory lay mostly in the Arctic drainage basin, giving this First Nation no direct access to salmon. Instead, dispersing across the landscape in family-based hunting bands, they became skilled and highly mobile hunters of big game. Moose, caribou, bighorn sheep, mountain goats and bears were their preferred prey. The Tse'Khene also relied upon beaver, marmots, hares and porcupines. In Fraser's time they still occasionally crossed the Rockies to hunt buffalo and elk, probably at the margins of old territories they'd been forced to abandon in the eighteenth century.

The people first met by Fraser would have been clad in moccasins, leggings and sleeveless shirt made from moose or caribou hide, or occasionally from rabbit skins or the pelts of other small animals. In cold weather people wore a fur cap, and might cinch a decorated belt over a cloak made from marmot or hare skins.

In summers, the rivers of the Rocky Mountain Trench were their highway. They used spruce bark to construct light and agile canoes for travel on the major rivers and lakes, where they caught suckers, whitefish and trout. Winter travel for the Tse'Khene was by snowshoe, and they lived in conical lodges that they covered with spruce bark.

Their hunting territories occupied the Rocky Mountain Trench from the Fraser River east of Prince George to the headwaters of the Kechika and Stikine rivers in the north. Their territory included the watersheds of the Omineca, Parsnip, Peace, Finlay, Back, Nation and Fox rivers.

Early fur traders noted the cultural and linguistic similarities between the Tse'Khene and the Beaver Indians east of the Rockies. Even in Fraser's time, fur traders surmised in their journals that the Tse'Khene were actually a branch of the Beavers who were driven to new territory when the Cree even farther east and the Beaver of what is now northwestern Alberta acquired guns.

The Tse'Khene were further squeezed by the powerful Carrier nation to the west and by the fierce Shuswaps to the south, who had massacred the Tse'Khene when they ventured into the North Thompson River country. This event occurred sometime in the generation before contact in 1793, because Mackenzie reported an account from a Tse'Khene woman enslaved at the time.

Never numerous because of the difficulty of subsistence in the terrain they inhabited, the Tse'Khene population had dwindled to about seventy people by 1916. Today the population is estimated at more than six hundred with concentrations at McLeod Lake, Fort Ware and Prince George.

CARRIER

Not surprisingly, the Carrier had their popular name bestowed upon them by outsiders. That's what they were called by the Tse'Khene, who met the fur traders before they did and provided a name that stuck. The term is said to be a translation of the Tse'Khene term *Agelh Ne* (the ones who pack), referring to a ritual in which widowed women carried some of the bones of their cremated husbands for a year after death.

Some Carriers dispute this claim. In her book *The Carrier, My People,* Lizette Hall, whose great-grandfather met Simon Fraser, says her father had never heard of the practice and told her that bones left after cremation were placed in a birchbark basket and hung in a tree. She says the term Carrier originated in reference to her people's legendary ability to transport goods over difficult terrain, occasionally using dogs for the purpose. In any event, the Yinka Dene Language Institute points out that the people known as Carrier prefer to be called by their own name, Dakelh, which translates loosely as "they who travel on water."

Athapaskan speakers like the Tse'Khene, the precontact Carrier occupied a territory that ranged from the headwaters of the Fraser River in the east to the Coast Range in the west and from near Anahim Lake in the south to roughly the 56th parallel in the north. Populations were concentrated around the lakes and rivers of the upper Skeena and upper Fraser, however, which sustained massive annual salmon runs.

Although the Carrier also moved in a seasonal round to exploit resources by hunting, fishing and gathering, their activities focussed on the salmon that they preserved by smoking and drying for the lean months of late winter and spring. Their ability to supply fur traders at isolated outposts with sufficient salmon and other game to survive the harsh winters made the Carrier crucial to the success of Fraser's commercial enterprise beyond the mountains. It's fair to say that without their decision to assist, there might be no British Columbia today.

Carrier culture was influenced by the rich and powerful tribes on the coast, particularly the Tsimshians of the lower Skeena and the Bella Coola. They adopted coast traditions like the potlatch, clan crests, social rank, regalia and totem poles.

While Carrier dress resembled that of the Tse'Khene and other Interior tribes—leather shirt, leggings and moccasins—for ceremonies they wore the decorated Chilkat blanket of the coast.

Carriers also borrowed housing design from their neighbours. They built pit houses similar to those of the Shuswap and Chilcotin in the south and rectangular plank buildings similar to those of the Tsimshian and Bella Coola in the north.

Anthropologists estimate that around the time of Fraser, the Carrier population was about 8,500. Judging from populations in the early fur-trade era, the majority was concentrated around Babine Lake and the upper Skeena and Stuart Lake and the Nechako.

The Carrier were devastated by epidemics and rapid economic change, like the Tse'Khene, with population falling to about two thousand by the 1930s. Today the Carrier number more than twelve thousand, however, and live in thriving communities scattered across the north central plateau.

CHILCOTIN

The name Chilcotin, according to anthropologist Diamond Jenness, translates as "inhabitants of Young Man's River," while Ives Goddard gives it as "people of the Chilcotin River." G.P.V. and Helen Akrigg give it as "ochre river people," not in reference to the colour but to the substance that was prized for use as a base for paint or dye.

The Chilcotin occupy the still-remote region that lies from west of present-day Williams Lake to the upper Kliniklini and Homathko rivers in the Coast Range and from the headwaters of the Dean River in the north to the upper Chilko River in the south.

Always something of a mystery to fur traders and anthropologists alike, the Chilcotin speak a distinct northern Athapaskan language but are the southernmost of BC's Athapaskan speakers. Anthropologists believe they migrated to the area they presently inhabit from farther north, but Chilcotin elders have no stories in their oral tradition that hint at such movement. In that respect, they may truly be said to have resided where they do since time immemorial.

Unlike their Carrier neighbours to the north, the Chilcotin did not rely primarily on waterways for transportation because the roughness of the terrain made them largely inaccessible by canoe.

Their territory was rich in big game. Using a combination of techniques that ranged from stalking to snares and deadfalls, the Chilcotin hunted elk, deer, caribou, mountain goats, sheep, marmots, hares, beaver, muskrats and porcupine. They also harvested salmon, whitefish and trout from the lakes and rivers.

Dress consisted of moccasins, a short leather apron and a fur robe for men, while women wore a knee-length leather skirt. Winter dwellings were rectangular structures with gable roofs made from poles, but in summer months they constructed temporary shelters of mats and boughs.

Although the Chilcotin had a reputation for being warlike, anthropologist Robert Lane suggests this arose less from a propensity to aggression than from their mobility and highly developed defensive tactics. They lived in dispersed small groups that made it difficult for enemies to surprise a whole community at once. Chilcotin mobility in difficult terrain and a strong sense of cultural identity meant that there was plenty of warning about intruders and a tendency toward a united response from dispersed populations. Furthermore, since potential enemies lived in permanent or semipermanent communities that the Chilcotin knew about, they were constantly vulnerable to retaliatory attacks.

Thus, Lane notes, "the Chilcotin were capable of devastating attacks against more 'powerful' but less mobile enemies."

Because of their remoteness, the Chilcotin were among the last of BC's First Nations to make contact with European culture. Their first known contact with a fur trader did not occur until 1815, and no post was built in their territory until 1821. The Chilcotin also suffered greatly from epidemics. Population dwindled to a scant 252 by 1823. Today more than eighteen hundred Chilcotin live in five communities scattered across their vast traditional territory between the Coast Range and the Fraser from Quesnel to Clinton.

SECWEPEMC

The territory of the Secwepemc, the Atnah of Fraser's journal, covered about 180,000 square kilometres and extended from west of the Fraser River to the Rocky Mountains. It reached from present-day Windermere in the south through the Yellowhead Pass to Jasper, Alberta, and north to a point in the Rocky Mountain Trench east of Prince George. In the west, their territory on the Fraser River extended from just above Soda Creek to just above Lillooet, and according to nineteenth-century ethnologist James Teit, included the lower Chilcotin River and Riske Creek.

The carrying capacity of the land suggests that as many as nine thousand people occupied this territory at the time of Fraser's visit. As a result of smallpox and influenza, the population had dwindled to about two thousand early in the twentieth century. Today it has rebounded to near first-contact numbers.

When Fraser met the Secwepemc for the first time at the end of May, 1808, he discovered he was not the first white person they had encountered.

"One of them had seen Mr. A.M.K. [Alexander Mackenzie] and even served him as a guide," he wrote. "It was through his means we were able to have any conversation with the others—I mean the Atnahs, whose language has not the least affinity with any of the different tribes with which I am acquainted."

The language that gave Fraser such difficulty was of the Interior Salish linguistic group, and the Atnah spoke two distinct dialects, western and eastern. In Fraser's time twenty-five bands were loosely organized into seven divisions: North Thompson, Shuswap Lake, Kamloops, Bonaparte around Ashcroft, Canim Lake, Fraser River around Williams Lake and Quesnel Lake, and Canyon on the west side of the river below Soda Creek and Pavilion.

Almost a third of these bands, including the entire Canyon division, disappeared after the last great smallpox epidemic in 1862, leaving seventeen bands today.

The Secwepemc of Fraser's day were nomadic hunters who travelled on a seasonal round to exploit resources. They dug roots, gathered berries, fished in lakes and rivers and hunted big game from the river bottoms to the subalpine mountain meadows.

Although the salmon resources of the Fraser River were of crucial importance, the Secwepemc considered hunting and sharing big game a more prestigious activity than fishing.

"They had bows and arrows both extremely well made, which they laid down on coming to us. Most of their bows were made of Juniper or Box wood and Ceader and covered with the skin of the rattlesnake, which they say are numerous in this quarter, and their arrows are pointed with stone of the flint kind but dark, and their clothing consisted of dressed leather, leggings and shoes with robes," Fraser wrote.

The Secwepemc had obtained horses in the late eighteenth century. By the time of Fraser's visit the horse had revolutionized travel, transportation, hunting and warfare, although for the most part the Atnah were on good terms with the neighbouring Kootenay, Cree, Okanagan, Nicola, Lillooet or Askettih, Chilcotin and Carrier.

The gold rush of 1858—and the depopulation caused by its accompanying smallpox epidemic—devastated Secwepemc culture and resulted in systematic alienation from their traditional lands and resources.

Although the colonial government under Sir James Douglas had originally set aside large reserves of land that the Secwepemc themselves identified as desirable, when British Columbia became a province, it reduced these reserves and permitted settlers to preempt Indian lands.

Only when the Secwepemc threatened a war was the problem addressed. The province laid out reserves totalling about four hundred square kilometres—less than 1 percent of the land over which they had ranged freely two hundred years ago.

The Secwepemc have played a key role in positioning the unresolved question of aboriginal title and native Indian lands at the forefront of BC's political agenda. Chief George Manuel became a key political player on the national stage as leader of the National Indian Brotherhood. For the past quarter-century, the Secwepemc have been leaders in promoting public education and the preservation of their language and culture.

ST'AT'IMC

Called the Askettihs by Fraser, the St'at'imc held territory extending from near the height of land that separated rivers emptying into the coastal inlets from the Lillooet and Bridge river watersheds in the west to the Fraser River between Leon Creek, where Simon Fraser abandoned his canoes during his 1808 journey, and Texas Creek just south of present-day Lillooet. Other territory included the Pemberton region, Seton Lake, Anderson Lake, Lillooet Lake and the upper part of Harrison Lake.

Fraser made first contact with members of the band occupying the river around Pavilion on June 12 when he travelled overland from Leon Creek.

"Seven Askettihs presented themselves before us with their bows and arrows in readiness for attack; they conceived us to be enemies, but upon coming nearer they discovered from our appearance and demeanour their mistake, laid by their weapons, joined us and we shook hands. However, we could not understand them." Fraser wrote.

"They looked manly, and had really the appearance of warriors," he said of emissaries sent from chiefs camped farther downstream. "The Askettihs dress the same as the Atnahs. They are civil but will not part with their provisions without difficulty. They have a variety of roots, some of which taste like potatoes and are excellent. Their bows and arrows are neat. Their mats are made of different materials, such as rushes, grass, watap [spruce roots]."

In the northern part of their territory, families lived in communities of pit houses during the cold winter months. These were occasionally fortified, and Fraser saw one in which the wooden palisades were about six metres high. Farther south, people lived in cedar plank houses that were smaller versions of those constructed by coastal peoples.

The St'at'imc were not a large or powerful nation and were pressured at the boundaries by their larger neighbours, particularly the Halkomelem-speaking peoples to the south and the Chilcotin to the north. There was also occasional conflict with the Nlaka'pamux and the Secwepemc. All of this explains the initial caution with which they met Fraser's expedition.

Although the St'at'imc subsisted by hunting big game, particularly elk, mule deer, mountain goat and black bear in the mountains, the band that Fraser encountered relied much more upon the abundant runs of salmon and other fish into the Bridge River, Seton and Anderson lakes and the lower reaches of the large creeks flowing into the Fraser River. A major fishery using traditional dip nets and racks for the wind-drying of salmon still takes place each summer at the confluence of the Bridge River and the Fraser River.

In fact just four years after Fraser had passed through their territory, the St'at'imc on the river became the main purveyors of the dried salmon provisions that sustained Fort Kamloops, established in 1812, and regular brigades of pack horses carried bales of the commodity there in trade. Contemporary arguments over the right of native Indians to both claim an aboriginal right to a share of salmon resources and to sell them for economic gain have their origins in these ancient commercial practices that predate the existence both of Canada and BC.

Like their neighbours, the St'at'imc were heavily affected by the gold rush and epidemics. Population fell from an estimated four thousand people in Fraser's time to about twelve hundred in the early twentieth century but has since rebounded to precontact numbers.

The St'at'imc have been at the forefront for redress, on behalf not only of their own grievances but also those of other First Nations. Early in the twentieth century, aided by ethnographer James Teit who had made extensive studies of the Interior tribes, the St'at'imc became active in an organization known as the Allied Tribes and later petitioned the government demanding restoration of lands taken from them.

A long history of militant political activism, including rail and road blockades, has characterized their frustration with the failure of provincial and federal governments to address grievances involving land and aboriginal rights.

For fifteen years, the Union of BC Indian Chiefs, an organization that advocated for aboriginal rights and opposed the treaty negotiation process, was led by Saul Terry of the St'at-imc's Bridge River Band.

NLAKA'PAMUX

The Nlaka'pamux, called the Hacamaugh by Fraser, inhabit the arid rain shadow of the Coast Range from just south of Lillooet to south of the United States border. Their traditional territory on the west side of the Fraser River included the Stein Valley and the east-flowing watersheds above Harrison Lake from Texas Creek in the north to Sawmill Creek, just above Yale, in the south. East of the river their territory extended up the Thompson River to Ashcroft, past Merritt and around Nicola Lake, then south to include Ross Lake in the US.

Fraser met his first Hacamaugh on June 16 in the company of two visiting Shoshone.

"All were exceedingly well dressed in leather, and were on horseback," he wrote. "They have a great quantity of shells and blue beads, and we saw a broken silver broach such as the Sauteaus [Saulteaux] wear, among them. They were kind to us and assisted us at the carrying place with their horses."

He met others at the Stein River and was greeted by twelve hundred at a camp near present-day Lytton, where he observed, "They have many chiefs and great men, appear to be good orators, for their manner of delivery is extremely handsome."

The next day, his party was overtaken by two men who were bringing a piece of iron (probably an axe head) that the explorers had accidentally left behind: "We considered this an extraordinary degree of honesty and attention."

Living in a sparse, desert-like terrain, the Nlaka'pamux relied heavily on salmon resources in the Fraser and steelhead runs into the Thompson. They used dip nets to catch salmon at strategic locations where fish would swim close to the riverbank using back eddies to conserve strength. They more often speared steelhead.

Ethnobotanist Nancy Turner has identified more than 120 species of plants that the Nlaka'pamux gathered for food. Hunters killed mountain goats, bighorn sheep, deer and black bears using stone-tipped arrows, spears, snares, deadfalls and nets.

Life among the Nlaka'pamux was remarkably egalitarian and democratic compared to the class-conscious society that came to supersede them as the dominant culture. According to David Wyatt, writing in the Smithsonian Institution's *Handbook of North American Indians,* every individual was a member of a family, local community and a band "but ruled by none, for each man had a voice in the informal councils where hunting, war and other matters were discussed. Leadership came from the wise and the experienced, and there might be different leaders on different occasions; women spoke and led in their own areas of expertise . . . . There were no classes . . . and ranking was informal, based on an individual's perceived wealth, knowledge and family origin."

Like their neighbours, the Nlaka'pamux were accomplished horsemen, capable of ranging widely across their territory, and engaged in trade that extended from the coast to the Rocky Mountains. The Nlaka'pamux suffered greatly as a consequence of the gold rush, which disrupted fishing on the Fraser and caused famine that winter. A short-lived but bloody war with largely American miners was ended by the intervention of a revered chief from Lytton.

The Nlaka'pamux have been politically active in seeking redress for grievances on the land question since they resisted the forcible incursion of miners in 1858. They sent delegates to plead their case in London and laid groundwork for the creation of the Allied Tribes of BC at a meeting at Spence's Bridge in 1915.

STO:LO

Simon Fraser made his first contact with the Halkomelem-speaking people of the Fraser River who call themselves the Sto:lo (people of the river) at Spuzzum on June 27, 1808. He called them the Ackinroe and was, he wrote, "hospitably entertained with fresh salmon, both boiled and roasted, green and dried berries, oil and onions"—a pretty good repast for voyageurs who had long ago cached or consumed their own rations of dried fish.

Sto:lo territory was extensive, ranging from just above Yale to near Cape Flattery on the Olympic Peninsula of Washington state. It extended from the lower Squamish River to Lake Whatcom and the upper watersheds of the Nooksack River. From the east side of Vancouver Island below Northwest Bay near Nanaimo to beyond Sooke, west of Victoria, the south shore of Juan de Fuca Strait as far as Port Townsend, the Canadian Gulf Islands and American San Juan Islands were all part of the territory.

This was a wealthy, powerful and highly organized society, as Fraser discerned during his visit. Anthropologist Wayne Suttles, who studied the people ethnologists call the Central Coast Salish for most of his life, divides them into several groups: the Upriver Halkomelem who greeted Fraser so hospitably; the Downriver Halkomelem who chased him back up the river; the Island Halkomelem, whose aggressive Cowichan tribe was feared on the mainland; the Northern Straits people who occupied the Gulf Islands and the area around Victoria; and the Clallam people first encountered by Spanish and British explorers in the last decade of the eighteenth century.

According to Suttles, the Upriver Halkomelem first encountered by Fraser comprised the Matsqui, the Sumas, the Nicomen, the Scowlitz, the Chehalis, the Pilalt and the Tait, who occupied the river between Hope and Yale. The Downriver Halkomelem that Fraser would have encountered were the Musqueam, the Kwantlen, the Coquitlam, the Katzie and the Nicomekl.

This social and political landscape was thrown into great upheaval and dislocation, however, after the smallpox epidemic of 1782–84. The Nicomekl and possibly several other groups on the lower Fraser simply vanished after the epidemic, for example, either killed by the virus or going as survivors to live elsewhere.

The rich salmon resources of the great river and their seasonal cycles were then central to the economic culture of the Sto:lo. This fact endures and permeates the salmon politics that continue to bedevil competing interest groups today.

As Fraser observed in his journal, the Sto:lo lived in large, well-constructed cedar plank buildings that could be organized in rows facing the shoreline and housed extended families and groups of families. These buildings were remarkable for their elaborately decorated house posts with carved human, animal and totemic figures. Fraser commented upon the great skill of the artists and artisans in shaping the wood.

Fraser also observed that people he visited on two occasions altered their appearance with the cosmetic use of paint, one group using red and another using white, while almost every social visit was accompanied by singing and dancing by the hosts.

On June 29, Fraser noted the weaving of different coloured "rugs" from dog hair. This practice was also observed by Capt. George Vancouver during his explorations of the coast in 1792. Vancouver saw packs of dogs among the Clallam that resembled Pomeranians, although larger.

"They were all shorn as close to the skin as sheep are in England; and so compact were their fleeces, that large portions could be lifted up by a corner without causing any separation. They were composed of a mixture of a coarse kind of wool, with very fine long hair, capable of being spun into yarn," Vancouver wrote.

Travelling painter Paul Kane recorded images of women spinning wool and weaving at their looms when he visited the West Coast in 1847.

Other materials used in weaving included mountain goat wool, fireweed cotton and the down of some waterfowl. Cowichan sweaters, although now knitted from sheep wool, are a direct descendent of this ancient technology.

Today the Sto:lo and their Halkomelem neighbours are a potent but pragmatic force in the politics of aboriginal rights. They have advanced the cause with a series of significant and successful court challenges that have altered the ways in which governments and mainstream society are required to deal with such issues.

THE BURNT WOOD PEOPLE

Simon Fraser's partners in the North West Company had created a sophisticated global trading network by 1806 that linked Asian, European and North American markets. His mission to north central British Columbia was intended—in addition to generating new sources of high-quality furs to replace those from depleted regions elsewhere—to secure the final transportation link necessary for the company to complete its ambitious business strategy.

Fraser sought a navigable route from the subarctic interior to the Pacific so that furs from the northwest could be shipped directly to lucrative markets in China. Tea, oranges, spices, porcelain and other high-value goods would be back-hauled from Asia for sale in Europe.

Then as now, viability for the whole commercial enterprise depended upon efficient transport. The crucial component in the North West Company's ability to extend its reach from Montreal to the Rockies was a group often overlooked or given cursory treatment in histories examining the origins of both British Columbia and the Canadian confederation with which it would eventually unite.

"If the Métis 'might be called the offspring of the Canadian fur trade,' their principal and characteristic function in that far-flung enterprise has been as movers of men and materials," writes Richard Slobodin.

"Indians were primarily harvesters of the renewable resources and Whites were primarily merchants, but there were Métis engaged in these activities while also dominating, in terms of manpower, the transportation function that was the lifeline of Euro-Canadian penetration of the North as well as the West," Slobodin notes in an essay for the *Handbook of North American Indians* published by the Smithsonian Institution in 1981.

The Métis gave the North West Company access to a large pool of skilled labour that was far less costly than that available to the rival Hudson's Bay Company, which imported many of its employees from Britain.

The Métis hired on as canoemen, packers, guides, hunters, and frequently *engagés;* this term came to mean men who contracted to stay at the remote frontier outposts throughout the year to do the necessary labouring jobs. They gathered construction materials, erected palisades and cabins, built canoes, made snowshoes and foraged for game and other foodstuffs.

Labour recruited in Britain and indentured to five- or seven-year contracts faced a steep learning curve, but not these Métis employees. They came with skill sets that were inculcated from birth and ideal for employment in the fur trade.

Furthermore, the Métis provided a bridge between the European culture of the fur traders and the indigenous cultures that trapped fur-bearing animals, prepared the pelts for storage and shipment and then traded them for new consumer goods.

Sometimes called *Bois-Brûlé* (burnt wood) for their darker complexions—or half-breeds or mixed-bloods—the Métis were the proud offspring of liaisons between European newcomers and native Indians. This melding of populations began almost as soon as colonies were founded in New France and New England, and explorers, merchants and traders began pushing beyond the first settlements.

Many French-Canadian coureurs de bois—seventeenth-century free traders who defied the colonial authorities to venture into the immense and uncharted *Pays d'en Haut* (upper country) around the Great Lakes—assimilated easily into the First Nations societies they encountered.

The Scots who entered the fur trade after the British conquest of New France, often in loose alliances with French Canadians, followed the same pattern. They likewise began largely as free traders defying the monopoly of the Hudson's Bay Company, eventually coalescing into the North West Company headquartered in polyglot Montreal, not imperial London. The Scots also came from a tribal society that had been marginalized. They held to traditions that were distinctly different from those of the English mainstream—including, as historian Sylvia Van Kirk points out in *Many Tender Ties,* her study of women in the fur trade—"disdain for the formalities of European marriage."

French-Canadian and Scottish fur traders took native Indian wives according to the customs of the tribes with whom they lived and traded. Often they wed in order to establish kinship obligations that would provide allies and protection from other hostile groups or to secure trading advantages with powerful chiefs. Duncan McDougall did this at Fort Astoria when he negotiated a marriage with the daughter of the Chinook chief Concomely.

Frequently they took native Indian wives because these women had skills—which women from European society lacked—essential to survival in the wilderness. They knew how to skin an animal and tan a hide, how to make clothes from what was at hand, how to snare small game and where to forage for wild fruits and vegetables. They were also invaluable for their ability both to interpret and to provide insights into the workings of a different culture.

Sometimes the liaisons represented only base exploitation by men who saw the relationships in limited terms of temporary sexual convenience. But sometimes the lonely young men who took female companions for unromantic reasons discovered they had come to love their wives so much they couldn't bear to be separated from them. Explorer David Thompson's marriage to Charlotte Small lasted fifty-six years. Daniel Williams Harmon, who succeeded Simon Fraser at Fort St. James, remained married to Elizabeth Duval for thirty-eight years. Peter Skene Ogden, who was at Fort St. James in 1835 after exploring much of what is now Washington, Oregon, Idaho, Utah and Wyoming, married Julia Rivet among the Nez Perce in 1818. That marriage—he had earlier been married to a Cree woman—lasted forty-six years.

It was from this cross-cultural commingling that the Métis nation was born and came to dominate much of the later fur trade across the northwest, particularly in New Caledonia. Métis employees, with their ability to span cultures, frequently rose to high rank in the fur trade and served as chief fur traders, factors responsible for trading posts and chief factors administering entire districts. A.C. Murray rose to take charge of New Caledonia and Fort St. James. Others became doctors, teachers, clerics and politicians.

The surnames of prominent Métis families—Beaulieu, Mercredi, Lafferty, Cardinal, Isbister, Jones, Fraser, Flett, Hodgson, Firth, Stewart, McKay and others—were stamped indelibly into the demographic landscape of the province.

The first first lady of British Columbia, Amelia Connolly—she had married fur trader turned colonial governor James Douglas in 1828—was Métis. So was Josette Legace, who married John Work, a chief factor with the Hudson's Bay Company about 1826. She was prominent in Victoria society as her husband and Douglas helped forge the new colony of British Columbia.

Today about forty-five thousand people in BC identify themselves as being of Métis descent, including Carole James, who served as leader of the official opposition for the New Democratic Party from 2003.

The Métis, as much as Scots fur traders, French-Canadian voyageurs and the First Nations who already occupied the landscape, can claim to have played a vital role in the rise of New Caledonia and the birth of the province we share today.

A Brief Note on Sources

Extensive fur trade bibliographies exist elsewhere, and since this book was not intended to be a scholarly research history, I have not included one here. Although I consulted more than three hundred and fifty texts, I found the most important sources to be first-hand accounts recorded in journals, letters, logs, fur company reports and other primary documents. Where primary sources were not available, I turned to ethnologists, anthropologists, historians and native Indian elders who had themselves heard and recorded first-person narratives.

For Simon Fraser's expedition, I relied most heavily upon two accounts:

The Letters and Journals of Simon Fraser, 1806–1808, edited and annotated by Dominion archivist W. Kaye Lamb in 1960.

Les Bourgeois de la Compagnie du Nord-Ouest: Récits de Voyages, Lettres et Rapports Inédits Relatifs au Nord-Ouest Canadien publiés avec une Esquisse Historique et des Annotations, published by L.R. Masson in 1889, in which Fraser's narrative was first published as *Journal of a Voyage from the Rocky Mountains to the Pacific Coast, 1808*.

Other first-person accounts consulted include:

Travels and adventures in Canada and the Indian Territories between the years 1760 and 1776: in two parts by Alexander Henry, published in 1809.

Vancouver's Discovery of Puget Sound: Portraits and Biographies of the Men Honored in the Naming of Geographic Features of Northwestern America, which includes Captain George Vancouver's 1798 narrative of his exploration of the Strait of Georgia and Puget Sound in 1792, edited and extensively annotated by Edmond S. Meany of the University of Washington in 1907.

Voyages from Montreal, on the river St. Lawrence, through the continent of North America, to the Frozen and Pacific oceans; in the years 1789 and 1793 with a Preliminary Account of the Rise, Progress, and Present State of the Fur Trade of that Country, published by Alexander Mackenzie in 1801.

The Journals of Lewis and Clark, edited by John Bakeless and extracted into one volume from the eight-volume report of the American expedition that traveled from St. Louis, Missouri, to the mouth of the Columbia River in the years 1804–1806.

Sixteen Years in the Indian Country: The Journal of Daniel Williams Harmon, 1800–1816, edited and annotated by W. Kaye Lamb in 1957 and republished by Heritage House in 2006 as *Harmon's Journal, 1800–1819* with a new introductory essay by Jennifer Brown of the University of Winnipeg.

The History of the Northern Interior of British Columbia, formerly New Caledonia: 1660 to 1880 by Father Adrian Gabriel Morice, published in 1901.

John Stuart's brief account of his sojourn at Rocky Mountain Portage House in 1805 and early 1806 I was able to examine in a copy held by the Fort St. John and North Peace Museum in Fort St. John, BC.

James Teit's ethnographies of the Thompson, Lillooet and Shuswap Indians, in which he records First Nations accounts of Fraser's journey for the Jesup North Pacific Expedition of 1897–1902, edited by Franz Boas and published in twelve volumes by the American Museum of Natural History. Teit's accounts were published in Volumes 1, 2 and 8.

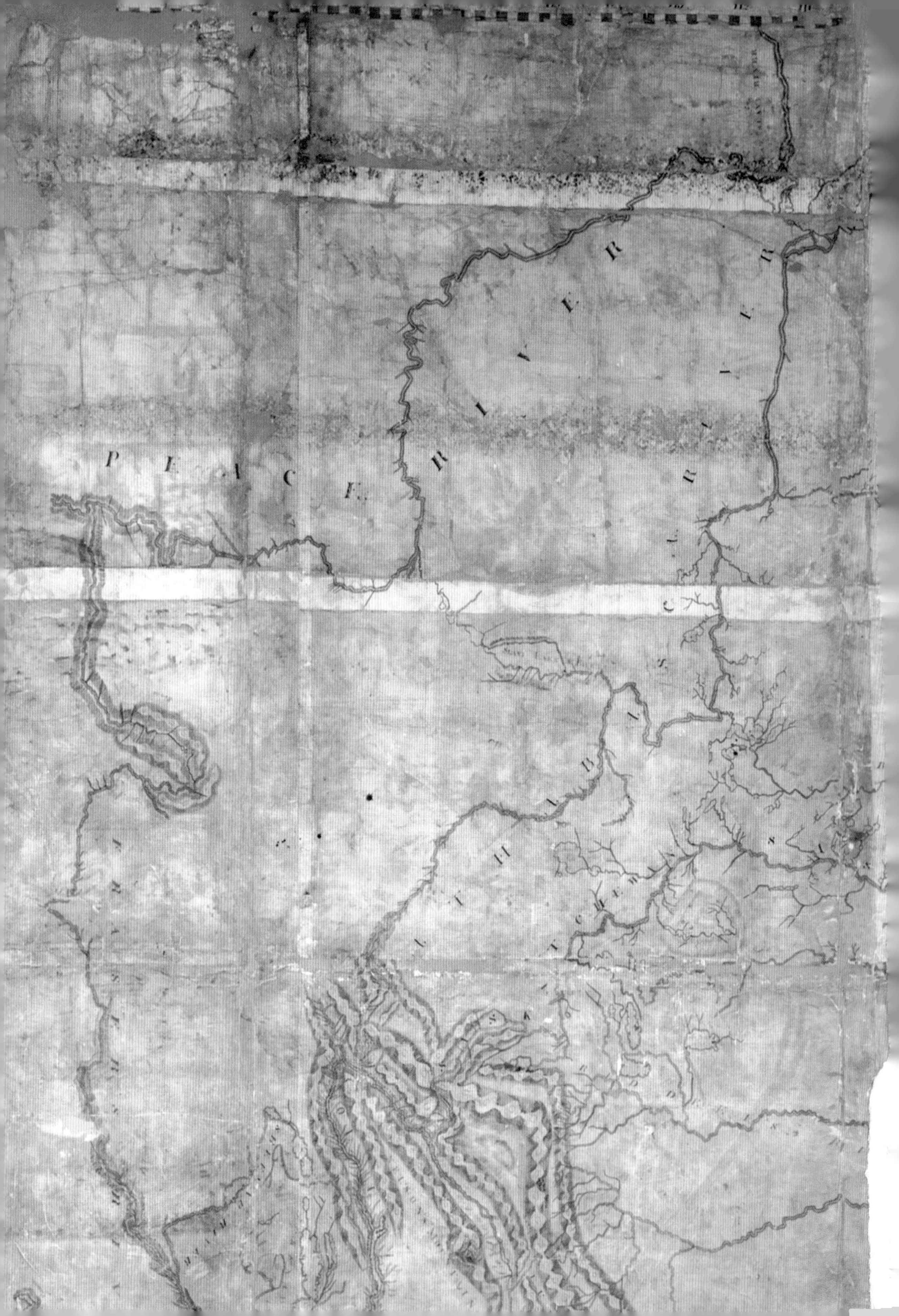
P E A C E R I V E R